THE
LOST BOOK
OF THE
GRAIL

"Any book written by these authors is worth noting, but this is a real tour de force. *The Lost Book of the Grail* takes us right into the heart of the Grail tradition. It addresses a key, very cryptic text ironically called *The Elucidation,* and step-by-step we are invited into its secret heart. We are shown the central act of wounding, which devastates the union between human beings, the sacred land, and the Sidhe, who are guardians of the secret life of the land. We are shown the branches of story that lead us into the restoration of the flowing life and love that are the hallmarks of the presence of the Grail. There is so much in this book; it's sure to become a classic work for all who seek to heal the wasteland and seek the Grail. Thoroughly recommended."

IAN REES, PSYCHOTHERAPIST AND
PROGRAM DIRECTOR OF THE ANNWN FOUNDATION

"This book is a wonderful new exploration of a little-known work in the rich cycle of Grail legends that elucidates with a new translation and commentary. A product of scholarly work that shows great erudition, it is also a pleasure to read and easily accessible to the general public. Caitlín and John Matthews are unparalleled experts on the Grail and Arthurian legend. Their work shows a whole range of insight that comes from a lifetime of study."

KREŠIMIR VUKOVIĆ, PH.D., POSTDOCTORAL FELLOW
AT THE CATHOLIC UNIVERSITY OF CROATIA

"I share the Matthews' view that *The Elucidation* draws in large part on authentic Celtic lore, as does the Grail legend. As Welsh scholar Sir John Rees suggested well over a century ago, the poem 'has a very ancient ring.' *The Lost Book of the Grail* not only illuminates but, I believe, rightly emphasizes the contemporary witness of the countryside being tragically subjected to relentless, irreparable destruction."

NIKOLAI TOLSTOY, AUTHOR OF *THE QUEST FOR MERLIN* AND *THE MYSTERIES OF STONEHENGE*

"You do not just read this book, you experience it as a seeker. Read it slowly and savor each page as it is a map into the mystery of mysteries. A literary tour de force by the authors."

DOLORES ASHCROFT-NOWICKI, AUTHOR OF *THE SHINING PATHS*

THE
LOST BOOK
OF THE
GRAIL

The Sevenfold Path
of the Grail and the
Restoration of the Faery Accord

Caitlín and John Matthews

With a New Translation
of the Thirteenth-Century Text of
The Elucidation of the Grail
by Gareth Knight and Caitlín Matthews

Inner Traditions
Rochester, Vermont

Inner Traditions
One Park Street
Rochester, Vermont 05767
www.InnerTraditions.com

Text stock is SFI certified

Cataloging-in-Publication Data for this title is available from the Library of Congress

ISBN 978-1-62055-829-4 (print)
ISBN 978-1-62055-830-0 (ebook)

Printed and bound in the United States by Lake Book Manufacturing, Inc.
The text stock is SFI certified. The Sustainable Forestry Initiative® program
promotes sustainable forest management.

10 9 8 7 6 5 4 3 2 1

Text design and layout by Priscilla Baker
This book was typeset in Garmond Premier Pro with Trajan, Gill Sans, Fritz
Quadrata, and Legacy Sans used as display typefaces

To send correspondence to the authors of this book, mail a first-class letter to the
author c/o Inner Traditions • Bear & Company, One Park Street, Rochester, VT
05767, and we will forward the communication, or contact the authors directly at
www.hallowquest.org.uk.

For all who still go on quest

*All those who travel the road can still see the
story there, sealed all in parchment.*

THE THIRD CONTINUATION OF THE GRAIL

Court of the Grail Guardians by Ari Berk

CONTENTS

ACKNOWLEDGMENTS

First and foremost, great thanks are due to the anonymous storyteller who gave us *The Elucidation*. Like a small shrine encompassing a great treasure, this text has given us waybread for the road as we researched. Many known and unknown Grail writers must also be thanked for leading us through the labyrinthine stories of this myth: they went there first; we merely followed their story, though our conclusions are our own.

It has long been our desire to prepare an edition of *The Elucidation* that any could read, with notes, commentary, and other supporting materials, without the dismissals with which this text has been greeted by many scholars who have failed to see its central importance. We are immensely grateful to Gareth Knight for the opportunity to work at last on a text that we regard as central to an understanding of the Grail and its teachings. Not only has he provided an excellent translation, to which we have contributed, but his vision in seeing this book through to the end has been inspirational.

Thanks to Nigel Bryant whose wonderful translation of the Grail Continuations has made this year's writing a great joy and comfort: his many other translations of the Arthurian corpus have made our hearts glad, as well as providing an extraordinary service to the world of Arthurian scholarship. To our Illyrian friend, Kresimir Vukovic, with whom we shared many mythic after-dinner conversations at various Oxford colleges: a big thank-you for your good companionship during this quest. To Ari Berk, much gratitude for his illustration of the Court of the Grail Guardians and for his enthusiasm and support over many years. To all our students and readers worldwide, thanks for your engagement with the quest, and your patience in awaiting this volume. A very special thank-you to all who participated in our public teaching of this text at *Voices of the Wells* at Hawkwood College in December 2016: what a wonderful weekend with your good help!

Revealing an Unknown Grail Story

[These are the] words our Hermes uttered when he hid his books away. "O holy books, who have been made by my immortal hands, by incorruption's magic spells, free from decay and incorrupt from time! Become unseeable, for every one whose foot shall tread the plains of this our land, until old Heaven doth bring forth meet instruments for you, whom the Creator shall call souls." Thus, spake he and, laying spells on them by means of his own works, he shuts them safe away in their own zones. And long enough the time has been since they were hid away.

Kore Kosmou

THE RETURN OF THE WELLS

Embedded within the Western mythic tradition is a long testimony of hidden texts that become revealed in due course. From the account of Hermes burying his teachings in the ground in the Hermetic *Kore Kosmou* text, right up to the Rosicrucian texts that seemed to spontaneously emerge and spread all over Europe in the seventeenth century, many wonderful teachings have come to light. Most recent is the discovery of the greatest cache of Gnostic texts ever found, revealed at Nag Hammadi in Egypt in 1945.

1

While we may marvel at the revelations contained within these texts, we wonder even more at the careful timing of their rerelease into the world, in an era when their teachings can be safely received and be heard once more. Any earlier discovery and these texts would have been regarded as heretical documents, fit only to be burned. As it was, the Nag Hammadi texts barely survived going on the fire of the Egyptian finder's mother, who was intent on cooking his supper with these very precious fragments used as kindling! Now these Gnostic texts form part of a recognized and major branch of scholarship.[1]

Like the hidden writings of Hermes that are buried for some future era to discover, some bodies of knowledge remain hidden until the right time arrives. That time has now arrived for *The Elucidation*. Back in the mid-nineteenth century, with rather less of a flourish of trumpets, the 484 lines that comprise the thirteenth-century French text called *The Elucidation* were first discovered, bound into the beginning of a manuscript known as the *Mons, Bibliotèque communale, no 4568*. Within this thirteenth-century French verse text, long seen as a prequel to Chrétien's *Perceval, ou le Conte du Graal,* are contained the most astonishing revelations, which are never quite elucidated.[2]

The title, *The Elucidation,* itself arises from a later 1530 French-printed edition in which the seven pages of a free-prose rendition of the original poem are titled *l'Elucidation de L'Ystoire du Graal,* or "The Elucidation of the Grail Story." Never was a name so ironically applied, many have thought, since the text purports to introduce us to Chrétien's *Perceval,* which is currently regarded as the first account of the Grail story. However, *The Elucidation* actually presents us with a myth that is entirely different from the one told by Chrétien. You might want to reserve your judgment about this very different myth until the book you are holding is done, as the text itself advises in its opening lines, for it is a multilayered exposition of a myth so essential that it is necessary to gather all the supporting material together first in order to see the vast canvas with which it presents us. Within the very small compass of its 484 lines, the totality of the Grail legend is mythically present.

The core myth around which *The Elucidation* dances gives us a completely different causation for the Wasteland from the one we are used to reading in the other Grail texts. Rather than the Dolorous Blow that is struck upon the Grail King, it details how the sacred hospitality of the earth was violated and what results from that violation; it hints at the restoration and healing of the earth but, most disquietingly, it also reveals what happens when that sacred hospitality is not taken to heart. The other astonishing thing that this small text does is to turn back through time, making it a prequel of a mythic order.

In our own era, we are very familiar with the idea of a prequel: Tolkien's three-volume *Lord of the Rings* books are prequelled by *The Hobbit,* while both are prequelled further in his *Silmarillion,* which details the mythology of Middle Earth from creation onward, in mythic fashion. The successive books of Tolkien's world nest within larger and larger boxes, starting initially with the story of an insignificant hobbit and his adventures after finding a ring; this action accidentally breaks through into a much larger world of men, elves, orcs, and dwarfs, which then ripples backward, into an ever-widening hinterland of epic story and deep myth.

Similarly, while the classic *Star Trek* TV series (1966–1969) has been followed by many other series that advance Star Fleet's intergalactic adventures into future centuries, it has also been accorded a prequel series of *Enterprise* (2001–2005), preceding the early adventures of the original series. Thus, the reader can run backward and forward in both memory and acquaintance with the themes and characters, while still being entertained with new scenarios and episodes from its mythic logbook.

That the Grail myth itself has been subject to a similar set of prequels and expansions may seem surprising to the reader. The general assumption among those unacquainted with the Grail legends is that there is one main Grail story, but this is not the case. Chrétien de Troyes's *Perceval, ou le Conte du Graal* (ca. 1180) was certainly the first surviving story to appear but, had he been a scriptwriter, his name on subsequent branches of the Grail legends would certainly have required a credit reading, "from an original idea by Chrétien," since it was closely followed by a variety of other stories that continued the adventure far beyond the original.

These stories, known as the *Continuations,* came about because Chrétien's *Perceval* was left unfinished, so that a series of writers—no doubt in response to many hearers' dismay at a truncated story—continued the story, expanding and changing it, with subsequent writers evolving the Grail quest into ever new adventures. This process, now so familiar to us from television and fiction, was going on within the Grail legends between the thirteenth and fifteenth centuries, almost unchecked. This is why there is not just *one* Grail story. In any case, the foreshadowing of the Grail legends begins much earlier, of course, as we will see.

A prequel has the power to range through time and space, presuming on our acquaintance with the original story as a foundational basis for understanding, while introducing new matter that interacts with characters and themes already actively in motion. This is certainly the case with *The Elucidation,* which is why we need to grasp this foundational basis from the outset, for this short poetic story has many windows through time where older and later themes are revisited or freshly introduced.

Medieval storytelling doesn't usually play much with time-lapse. Narratives usually unfold from beginning to end, in order. That we find such a thing in the Grail legends is due to the way it deals with the primal questions evoked by this key myth: Why are things like this? What caused this? Whom does the Grail serve? What will cure these ills? The cause of unheeded or violent actions upon the world cannot be healed, we are told, "as long as the world lasts."[3] The solution, then, is to step *outside time* in order that the restoration can be made: which is precisely what a myth does, empowering us to be active in situations that have become stalemated in time.

This is how the quest for the Grail comes into being. Within the Grail legends it is the knights of Arthur who are the active agents of the solution, sometimes blundering about and making things worse, sometimes fortuitously falling through and beyond time and space into liminal, otherworldly places. In an unknown castle, in another world, Perceval views the procession of holy and mysterious things and sees portrayed, in one extraordinary scene, the very heart of a lamentation for the world's sorrow. The begged question is: Why on earth is this happening? But because his mother has instructed Perceval that curiosity is ill-bred, he neglects to ask why, and so the sorrow and pain, which is central to the Grail mystery, is not halted at that very moment.

In the words of Dai Great-Coat, the soldierly protagonist of *In Parenthesis,* the great mythic poem of World War I, written by the Anglo-Welsh poet David Jones: "You ought to ask . . . what's the meaning of this? / Because you don't ask . . . there's neither steading—nor a roof-tree.⁴ In the Grail quest, *not asking* gets you nowhere and merely repeats the cycle of suffering. From the beginning we need to ask questions; it is the only way of navigating the landscape of the Grail.

WHAT IS THE GRAIL?

We all think that we know and understand the Grail. Many people, when asked about it, will assert that it is "the *Holy* Grail," with their minds full of the Cup of the Last Supper. Others will immediately go into a riff of the film *Monty Python and the Holy Grail,* telling us that they "have one already" and that "it is vairy nayce," in a phony French accent! Very few will associate it with the two cruets of water and blood brought by Joseph of Arimathea to Britain, which is the foundation myth of the Glastonbury Grail legend. But even fewer will know of the cup of hospitality that is brought forth by faery maidens to travelers—no, we have really not invented this—as you will read in *The Elucidation!*

The word *graal* appears in Chrétien de Troyes's *Perceval, ou le Conte du Graal,* where it appears as a serving platter, the kind of wide dish in which pages presented food at table, as the custom was, bringing it first to the lord at the high table and from thence served to everyone else in order. The Bleeding Lance that accompanies it has clear connections with the Passion of Christ. In *Perceval,* we are told that the rich Fisher King is the son of an older king who is served from the Grail: "Do not think that he is given pike, lamprey, or salmon; he is served with a single host, which is brought to him in that grail. Such a holy thing is the grail that it sustains and comforts his life."[5] It also keeps him alive for twelve years. Note too that Chrétien, who did not invent the word, does not call the Grail "the Holy Grail," but "a holy thing," or a hallow—a sacred object.

The early thirteenth-century Grail writer, Robert de Boron was the first to explicitly associate the platter of the *graal* with the chalice of the Last Supper. It is not until the *First* and *Third Continuation,* written by writers who extended Chrétien's *Perceval* into a longer cycle, that we hear how Joseph of Arimathea brought the Grail with him, a vessel that had nurtured him in prison, after his captivity in Rome (see page 168).

Scholars and writers alike have attempted to make of the Grail something completely other, from the Grail scholar A. C. L. Brown, who saw the vessel's origins as a *criol,* or Irish cup of plenty,[6] to Baigent, Leigh, and Lincoln's *Holy Blood, Holy Grail,* where it becomes the bloodline of Merovingian kings[7]—a theory that has since spawned an entire industry of speculation.

Nor has the literary evidence for the Grail stayed just upon the page. Several actual sacramental or healing vessels around Europe have been claimed as "*the* Grail." From the Santa Calix of Valencia, which is made of one piece of agate, to the humble wooden bowl of the Nanteos Cup in Wales, several vessels have been promoted as "the one true Grail."[8]

This book is not about a quest to find such a historic relic or archaeological artifact, but about something much greater, since the Grail is not an object to be excavated and finally curated in a museum. It is rather about the ever-living hallow or sacred vessel that passes in and out of time and place, but which abides beyond both, in eternity and space. In this book we are concerned with the myth.

Myth is a word that has become demoted to mean "an imaginary thing that is without truth." Here, in this book, we are using *myth* in its original, primal sense as "that which is the truest thing of all." Myth is the means by which we live well, with understanding and compassion. As the fourth-century Greek philosopher Sallustius remarked in his *Concerning the Gods and the World,* "myth is something that has never happened and is always happening."⁹

As with the myth of King Arthur, the Grail myth itself is made up of many individual and different stories, with a central core that is given various treatments and interpretations in the many texts that relate its finding. Like the Arthurian legends themselves, the Grail is a catalyst and attractor of other myths that become accreted to it.

The many hands that have been at work on the Grail, extending and expanding, collapsing and eliding themes together, have crafted and grafted until a story from Britain has become the lode-bearing deposit of many myths, wherein Passion narratives, faery lore, chivalric adventures, gnostic secrets, and salvific legends all meld together to create a rich mélange. This fusion of myths into one story belongs to neither one individual, nor to a specific group, but has become a myth from which anyone may learn. The Grail writers, by leveling cultural and spiritual themes with a delightful lack of distinction into one timeless narrative, enable any quester to discover how the relics of the Passion, faery hospitality, knightly honor, and gnostic lore may become part of a day's quest.

As we approach *The Elucidation,* this continual unfolding and blending of themes is worth bearing in mind, because then we can find refractions and echoes that enable us to understand and illuminate the text.

WHERE DOES *THE ELUCIDATION* FIT?

It is often considered important to trace the origins of a myth, to track it back with relentless pursuit, to one single place of origin. However, the Grail's origins do not lie in one place, since they belong to a much wider, mythic commonality, whose many strands we will be exploring in this book.

The written legends of the Grail emerge between the end of the twelfth century and the beginning of the thirteenth century, in a time of great ferment and spiritual creativity. During this same time the nations of Western Europe were coming together as representatives of Christendom to defend what they saw as the birthplace of their spiritual heritage, the holy places in Jerusalem. The great cathedrals of Europe were being exuberantly erected, while all over France, the cult of the Black Virgins and Romanesque Madonnas was flourishing. The times were ripe for a deeper exploration of the apocryphal and mystical elements of Christianity.

We have to thank Chrétien de Troyes for inseminating Europe with the Grail story in his *Perceval*. Other anonymous storytellers also played their parts, but he is the one who first told it to a large and international audience. In fact, he begins his *Perceval* with this very image in the prologue, "Who sows little reaps little, and whoever wants to reap a harvest scatters his seed in those places where God yields a hundredfold; if the good seed falls on dry ground, it will thirst and come to nothing."[10] The harvest has indeed been great.

Chrétien's patron was Count Philip of Flanders (1143–1191), whose second wife, Sibylle of Anjou, was the daughter of Count Foulques of Anjou and sister to Geoffrey Plantagenet, the father of Henry II of England. Philip's own father, Thierry of Alsace, had been rewarded with a special gift for his services in the Second Crusade: the phial of Holy Blood, a relic of which can still be seen processed at Bruges in Belgium every year. So, we can immediately understand how Philip, who is mentioned in *The Elucidation* as the one who gave Chrétien the story of the Grail, is a plausible candidate both as a patron and as one with a vested interest in the Grail story. To complete the picture we need to know that Philip of Flanders married Elisabeth of Vermandois, who was a niece of that great patroness of the arts, Eleanor of Aquitaine. Philip's well-connected court, with its network of relationships and influences, connected Europe with the Kingdom of Jerusalem, becoming fertile ground for teaching the whole of Christendom about this myth.

To give a sense of where *The Elucidation* fits within these many Grail texts, here is brief breakdown of the earliest Grail texts that were written between 1180 and the 1230s.

1. Chrétien de Troyes wrote about the Grail first in *Perceval, ou le Conte du Graal* in the 1180s, but because he left it unfinished, it was continued by

2. the anonymous *First Continuation,* written about 1190, followed by

3. the *Second Continuation,* attributed to Gautier de Denet, sometimes called "Wauchier de Denains," written in about 1220, followed by

4. *Gerbert de Montreuil's* [unnumbered] *Continuation* of the early thirteenth century, followed by

5. the *Third Continuation* of Manassier about 1220–1230;

6. *The Elucidation* of the early thirteenth century; and

7. the anonymous story of *Bliocadran,* which was found bound in with *The Elucidation.*

The anonymous author of *The Elucidation* had closest knowledge of the *First Continuation* text and its successors, like *Gerbert de Montreuil's Continuation,* which seems to bear the influence of Robert de Boron. There are many other intertextual connections. We will explore some of the possible sources for Chrétien in the ensuing chapters but we must bear in mind that the Grail myth was first seeded in earlier times and cultures whose folk traditions also flow into the main confluence.

The main Grail texts that flowed from the initial outpouring include the following:

• Robert de Boron, *Li Romanz de l'estoire dou Graal,* circa 1200.

• *The Lancelot-Grail, the Old French Arthurian Vulgate, and Post Vulgate Cycle,* which is a vast series of texts that connect the Passion with the Arthurian legends in an authoritative way; written in five parts, with occasional codices that extend them. These were written between about 1215–1235.

• The *Estoire del Saint Grail* (History of the Holy Grail) relates how Joseph of Arimathea and his son Josephus brought the Grail to Britain.

• The *Estoire de Merlin* (also called the Vulgate or *Prose Merlin*) tells us about Merlin and the early history of Arthur. The Vulgate *Suite du Merlin* (Vulgate Merlin Continuation) acts as an appendix to this part of the Vulgate, continuing with Arthur's early adventures.

- The *Lancelot* or *Lancelot Proper* is the longest text, making up half of the entire cycle. It details the adventures of Lancelot and the other Knights of the Round Table and the love between Lancelot and Guinevere.
- The *Queste del Saint Graal* (Quest for the Holy Grail) relates the Grail quest and its achievement by Galahad.
- *Perlesvaus*—a more elaborate version of Perceval's quest, working it into a dreamlike set of adventures.
- The *Mort Artu* (Death of Arthur) relates the king's death at the hands of Mordred and the decline of the Round Table.

These texts were followed by the *Post-Vulgate Cycle,* a work based on the *Lancelot-Grail* but differing from it in many respects.

While it isn't essential, you may find it useful to read for yourself *Perceval, the Story of the Grail*—several excellent editions of which are mentioned in the bibliography. The whole text can also be read online, and a brief breakdown of its story appears on pages 19–21.

THIS EDITION AND OUR METHOD

The Elucidation primarily tells us about itself through its unfolding story, so we have closely followed its themes to see what is revealed. Throughout, we have tracked the myth, drawing upon parallel myths and stories in the Grail canon, respecting the myth to show us what is remembered and represented. We have also consulted the earlier Celtic parallels and other originating medieval materials that form the matrix of the Grail legends. While we have respected the historical context of this myth, we have also examined it through the perspectives of eternal understanding, the timeless myth that the Grail evokes.

This is particularly important when we come to regard the view from the faery side of things. The Maidens of the Wells who offer hospitality in *The Elucidation* are not human beings. They live outside of time and space, remembering and representing a paradisal union and accord that humans, who live through serial time, have often chosen to set aside as "imaginary."

What the Grail represents is not a fantasy, however: it brings fellowship, plenty, and peace, a union of spirit that is entirely encompassing of all faith traditions and is nearer in kind to what Christ spoke of in the Gospel of Thomas as "the Kingdom," whose presence is all about and within us. The Grail reunites us with a state of consciousness that brings everything together in an essential sacred continuum. That primordial state of being demands that we engage with it and is ultimately the basis of "the Joy of the Court" that is sought by the Arthurian knights in this text.

The first chapter provides a literary and historical context for the Grail legends, including a breakdown of *Perceval,* so that the reader has a prior sense of its shape before moving on to its prequel. A prose version of *The Elucidation* poem by Gareth Knight can also be found in chapter 1, so that you can grasp the story's outline from the outset.

The original text in translation can be found in chapter 2 with commentary. We have clarified any narrative ambiguities within the text by the occasional and judicious use of bracketed amplifications only where the action is unclear, due to the pile up of possessive pronouns that often occur within the verse. We have made no attempt to replicate the prosody in our translation; the verse consists of four-line stanzas of rhyming couplets, giving it a tripping simplicity. The poem has been numerated by line and divided under new headings with a brief commentary beneath each section for ease of reading and study.

Chapter 3 explores the role of the story and its storytellers, while chapter 4 delves deeper into the matter of the Wells and the maidens who live in them. Chapter 5 speaks of the Land of Women and the way in which this otherworldly land finds its parallel in the Grail legends. In chapter 6 we discover the role of the Grail family and of the anti-Grail Kings who are responsible for the causes of the Wasteland, seen in context within chapter 7 where these implications are further explored.

The mysterious Courts of Joy are entered in chapter 8, and the restorations provided by the Grail are shown in chapter 9 where an appreciation of the quest's trajectory is discovered. A bibliography and thematic index follow with a verse version of *The Elucidation* for those who want to have some sense of its poetry.

We are ever mindful of the prophecy within *The Elucidation,* and of our part in their transmission:

> *And if I tell you one by one—*
> *For he wishes to show each of you*
> *In what way the Grail served—*
> *For the services that it gave*
> *Were revealed to him by a good master.*
> *[This service] has been known but hidden.*
> *The good that it served will openly*
> *Be taught to all people.*[11]

May we wish you well as you set out on this quest into the heart of the Grail myth, hoping that you find within its terrain the hospitality and wisdom that will nourish the whole world.

1

THE STORY OF
THE GRAIL

The kindly abbot showed the Count around the abbey,
leading him to a tower where, some years before, hidden
within a wall full fourteen feet in depth, workmen had
discovered a hidden cupboard. . . . It contained a book . . .
PERCEFOREST, BOOK 1, CHAPTER 2

THE WORLD OF THE MEDIEVAL
GRAIL LEGENDS

ven within the Middle Ages the source and provenance of a good story could itself provoke an intriguing mystery, like the mysterious discovery of a book that is the source for the story of *Perceforest*, a little-known but mighty text that traces the prehistory of King Arthur's Britain.[1] Like the count in the epigraph above, we all want to know where the book or story came from and how it came into being.

With the Grail legends we do not have such an easy answer. Chrétien de Troyes's unfinished *Perceval, ou le Conte du Graal* (ca. 1180–1195) was the very first medieval account of the Grail legends, and it seems to have arisen without much warrant from a prior text. There are no mysteriously boarded-up cupboards from which this story leapt forth, although Chrétien does profoundly thank his patron, Count Philip of Flanders

(1143–1191), for giving him the book in which the Grail first appears: alas we have no more than Chrétien's word on this literary source.

Any origination legends for the Grail story are often introduced as a literary device that enables the storyteller to give an authoritative source for his telling.

To demonstrate how much credence we should place on wondrous literary antecedents found in any text, we only have to turn to the end of the *Quest of the Holy Grail,* dated to about 1220, which cheerfully tells us that

> so, when Bors had related the adventures of the Holy Grail just as he had beheld them, they were committed to writing and kept among the rolls at Salisbury. Master Walter Map got them from there to make his book of the Holy Grail for love of his lord King Henry, who ordered the story to be translated from Latin into French.[2]

Since Walter Map died before 1210—ten years *before* the *Quest* was written—this attribution is highly unlikely! But we do appreciate the imaginative audacity that makes Bors, the only Grail-questing knight to return to court, into the narrator or preserver of the text. As we will see in chapter 3, a similar literary device in found in *The Elucidation.*

Whenever we approach a text like *The Elucidation,* written so far away in time as the early thirteenth century, it is important to stop and assess its context, so that we do not try to read and judge it by contemporary values but have some sense of where it stands within the Grail mythos.

The first Grail story arose after the first two Crusades, when medieval Europe was profoundly impacted by what was seen, by Christians, as the plight of Palestine and the necessity to liberate the holy places of Christianity. Count Philip of Flanders might well have brought back any number of relics or books from the Holy Lands, as did his father, Thierry of Alsace, establishing the cult of the Holy Blood of Bruges in a church built between 1134 and 1157 to house the Holy Blood relic that had been given to him by the crusader king of Jerusalem, Baldwin III. Chrétien would have been most familiar with this relic and its veneration, including the religious processions in which the faithful participated, but to whom it would have been powerfully mysterious. The Holy Blood continues to be processed to the present time on Ascension Day in Bruges.

Relics, particularly those of the Passion of Christ, were highly prized, as the many pieces of the True Cross displayed in shrines all over Europe testify. Apocryphal biblical sources, including works like the fourth-century Greek text, the Gospel of Pilate, suggest a singular fascination for anyone who was present at the Passion, who might have handled these relics personally: this text provides us with the core of the British myth of Joseph of Arimathea, renowned for relinquishing his own tomb in order that it might receive the body of Christ. In the subsequent myth we learn how Joseph brings two cruets filled with water and blood, taken from the side of Christ, to Glastonbury.[3] However, it is not these two vessels of the Passion that are central to the Grail story, which rapidly transmogrify into a miraculous vessel, changing from a relic of the Passion, to the Eucharistic cup of the Last Supper in the later legends.

Chrétien certainly did not invent the word *graal:* it appears in a Venetian manuscript of the *Roman d'Alexandre* composed some ten years before Chrétien wrote the first part of his *Conte du Graal.* In line 618 appears a reference to a dish or platter, *Ersoir mangai o toi a ton graal,* or "this night partake from your grail."[4] Nor is this the only such early reference.

The *Libre de Gamaliel,*[5] written by Pere Pasqual, Bishop of Jaen, sometime before his death in 1300, is a version of the fragmentary Gospel of Gamaliel, dating from the fifth century or earlier, which brought together parts of two other surviving apocryphal gospels: the Acts of Pilate and the Gospel of Nicodemus.[6] These, as we shall see, provide another primary source for the Grail story that Robert de Boron and possibly Chrétien drew upon when composing their works. The *Libre,* composed in Catalan at the end of the thirteenth century and deriving from an earlier, now lost, text in Occitan, which purported to be written by Joseph of Arimathea, Nicodemus, and Gamaliel himself, brought together the narrative of the Passion and the life of Joseph of Arimathea in a form that was to be repeated with variants throughout the Middle Ages, particularly within the sphere of the Grail romances.

The single most significant aspect of Pasqual's translation is the use of the word *gresal,* which shares its origins with *gradalis,* Medieval Latin for "a flat, shallow dish." Having described the events of the Crucifixion and the healing of Longinus with the blood running down the lance, Pasqual adds:

> Then Joseph of Arimathea took a *gresal* in which he put the blood of Jesus Christ, and he kept the lance; and they all returned to the city, save for the relatives of the mother of Jesus Christ and the others who were with her, Saint John the Evangelist and Joseph of Arimathea.[7]

This is the only known instance so far discovered of a word that clearly shares its origin and meaning with the word *grail* being used by an ecclesiastical writer, nor can we be certain that the anonymous author of the original Gospel of Gamaliel used it; however, we can see that in using this word, Pasqual demonstrated an understanding of the connection between the vessel used to collect the blood of Christ and the story of the Grail. It bears witness to that fact that, as noted by Allen Cabaniss, Grail literature was in its turn beginning to affect the interpretation of the liturgy. To read more about the Grail's origins, see "The Grail before the Grail" by John Matthews.[8]

Within *The Elucidation,* we see two different, though related, forms of the Grail: the cups by which the mysterious Maidens of the Wells offer hospitality to travelers, and the Graal of the Grail procession, from which everyone seated at table receives a banquet. Both vessels bestow food and plenty, but neither is depicted as a sacramental chalice: rather, they are concerned more with communal feasting than with communion. In Chrétien's *Perceval,* a spear dripping blood, a *graal* (a kind of platter), and a *tailleor* (a casket or tabernacle) pass by in the procession witnessed by Perceval. Apart from the spear dripping with blood, which is a clear reference to the Lance of Longinus that pierced the side of Christ while he hung on the cross, the other vessels are nonsacramental.

The two vessels provide the same function, as we shall see in chapter 3, representing a tradition that is present under two forms in *The Elucidation.* Within this book, we will term these two appearances of the Grail, "the Faery Grail" and "the Holy Grail." These are not two different vessels but rather two appearances of the same Grail. The Faery Grail represents the earlier, folk tradition of the cup, which is entirely to do with the relationship of humans with faeries and the earth: we will explore its context and antecedents in chapters 4 and 6. The Holy Grail represents the Arthurian cup, which has taken on Christian coloration, and with which most people are more familiar.

LISTENING TO THE STORY

For those who are well educated it is no great matter to go to a shelf, take down a book, and read without a second thought. It is just something we can do. But for most people in the Middle Ages this was not a given. Only clerics read fluently and even they might not have read very easily at times.

Even for those who could read, words were usually read aloud or muttered under the breath, since few people could read absolutely silently—this was regarded as a rare skill in the Classical period. Plutarch tells us that Julius Caesar could do it. In the fifth century, Saint Augustine was astounded that Ambrose, Bishop of Milan, could read *tacite,* or silently.[9] In the Middle Ages, reading may have fallen into three categories: reading *in silentio* (not moving your lips), reading *sotto voce* (under your breath) when memorizing or as an aid to meditation, and reading in public (projecting your voice) such as monks did at mealtimes when reading martyrologies to their fellow monks while they ate in refectory.

In the *First Continuation,* the narrator (who is believed to have been Gauchier de Denains) gives us a little glimpse of what it was to be reciting the Grail story. Having got to the part of the story where Gawain kills an unknown knight and leaves him to be mourned by tender-hearted people at court, Gauchier says, "At this point, we should say a pater noster for the departed, and before I continue the story you can call for wine."[10] This unprecedented glimpse into the process of reading aloud in public to an assembly neatly combines the readers' suspension of disbelief with a wine-and-comfort break.

Reading, or the audition of a story, was not seen as a merely recreational activity, but was expected to elevate the mind and improve the soul. The improvement that might be drawn from a story—not quite the therapeutic self-help stories of our own time, but with more emphasis on the moral strength that might be derived—was praised by the knight, Geoffrey de La Tour Landry who, writing as the widowed father of three girls in the fourteenth century, announced that

> it is a good, noble and a faire thinge for a man or a woman to see and beholde hemself in the mirror of stories, the which hath been written by oure aunsetters [ancestors] forto they give us good ensaumples that they dide, to live and to eschewe the evil.[11]

It is to many such ancestral sources that we need to look in order to pursue our theme. Over the years, in our own writings, we have suggested some of the mythic themes and narratives that lead up to this first appearance of the Grail in literature, which include the wonderworking cauldrons of Celtic tradition, the Platonic and Hermetic vessels from which life spills into being in a variety of esoteric traditions, and early Hebrew and gnostic myths.[12] While none of these sources alone are responsible for the profusion of Grail texts that arise from 1180 to 1350, they demonstrate a continuously evolving understanding of the vessel of grace.

PERCEVAL, OR THE STORY OF THE GRAIL

Before we proceed to the story of *The Elucidation,* here is a brief outline of Chrétien's *Perceval, ou le Conte du Graal,* so that you have a baseline from which to operate. Composed by the poet Chrétien de Troyes in circa 1180, and left unfinished by him at his death, this text contains what may be called the foundational story of the Grail. With one or two exceptions, all of those texts written subsequently draw upon Chrétien's version, either elaborating or adding to it according to their own understanding. Debate still rages over Chrétien's own sources. He may have been the first to write down the events of the quest and, for good or ill, left his mark on all that followed, but the core of the story almost certainly did not originate with him.

Perceval is brought up by his mother in the forest where, in ignorance of the ways of the world, he happily hunts game with roughly made throwing spears. Then one day he meets three knights in the wood. Thinking them angels because of the brilliance of their armor, he questions them concerning their origin. Learning from them of Arthur's court and the institution of knighthood he vows to go there in search of adventure, and ignoring his mother's anguished request that he should remain with her, he rides off on an ancient nag to find his way in the world of chivalry. Before he departs, his mother gives him last-minute advice, but without the context for Perceval to fully comprehend it: always to give help to any women in distress, but take no more from them by way of reward than a kiss—though if one should also wish to give him a ring, let him take that also. Also, if he meets with anyone on the road he should not part from them without knowing their name, for those who conceal such things are of no good to anyone. She advises him to seek out worthy men and to pray whenever he sees a church.

Armed with this advice, the first person whom Perceval encounters along the way is a beautiful woman in a scarlet pavilion, whose ring he takes and whom he kisses, but against her will. He then proceeds to Arthur's court where he enters in time to witness the arrival of a red knight who spills wine in the queen's lap and carries off her golden cup. Still mindful of his mother's instructions Perceval pursues the knight, kills him, and returns the cup to the queen. He attempts to acquire the red knight's armor on the way by the simple expedient of pulling it off, until shown how to untie it from the body.

From the court he then sets out on further adventures, meeting with a nobleman who gives him training in chivalry and counsels him not to be talkative. Perceval arrives at the castle of the Fisher King, whom he finds presiding over a hall in which a nobleman lies upon a couch: this is the Fisher King who presents Perceval with a sword, which he accepts unthinkingly. A procession passes through the hall, led by a squire carrying a spear from which blood drips upon the ground, followed by two squires each carrying a ten-branched candlestick. After this comes a damsel carrying a "grail" that blazes with a light so bright that it puts out the light of the candles and of the stars.

Following her is another maiden carrying a talleors (variously translated as a dish, a bowl, a casket, or a tabernacle). Perceval watches all this but fails to ask its meaning. He retires for the night and on waking finds the castle deserted. Thinking the company has gone hunting, no sooner has he crossed the moat than the drawbridge descends. Perceval then encounters a damsel cradling the body of a knight in her arms and lamenting bitterly. She is his cousin and tells him that the Fisher King has long since received a wound in the thighs, which has never healed, though it might well have done so had Perceval asked about the procession of the Grail. She also informs him that the sword that he was given at the castle will break if he is not careful, but that in such a case he can restore it by dipping it in a lake near which its maker, the smith Trebuchet, dwells.

Returning to Arthur's court, Perceval is upbraided by a hideous damsel who appears from nowhere to mock him for so foolishly failing to ask the question that would have healed the king and made his country prosperous again. Determined to right this wrong, and to learn more of the mysterious Grail, Perceval sets forth again and after many adventures meets with a band of pilgrims who reproach him for bearing arms on Good Friday. Five years have passed since he left Arthur's court and in his eagerness to discover more about the Grail he has forgotten God. Perceval confesses his sins to a forest hermit and learns from him that his mother died of grief after he left her. He also learns that the Fisher King is the son of an older king who is served by a single host from the Grail that keeps him alive.

He feels great remorse but has still not rediscovered the Castle of the Grail. Here the story changes course to deal with the adventures of Gawain, whose quest is to free an imprisoned damsel. By way of reward, she shows him an underground crypt where the Sword of Judas Maccabeus is kept, now called the Sword of the Strange Girdle. Continuing his adventures, which at this point have nothing to do with the Grail, Gawain is ferried over a rise to a magical Castle of Maidens where many damsels are held prisoner awaiting the one who will deliver or marry them, thus putting an end to the enchantments of the place. Gawain undergoes many trials and tests in this place, including the adventure of the Perilous Bed, which is so designed that anyone who sets foot upon it or attempts to lie down is at once assailed by invisible opponents, who fling spears and fiery arrows at him, and is then attacked by a lion. But Gawain overcomes them all and is proclaimed lord of the castle. Gawain sends a messenger to Arthur's court to explain that he has been delayed and will return thither.

Here Chrétien's narrative breaks off, in midsentence, and there perhaps the story might have ended, but it exerted such a powerful hold over the imagination of medieval Europe that others felt drawn to try to solve the problems left by the unfinished poem. The surviving attempts to "finish" what Chrétien began are called the *Continuations*.

THE GRAIL'S DEVELOPMENT

In the *Second Continuation* of the Grail stories we hit upon a passage where the narrator's voice leaps up out of the story: it tells us that many would-be storytellers are going about who are twisting the good stories, distancing them from their sources and adding so many lies that the stories are killed and the good books are dishonored. And those who hear and listen to them don't know what good stories are; no, when those minstrels sit in their houses for the night and they get them to relate some adventure—unrhymed—they think they've heard the whole story; but they'll never hear it in their lives.[13]

This tells us that many hands were at work in the creation of the Grail legends, to the irritation of the author of the *Second Continuation!*

The beginnings of the Grail myth go back to the very dawn of human consciousness, and to a desire of human beings to make some kind of direct contact with the divine, to receive healing, and to make right the wrongs of the world. The Grail appears as a vessel of mercy that, through different spiritual agencies, offers an opportunity to those qualified by courage and belief to bring that mercy. Whether we look to ecstatic and initiatic drinks of the ancient mystery cults, or to the miraculous manna found by the Israelites in their desert wanderings, or to Celtic myths of cauldrons that provide plenty, wisdom, or eternal life, we find a collection of vessels from many cultures; each contains a substance that enabled those who discovered it to be healed, nourished, or experience divine communion.

But the story, as we know it best, can be said to begin with Chrétien. He it is who lays out the story of Perceval's adventure and gives us the first description of the mysterious vessel and its even more mysterious guardians in its medieval Arthurian context. The *Continuations* and preludes like *The Elucidation* extended it far beyond Chrétien's unfinished fable, but it was left to others to develop the growing mythology of the Grail. The twelfth-century Burgundian soldier-poet Robert de Boron first connected it to the mystery of the Passion by naming it the "Holy" Grail and specifying its links with the story of Christ and the sacred blood in a cycle of texts including the *Roman de l'Estoire dou Graal* of circa 1200, a *Merlin* and a *Joseph of Arimathea* and possibly a version of the Perceval story nowadays identified as the *Didot*

Perceval. In these he wrought a highly religious account of the quest for the Grail.[14]

A mere twelve years later the German poet Wolfram von Eschenbach (1117–1220) produced his *Parzival*, a vast, rambling poem that began by stating that Chrétien had got the story wrong and citing as his source a Provencal writer named Kyot, who in turn had gotten it from an even more mysterious personage named Flegetanis, an astrologer of possibly Jewish descent. For Wolfram, the Grail was a stone, an emerald fallen from the crown of the fallen angel Lucifer, which granted plenty to those who encountered it.[15] This was followed, soon after, by the massive compilation of stories nowadays known as *The Lancelot-Grail* (1215–1235), which brought the story firmly into the world of Arthurian literature, stretching the story backward to the time of Christ and forward to the end of the Arthurian dream with the death of the king himself.

This huge collection gathered up a prose *Perceval,* following but again extending Chrétien's version; then a prose rendering of the story of Lancelot, drawn in part from Chrétien's *Chevalier de la Charette* (Knight of the Cart); the *Quest del Saint Graal,* which picked up de Boron's Christianized account and elaborated it with an extensive theology; an *Estoire du Merlin,* which drew upon older stories of the great enchanter, and wove his story into the web of cross references; and a *Mort Artu* (Death of Arthur), which chronicled the events leading up to the destruction of the Round Table fellowship and Arthur's departure for Avalon.

It was this cycle that became the source for what is still arguably the greatest medieval Arthurian retelling—the *Morte d'Arthur* of Sir Thomas Malory, written between 1470 and 1480 and published five years later.[16] Malory stripped out most of the theology he found in the *Lancelot-Grail* and provided us with the most luminous and human account of the Grail quest, sought after by the Fellowship of the Round Table and achieved after long years of searching by three knights: the saintly Galahad, son of Lancelot; Perceval, now relegated to second place; and Bors de Ganis, Lancelot's cousin, who represented the simple man of faith.

This was all a far cry from Chrétien's simple tale of the poor knight who wandered into the mystery of the Grail, failed to understand it, and who was left with no certainty of achieving his quest in the unfinished ending of his final work. Through the sprawling edifice of the *Lancelot-Grail,* the winding and mysterious avenues of Wolfram's *Parzival,* and the glowing vision of Robert de Boron, the Grail story grew into a myth of stupendous proportions. Yet it never really moved far from the work of the poet who began it all—Chrétien de Troyes— and the anonymous author of *The Elucidation,* as well as those who wrote the *Continuations,* and who set themselves the daunting task of explicating the mystery.

Chrétien's own motivations for writing *Perceval* are intriguing. A clue to its writing may lie in Chrétien's own name, which is an unusual one for a man in France at this time, who would most often be named after a saint. The name of "Christian" is one that is most often given or taken by someone whose first religion was not Christian. If Chrétien had a Jewish background, then the central premise of the Grail feast as a meal in which all partake equally makes better sense. For Jews, the sight of a Christian communion, with congregants going up to an altar to have a piece of wafer placed upon their tongues, is utterly at odds with the Sabbath table around which everyone sits together and where stories, songs, and good food are shared.[17] Despite the accretion of Christian Passion narrative elements to the Grail story, this is not a story of a sacramental meal such as might be authorized by the church. The Grail legends remain extracurricular to Christianity, having no belonging or warrant in orthodox belief. They remain in a mythic terrain all their own where the imagination may find its own understandings in the secret places of the heart.

THE PROSE VERSION OF *THE ELUCIDATION*

We continue our storytelling with the following prose edition by Gareth Knight of *The Elucidation,* presenting it here first so that you can appreciate the flow of the story at the outset, just as if you too were a listener at the court. This story tells what happened before Chrétien's story of the Grail and the consequences that were experienced in the realms of Logres, the land of Arthur. The original poem in a line-by-line translation follows in the next chapter, where we supply a full commentary. The numbers in brackets here refer to the lines of the original poem. If you wish to read a verse translation, please see the appendix (pp. 294–310) where a version is provided.

[1] By noble command was this romance worthily begun. The most pleasing story ever told, that of the Graal, but about which we may not tell the secret, or sing of it, for that would allow the story to spread before all was revealed, and many who had not so transgressed would be sorry for that. So the wise thing is simply to leave it out and pass on. For if Master Blihis was right—the secret may not be told. As for myself, I hope to tell a story that is pleasing to the ear, for the seven guardians of it are those who rule over all good stories told throughout the world.

[17] Thus these writings will tell who the seven guardians are, what ends they seek and how. For one must listen to them before speaking true in the telling. For you have never heard the great noise and rumor truly related about how and why the rich country of Logres was destroyed. Many knew and spoke of it in times gone by. How the kingdom turned to loss, with the land dead and deserted and not worth two hazelnuts, when they lost the voices of the wells and the maidens that dwelt within them, by whom great things had been served.

[35] For none who went by the forest ways, be it by evening or morning, whether to eat or to drink, could now be seen to change his route to find one of the wells. Now no one was asking for a fine meal to please him, whatever his right might be. For once, it is my belief, one could not have asked for anything more beautiful than a damsel from a well, carrying a golden cup in her hand with meats and pies and bread, followed by another maiden bringing a white napkin and a dish of gold and silver on which was the meal that had been requested. For many

at the wells were well received, and if the meal did not please, others would be brought, as desired, with great joy and plenty. The maidens served gladly and all who traveled the forest ways came to the wells to eat.

[63]   King Amangons ruined it first. He did the evil in cowardice and wickedness that other hands repeated from the example he set. The king, who should have protected and guarded the maidens in peace, violated one of them, deflowered her against her will, took her golden cup, and made off with her to serve him ever after, from which much ill would befall. For the rest of the king's men followed their master's example. And now no maiden served a well or came forth for any man who came and sought to eat.

[80]   God, was there no honorable man then to be found? When they saw how their lord raped whatever maidens he found beautiful, the others raped them too and took their golden cups. Since then, nothing has come from the wells. No maiden, nor service.

[90]   Know this truly, sirs, for thus it happened that the country went into decline. The king came to a bad end and all the others with him, and so were many punished. The kingdom was laid waste, with no wells, nor tree in leaf. The meadows and flowers dried up, and all the brooks were diminished.

[99]   Nor from now could the court of the Rich Fisher be found, who had made the country resplendent with gold and silver, furs and rich brocaded silks, with meat and clothing, and gerfalcons, merlins, goshawks, sparrow hawks, and falcons. Once, when the court could be found, there were, throughout the country, riches and the great plenty I have named, so that all were amazed, both rich and poor, by the great wealth. But now all was lost from the kingdom of Logres that once had all the riches in the world.

[116]   In the time of King Arthur the Knights of the Round Table came, since when no greater knights have been seen, so worthy, strong, and

proud, so vigorous and hardy, wherever they are heard of and their adventures are told.

[124] They vowed to recover the wells and swore zealously to guard any maidens who came forth, along with the cups they carried. And to destroy the descendants of all who had done them harm, and any such remained who had stopped the maidens from coming out of the wells. When they could find one they killed or hanged him, gave alms and prayed God to restore the wells to such condition as they had been in before, with all the riches that came out of them as their service required. But no matter how they searched they were unable to find them. No voice could be heard nor maiden seen.

[145] But some found adventures, which made many marvel. They found maidens in the forest, more beautiful than had ever been seen, and well-armed knights on chargers wherever the maidens were, and who fought with any who wanted to take them away. Many a knight was killed for the maidens in many battles throughout the land. King Arthur would not recover from the loss of many good knights, but gained many fine ones from it, as the stories tell.

[161] The first knight overcome was Blihis Bleheris, beaten by Sir Gawain through the great prowess he had. He was thus sent mounted to give himself up to King Arthur, not to delay but go straight to the court of which he knew nothing, nor of the king. But he knew such good stories that no one could be wearied of hearing them told. And some of the court asked him about the maidens who rode through the forest, and to tell what he knew of them. And many who heard him stayed up many nights to hear and ask about the maidens and the knights.

[183] And he said to them, "You wonder greatly about the maidens you have seen going through the forest, and keep wanting to know in what country they were born. I will tell you truly. All were born of the maidens, and you will never see more beautiful, that King Amangons raped. A harm that will never be repaired as long as the world shall last."

[194] The Knights of the Round Table, by courtliness and honor, by prowess and by strength, swore to recover the wells by force.

[200] "I would like to tell you of all the squires, knights, and worthy men that one hears of, together with the maidens who wander this land. They must so wander until God allows the court to be found, from which great joy will come, and from which the country will be made resplendent. Adventures will come to those in the court who seek what has never been found in this country, nor ever told before."

[213] All were greatly pleased about what they had heard Blihis tell, after which it was not long before a great parliament was held of the good knights of the court, where each one had his place. Then they sought with great vigor the court of the Rich Fisher, who knew much magic and could change his appearance a hundred times. Some sought him in his one shape, others under other forms.

[225] Sir Gawain discovered the court in the time that Arthur reigned, and was at that court in truth. This will be told later, of the joy he found there by which all kingdoms were restored. But before him the first to find it was a young knight of very tender age, though none stronger or more courageous could be found in all the world. Thus, this young man of whom I speak, whose prowess surpassed by the height of a mountain all who were there, came to the Round Table. Thought at first to be of low degree, but then of noble character, he searched throughout the land to find the court and truly found it, as many of you know.

[247] It was Perceval de Galles who asked whom the Graal served, but when he saw it, did not ask about the lance and why it bled, nor of the sword of which one half the blade was missing, with the other resting on the dead body on the bier. Nor the way of the great vanishing. But I tell you that he certainly asked whose corpse it was that lay in the hall, and about the rich silver cross that was processed before all.

[261] For three hours, three times in the day, there was such lamentation that no man who heard it would be so hardy as not to be frightened.

Four censers and four rich candelabra hung at the corners of the bier when the service was done. Then all crying ceased and everyone vanished. The hall that was so great and wide remained empty and frightful; and a stream of blood ran from a vase where the lance stood, through a rich silver tube.

[276] Then all the people returned to the palace with the knights, and the finest meal that anyone had seen came out. The king, all adorned, had not been known before, came from a room, dressed in such noble attire that none had ever seen or known, all was so very rich. He had a fine ring on his finger, and his sleeves were tightly laced, while on his head was a gold circlet, and jewels worth a treasure on a belt with the buckle before. No such fine a living man could ever be found, and many might be puzzled if they had seen him dressed as a fisherman by day.

[297] As soon as the king was seated, bread was given out to all the knights seated at other tables and wine set before them in great gold and silver cups. After that the Graal was seen, with neither servant nor seneschal, coming through the door of a room, and many were henceforth served in rich golden dishes each worth a great treasure. The first was set before the king and then to all the others around that place, and never were such marvelous meals brought to them as the food that they were given.

[315] Then came a great marvel for which none could be prepared. But I cannot now speak of it, for Perceval must tell it further on in the middle of the tale. It would be a great villainy and shame to force such a good story beyond where it should go. When the good knights come, who will find the court three times, then may be heard, point by point and without invention, the truth about whom the wells served and who the knights were, and why the Graal was served, and of the lance that was bleeding.

[333] I will tell you the entire way of it, and why the sword was on the bier. I will tell you all omitting nothing. The mourning, the vanishing, all will be revealed to the people who hear it told, and how the story must unfold.

[339] Sirs, it is proven truly that the court was found seven times, as seven branches of the story, but if you do not see what this means, realize that the seven branches are really seven guardians. Each of the guardians will tell you a place where the court was found. This was not allowed to be told before but now I will reveal it in this writing, and name the seven guardians, omitting nothing. Thus, they will be well named and described, in order, from beginning to end.

[353] The seventh branch pleases best. It is about the lance with which Longinus struck the side of the King of Holy Majesty.

[357] The sixth, without fail, is the story of the great battle.

[359] The fifth, in turn, is of the anger and loss of Huden.

[361] The fourth possesses the stories of the Swan, for he was no coward, the dead knight in the skiff who first came to Glamorgan.

[365] The third is of the hawk, of which Castrars had great fear. And how Pecorins, the son of Amangons, carried the wound on his forehead all his life.

[370] The second is not found in the testimony of good storytellers, it is the story of the Great Lamentation, how Lancelot of the Lake came there when he lost his strength.

[375] And this is the last, that since I have started it with such great effort I have to tell you the rest without delay. It is the adventure of the Shield. There was never a better.

[381] These are the seven true stories that depend from the Graal.

[383] This adventure brought about the joy whereby the people multiplied (in numbers) after the great destruction. Through these adventures the court and the Graal were truly found. The kingdom was repopulated, the streams that had not flowed and the fountains that had sprung up but then dried were now running through the meadows. Then were the fields greatly flowering and the woods dressed in

green. On the day the court was found the forests became so great, so verdant, so fine, and well grown, that all marveled who traveled throughout the land.

[401] Then came a people full of ill will, who came forth from the wells but were not recognized. Then were castles and cities built, towns, boroughs, and strongholds too. The rich Castle of Maidens was built for the damsels, the Perilous Bridge and the great Castle of Pride, of nobility, and lordship, with an Order established for peers and rich courtiers, set up in vanity against the Round Table. It was well known by all that each had a lady love therein, and many led a fine life. There were 366 who maintained the castle, and each of these had 20 knights who were their leaders, to the number no less than 7600 plus 4 times 20 and 6 [=7,686]. Those who deny that such things happened know this, although through all the world they will not find any such today.

[429] They rode through the country and made war on King Arthur. Many went from the court of the good knight to put them to the test. This I know well, when they captured one, they held him captive without parole. King Arthur wanted to ravage and destroy the castle but all those who hated him attacked him at every point and engaged him in wars, so that none could go on the quest in a war that lasted for more than four years, as the stories tell us, as does he who writes this book.

[445] And if I tell you one by one, and wish to show each of you in what way the Grail served, and the services it gave, as revealed by the good master, as had been known but hidden, and of the good that it served openly, to be taught to all people as you have heard it from me. About King Arthur who, as I told you, spent four years in war against the people of his country, but that all came to an end so there was no man or neighbor who did not them do his will. Thus, by force or agreement, all truths were proved. But know that it was named, to the shame of them, and the honor of the king, as most people know. Then in that day the court was abandoned and the Rich Company went hunting in the forest, hawking and following the good rivers, just so are people

of good upbringing, some playing court to the ladies, others preparing themselves for it, to take their ease there in winter until summer.

[475] Now will Chrétien tell this moral tale that has been heard, which effort will not be neglected by Chrétien who strove and labored to put into verse the best story by order of the count, which is the story of the Graal, of which the count had the book, that it may be told in all royal courts. Let us pray he acquits himself well.

Immediately we can see how different *The Elucidation* is from Chrétien's *Perceval:* we have similar protagonists, but now we have acquired a prequel story that changes everything, opening windows onto other, older worlds. *The Elucidation* provides us with a whole sequence of stories, some of which are mentioned, others merely hinted at, while others open into a deeper myth from whose depths many roots are nourished. It is a story whose mysterious branches reach into every Grail text. Let us now follow them.

2

THE ELUCIDATION OF THE GRAIL

Translation and Annotated Analysis

I found a little child in a great leafy tree, sitting up high on a branch . . . he told me no secrets . . . [but] that I would encounter something very pleasing to me. And that was indeed true; what I saw and heard delighted me, for there are many wonders there.

SECOND CONTINUATION OF THE GRAIL

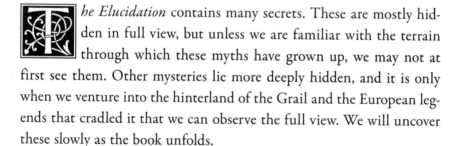he *Elucidation* contains many secrets. These are mostly hidden in full view, but unless we are familiar with the terrain through which these myths have grown up, we may not at first see them. Other mysteries lie more deeply hidden, and it is only when we venture into the hinterland of the Grail and the European legends that cradled it that we can observe the full view. We will uncover these slowly as the book unfolds.

A complete line-by-line translation, by Gareth Knight and Caitlín Matthews, of the thirteenth-century French poem of *The Elucidation* is given here in sections; following each section is a short commentary on matters that need some immediate explanation. We have chosen to explore the major themes of this story more deeply within the chapters that follow. We are responsible for providing the headings that divide this poem into sections for ease of study; these are not present in the original. If you wish to read a freer verse translation, one is provided as a reading version in the appendix.

THE PROLOGUE

By noble command,
Was the romance worthily begun
Of the most pleasing story there is:
Which is of the Graal, about which we may not
5   Tell the secret or even sing of it;
For that would reveal the story
Before all was said,
That some might be sorry for,
Who had not been at fault;
10   For the wisest thing is to leave it
And simply pass over it;
For if Master Blihis did not lie,
No one should tell the secret.

Explanation of the Prologue [lines 1–13]

The prologue tells us that this text was brought into being "by command," but by whom? Chrétien's *Perceval* was dedicated to Philip, Count of Flanders (1143–1191), whom he thanks profusely for providing him with the book he adapted into the "best tale ever told in a royal court." Scholars have linguistically analyzed *The Elucidation* and noted that the manuscript was copied in the Picard dialect, and that it was housed and discovered in Mons, but we cannot be more precise than this.

[6]* *Reveal the story:* this is the first warning about not revealing the story before its due time.

[8–9] *Some might be sorry for:* this proverb, which speaks of some innocent bearing the fault of others, echoes Chrétien's story of *Cligès*

---

*Numeration is specific to the lines commented upon.

where he speaks of "A person free of blame of guilt often pays for another's sins" (v. 558–59). This could be seen as a reference to the Atonement of Christ, who is believed to have redeemed the sin of humanity by his own death.

[12] Master Blihis: he also appears in *The Elucidation* at lines 161– 212, and at 449, as the guardian of the earliest levels of the Grail story. He is discussed in greater detail in chapter 3.

THE FOOD YOU MOST DESIRE [LINES 14–62]

Now listen to me, all and some,
15 And you will hear told a story
That is easy on the ear;
For the seven guardians of it will be
Those who rule throughout the world
All the good stories ever told,
20 As these writings will relate.
Who the seven guardians are,
Their acts, and what ends they will reach,
For you have never heard told
Nor truly related this story,
25 Of how there was great noise and rumor,
About how and why was destroyed
The rich country of Logres;
Many knew this in times gone by.
The kingdom turned to loss,
30 The land was dead and deserted,
So that it was not worth a pair of hazelnuts;
That they lost the voices of the wells
And the maidens that were within them;

For by them great things were served,
35 That no one who wandered the byways,
Be it in evening or morning,

Whether to drink or to eat,
Would need to change his route,
Save he who turned toward the wells.

40   He could request nothing
By way of fine food that pleased him
That would not be given to him,
Provided he asked reasonably.
Then would arise, as I understand,

45   A maiden from out of the well
He could not have asked for one more beautiful—
Carrying a golden cup in her hand,
With meats, pies, and bread.
Another maiden bringing in turn

50   A white napkin and dish
Of gold and silver in which was
The meal that had been asked for,
By whoever had come for the meal.
At the well, many were well received;

55   And if the meal did not please him,
Many others were brought him
[textual lacuna] . . . all as desired
With great joy and great plenty.
The maidens together

60   Served well and gladly
All those who traveled the ways
And came to the wells to eat.

Explanation of The Food You Most Desire [lines 14–62]

The service of their amazing roadside hospitality the Maidens of the Wells offer to all travelers takes place at a time long before King Arthur's court comes along. Later Grail texts, like the *Lancelot-Grail,* speak of "the food that is most desired" being provided to those seated at the Grail feast.

[17] Seven Guardians: these individuals are revealed in more

detail in lines 339–82. We discuss these more fully in chapter 3.

[27] Logres: Logres is the name used in the Arthurian tradition to denote the realm of England. It derives from the Welsh *Lloegr,* a term used since the tenth century in the *Armes Prydein,* a Welsh prophetic poem about the restoration of the Cymru, the native people of Britain. Logres is specifically used throughout the Arthurian legends, with Geoffrey of Monmouth deriving it from Locrinus, one of the descendants of Trojan survivor Brutus. It is clear that the French Arthurian writers found their own soundalike echo to Logres in Castle Orgueilleux or "Proud Castle."

[32] Voices of the Wells: these mysterious voices are also lost, as well as the maidens. For more about this potent image and to consider whether the voices and the maidens are recoverable see chapters 4 and 8. Here we must pause, however, because there is a possibility that "wells" might be "hills," because Old French *puis* is "wells" or "depths," but Old French *pui* is "hill, mountain, or height," as in the vertiginous hill city of Le Puy en Velay, in the Auvergne, France. So, the maidens might equally be "within the hills" (see chapter 4).

[34–62] Great things were served: the wells show us the first and most basic function of the Grail, the giving of hospitality. Importantly, it reveals how the Grail gives the food that is most desired (see chapters 4 and 6).

VIOLATING HOSPITALITY

> King Amangons violated it [their hospitality] first,
> Behaving wickedly and cowardly;
> 65 Afterward, other hands did likewise,
> By the example they took from him,
> From the king who should have protected them
> And kept and guarded them in peace.
> He violated one of the maidens,
> 70 And deflowered her against her will,
> And took away her golden cup,
> And carried it and the maiden off with him;

Then made it ever after to serve him.
From which much ill was to befall;

75   For thus no maiden served a well,
Nor came forth from a well,
Not for any man who came there
And requested to eat.
And all the rest [king's men] followed [his example].

80   God! Why was there not then seen
Any honorable vassal?
When they saw their lord,
Who raped the maidens,
Whichever he found most lovely.

85   All the others also raped them
And took away their golden cups.
Thus, since then, none came out of the wells,
Not one maiden served again;
Know this most truly.

Explanation of Violating Hospitality [lines 63–89]

[63] Amangons: this villainous king lives in the time long before King Arthur, and it is the action that causes the land to become a Wasteland. For more about him, and the other anti-Grail Kings see chapter 6.

[69] The rape by Amangons: this dual assault—on the bodies of the maidens as well as the stealing of their golden cups—is a primary loss for all who come after this time.

[82–86] The others also raped them: Amangons's rape and theft of the cups serves to encourage his men to do likewise.

THE WASTELAND AND THE RICH FISHER

90   Sir, thus it happened:
The country went into decline,
And the king came to a bad end

And all the others after him,

And so were many punished.

95   The kingdom was laid waste,

With no wells nor tree in leaf;

The meadows and the flowers dried up,

And the brooks diminished;

Nor could be found from now on

100   The court of the Rich Fisher

Which had been making the country resplendent

With gold and silver, furs, gray fur,

Rich brocaded silks,

And meat and clothing;

105   Of gerfalcons, merlins,

Goshawks, sparrow hawks, falcons.

Of old, when the court could be found,

There was throughout the country

Riches and great plenty,

110   Such as I have named,

That all be amazed,

Both poor and rich, by the wealth;

But now all was lost.

In the kingdom of Logres

115   Were all the riches of the world.

Explanation of The Wasteland and the Rich Fisher [lines 90–115]

[95] The Wasteland: the land is deprived of its moisture and greenness, leaving it dry and barren. There is no mention of the Wasteland in Chrétien's *Perceval;* however, since it is first instanced in the *First Continuation,* we can guess that *The Elucidation's* author was aware of it from there and has either created a wholly different causation for it, or is drawing upon another scenario entirely (see chapters 4 and 6).

[99] The court of the Rich Fisher: this court, from which derive all the good things of the country, is also lost.

[114] Logres: see note for line 27 above.

THE ROUND TABLE KNIGHTS
VOW VENGEANCE

The knights of the Table Round
Came in the time of King Arthur;
Since when no greater have been seen.
These were such good knights,
120   So worthy, strong, and proud,
So vigorous and hardy,
That as soon as they heard
The story of this adventure,
They vowed to recover the wells.
125   All swearing together
To zealously guard
The maidens who had come forth,
And the cups they carried,
And to destroy the lineage
130   Of those who had done them harm,
Who had stopped them
Coming out of the wells, whence they came no more.
When they [Arthur's knights] could take one [of
         Amangons's men],
They killed or hanged him.
135   They gave alms and prayed
To God that he restore as before
The wells in such condition
As they were at first;
And for the honor that they would pay them [the
         maidens]
140   They would request their service,
But no matter how they searched,
They were unable to find them;
Never voice could be heard
Nor maiden seen to emerge.

Explanation of The Round Table Knights
Vow Vengeance [lines 116–44]

[129] Vowing to destroy: as we will see below, there is a distinct problem about this particular vengeance quest that causes its trajectory to be deflected.

[136] To restore as before: the restoration of the wells is likewise troubling.

[143–44] Never voice could be heard: what was previously known cannot be restored as it originally was, and the quest has to go forward, not backward.

WHAT THEY FOUND IN THE FOREST

But such adventures they found,
Which made many marvel.
For in the forest they found maidens—
You could not ask for any more beautiful—
And with them knights,
150   Very well armed on their chargers,
There where the maidens were;
Together they fought with any
Who wanted to take them away;
Many a knight was killed.
155   Because of the maidens, I would say,
Were many battles fought throughout the land.
King Arthur could not help
Losing many a good knight,
But he gained many good ones from it,
160   As the stories will tell you.

The first knight captured
Was called Blihis Bleheris;
Beaten by Sir Gawain
Through the great prowess he had;

165　He was sent to give himself up to King Arthur.

He mounted up without delay.

To the court he surrendered himself.

By no one was he known,

Nor did the king recognize him,

170　But such good stories did he know

That no one could be wearied

On hearing them told.

Some of the court asked him

About the maidens who rode

175　Through the forest, since they [the court] had not been
　　　there.

So they quite rightly

Asked about them.

And to tell what he knew of them,

And many willingly heard him,

180　And stayed awake many nights,

Learning about the maidens, and knights,

To hear and question him.

He (Bleheris) said to them: "You wonder greatly

About the maidens you have seen

185　Going through that forest,

And you can't stop asking

In what country they were born.

I will tell you truly:

All of us are born of the maidens—

190　Never will there be more beautiful in the world—

That King Amangons raped.

That harm will never be

Made good as long as the world lasts."

The knights of the Table Round,

195　By courtliness and honor

And by prowess and strength,

Swore to recover by force

The wells—of the bachelors,

The knights and worthy men—

200 "I would like to tell you of all—

Those who travel together, [the knights guarding the
maidens]

And the maidens likewise

Who wander about this land,

Throughout the forests and the country—

205 That they must wander so,

Until God allows them to find

The court from which joy will come,

By which the country will be resplendent.

Your adventures will come

210 To those of the court who will seek,

What has never been found

In this country, nor told before."

Explanation of What They Found in
the Forest [lines 145–212]

[155–56] Battles because of the maidens: here we are given the hint that
the subsequent wars, which we hear about in lines 445–74, are consequent upon the jealous guardianship of the maidens.

[161–62] Blihis Bleheris: this knight is a storyteller who is able to
explain about the provenance of the maidens and knights that are found
in the forest (see chapter 3 for a full discussion).

[189] All of us are born of the maidens: Blihis reveals that his company are all descended from the Maidens of the Wells and born of the
rape of Amangons and his men. This means that the Round Table
knights cannot kill the descendants of Amangons without killing the
children of the maidens!

[201–8] The wandering: Blihis and his companion knights and
maidens are fated to wander and not settle anywhere until the Court of
Joy is found (see chapter 7).

SEEKING THE COURT OF THE RICH FISHER

Great gladness they all made
About what they had heard him relate.
215   No great time elapsed
Before they held a great parliament
Of the good knights of the court,
Where each one had his place;
They sought with great vigor
220   The court of the Rich Fisher
Who knew much magic
And could change his appearance—
Some sought him in one shape,
While others under another form.
225   Sir Gawain found it [the court]
In the time that Arthur reigned,
And was at the court, in truth.
This will be told later on—
The joy that he found there,
230   By which all the kingdoms were restored.

But the first to find it before him
Was a young knight
Of very tender age;
But none more strong or more courageous
235   Could be found in all the world.
There came then to the Table Round
The young man of whom I speak,
Whose prowess surpassed
All those who were or are
240   By the height of a mountain.
Thought at first of low degree,
Then of noble character,
He searched throughout the land,

Among those who sought the court.
245 It is he who found it, truly,
As many of you know:
It was Perceval the Welshman.

For he asked who the Graal
Served, but did not ask
250 About the lance, why it bled
When he saw it, nor of the sword,
Of which half the blade was missing,
And the other lying on the bier
On the dead body; nor the manner
255 Of the great vanishing.
But I tell you in no uncertain terms,
That he asked whose was
The corpse in the hall,
And about the rich silver cross
260 That was processed before all.
For three hours three times in the day
There was therein such lamentation
That no man would be so hardy
Not to be frightened when he heard it.

265 There hung four censers
And four rich candelabra
At the corners of the bier,
When the service was done.
Then all crying ceased,
270 When everyone vanished.
The hall that was so great and wide
Remained empty and frightful;
And the stream of blood ran
From a vase where the lance was,
275 Through the rich silver tube.
Then all the people returned

To the palace, and the knights.
Then were the finest meals
That anyone had known.

280   Then there came out, all adorned,
The king who had not been known;
Coming dressed from a room
In such very noble attire
That none had ever seen or known

285   The robe nor the adornment,
All so very rich;
He had a very fine ring on his finger,
And his sleeves tightly laced,
And on his head a gold circlet—

290   The stones were worth a treasure—
A belt with the buckle before.
No such a fine living man
Could anyone find.
Many might be puzzled by this

295   If they had seen him by day
Dressed as a fisherman.
As soon as the king was seated,
Then was seen at other tables
The knights who were all seated.

300   Then the bread was given to them all,
And the wine set before them
In great gold and silver cups.

Afterward, the Graal was seen,
Without servant or seneschal,

305   Coming through the door of a room
And many were properly served
In rich golden dishes,
Each worth a great treasure.
The first course was set

310   Before the king, and then served
       To all the others around in that place;
       And never were such marvelous
       Meals as were taken to them,
       And the food that they were given.
315   Then came the great marvel,
       For which none could prepare.
       But I cannot now speak of it,
       For Perceval himself must tell it
       Further on in the middle of the tale.
320   It is a great villainy and shame
       To dismember such a good story
       Before it has run its road.

       When the good knights will come,
       Who found the court three times,
325   Then may be heard,
       Point by point, without making anything up,
       The truth of whom the wells served,
       And who the knights were,
       And why the Graal served,
330   And of the lance that was bleeding.
       I will tell you the entire way of it
       And why there was on the bier
       The sword. I will tell you everything,
       And will omit nothing—
335   The mourning, the vanishing—
       All will be revealed to the people,
       Who will thus hear it told,
       How this story will unfold

Explanation of Seeking the Court of the Rich Fisher [lines 213–338]

[216–20] The oath of the knights of the Table Round: this second oath to find the court of the Rich Fisher, replaces the Round Table knights' first

one [line 124] to wreak vengeance on the descendants of Amangons and his men. They sensibly decide to concentrate on rediscovering the court of the Rich Fisher instead.

[220] The Rich Fisher: this figure, known to us from *Perceval* as the Fisher King, from the confusion between the French of *pécher* ("to sin") and *pêcher* ("to fish"). It is to his castle that Perceval arrives and where he sees the Grail procession (see chapter 6 for more about this mysterious figure).

[225] Sir Gawain: Gawain appears in *Perceval* as the senior and mentoring knight who guides Perceval. As a chief protagonist in the mysteries of the Goddess, Gawain is first on the scene in a variety of quests regarding ladies and their rescue, so it is no surprise to discover that he finds the court.

[228] This will be told later on: unfortunately, it is not.

[231–32] The young knight: this is Perceval himself, also called "the Welshman."

[248–55] The questions: Perceval is famed for not asking about the Grail procession in Chrétien's story, but here he asks questions about some things, but fails to ask about others.

[252] The broken sword: the theme of the broken sword appears in *Perceval* (line 3670) where Perceval is told by his female cousin not to rely upon his sword, which is likely to break in pieces; if it does, she advises him to go to Trebuchet, a smith who lives at Cotoattre in the middle of a lake (identified as Scottewatre, the medieval name of the Firth of Forth). In the *Gerbert de Montreuil Continuation*, Perceval is told that the smith who mends that particular sword will die when it is reforged,[1] which is why his gate is guarded by serpents.

[258] The corpse in the hall: in *Peredur*, the Welsh *Perceval*, Peredur's quest for the Grail begins with the sight of a head in the dish, which turns out to be his cousin, for whom he vows a vengeance quest. The unnamed corpse with the cross that is processed before it in *The Elucidation* remains unknown. The scene resembles a Good Friday liturgy except that the lamentation attending it happens three times a day for three hours. In the Orthodox liturgies, an effigy of Christ's deposed body is lamented.

[273] The stream of blood: the bloody dripping spear is based upon

the Lance of Longinus, the Roman soldier who pieced the side of Christ to establish his death on the cross. This relic was held by the kings of Jerusalem and passed on to Constantinople until its fall. Sultan Bayezid II gifted it to Pope Innocent VII in 1492, and it has remained since in the Vatican. Several other fragments of the lance exist, including one at Vienna (see chapter 3).

[276–79] After the procession: everyone stops lamenting and sits down to dine.

[280–96] The coming of the Rich Fisher: the Rich Fisher is one who is kingly by night and by day a fisherman. This sounds like a rationalization of the Fisher/Sinner King.

[303–5] The Graal was seen: it comes without attendants and after it has appeared, many are served in golden dishes. The wording makes it unclear whether the food comes from the Graal itself, but the implication seems to make this possible. This is precisely what the Grail does in Wolfram's *Parzival,* and other texts, serving the food that is most desired without a servitor.

[317–22] But I cannot speak of it: whatever revelations are to be given, only Perceval can speak of them, and we receive another warning about precluding the story by telling it here.

[323] When the good knights come: not one but three knights find the court.

[331] I will tell the entire way of it: unfortunately this pleasant promise is not borne out in *The Elucidation,* and is one of the reasons why its title is so ironic and frustrating.

[336–38] All will be revealed to the people: this promise, too, seems not to be fulfilled, but it is the first that makes clear that the Grail secrets are intended to be somehow revealed to everyone, not just to specially qualified people.

THE SEVEN BRANCHES OF THE STORY

Sir, it is truly proven

340   That the court was found seven times

As seven branches of the story;
But you do not know what this means!
Know that the seven branches
Are really the seven guardians;
345 Each one of the guardians will tell
The place where the court was found;
Before, it was not allowed to be told;
Now I reveal it in this writing
And name the seven guardians;
350 And will omit nothing from it,
Thus they will be well named and described,
All in order, from beginning to end:

The seventh branch that pleases best,
It is all about the lance
355 With which Longinus struck the side
Of the King of Holy Majesty.
And the sixth, without fail, is
About the great strife of the toil.
The fifth I will tell you in turn:
360 The anger and loss of Huden.
The Stories of the Swan are the fourth,
For he was no coward,
The dead knight in the skiff,
Who first came to Glamorgan.
365 The next is the third, of the hawk
370 The second is not found
In the testimony of good storytellers:
It is the Story of the Great Lamentation,
How Lancelot of the Lake came
To the point where he lost his strength.
375 And finally, there is the last story:
Since I have started this with great effort,
I have to tell you all of it—

You'll not hear me extenuate—

It is the Adventure of the Shield:

380   There was never a better.

These are the seven genuine stories

Which proceed from the Graal.

Explanations of The Seven Branches of the Story [lines 339–82]

The naming of most of the seven branches of the story, dealt with in reverse order, is very frustrating for the Grail scholar who would like to know a lot more about how these stories were shaped. Unfortunately, we do not have a lot of information about the ones hinted at here (see chapter 3 for a fuller explanation of the parts of the stories that we do know).

[340] The court found seven times: the court of the Rich Fisher is accessed seven times: the implication being that this happens in each of the subsequent stories. Early in line 323, we are told that it is found three times.

[343–45] The seven story branches are the seven guardians: the word *branch* is used here in a literary way, as a bough upon a larger tree of the story. Each of the branches is also one of the guardians of the whole Grail myth. The only other Grail text to use this manner of division is *Perlesvaus.*

[353] The seventh branch: the story of Longinus and his spear as the relic of the Passion is told in several stories, including in the *Suite du Merlin.* The spear is often described and is shown to have catastrophic effect upon the fertility of the land. The soldier is unnamed in the gospels, but called Longinus in the apocryphal Gospel of Nicodemus, which is appended to the Acts of Pilate.

[358] The great strife of the toil: this may refer to the Battle of Camlann, which is described in all British accounts as a *gueith,* or strife/toil, the British name for civil war. This is the nearest we come in Arthurian literature to the implication that the mortal wound that Arthur receives at this battle and that causes him to retire to Avalon to be healed, puts him in the category of a Wounded King!

[360] *Huden:* Huden is known as Tristan's dog, sometimes also called Houdenc or Housdenc. When Arthur and his men enter the castle of Brandelis, a brachet (a hunting dog) runs into the hall and Kay begs it as a gift, to be a companion to Huden. It has been suggested that this may be connected to an episode in the *Prose Lancelot* where Gawain's brother, Gaheriet, fights against a Guidan who chooses to drown himself rather than be captured.

[361] *The Stories of the Swan:* while some translations refer to the "stories of heaven" this line might be better translated as "the stories of the swan" since it clearly deals with an incident from the *Pseudo-Wauchier Continuation* in which a sleepless Arthur is watchful by the sea and sees a skiff brought to shore by a swan. In it lies a dead knight with a lance. A letter with the body says that the corpse should remain in the hall and that whoever drew out the lance would be as dishonored as the cowardly Guerrehes who neglected to strike the murderer in the same part of the body as the corpse was killed. Guerrehes's dishonor is to become a weaver if he refuses to return within the year and kill the Little Knight (see chapter 3). Later, while the corpse is still lying unburied, Guerrehes accidentally touches the lance that slips from the body. He returns and kills the Little Knight, and a maiden who recognizes the spear blade tells him his duty is fulfilled. Knight and maiden return in a swan-drawn skiff to Arthur's court. This takes place at either Carlion or Glamorgan, according to variant texts.[2] Swan-knight stories also feature in Wolfram's *Parzival* and in the anonymous *Sone de Nansay,* most notably in *Lohengrin,* the son of Parsifal's half brother, Feirefiz, and the Maiden of the Grail (see *Temples of the Grail* by John Matthews and Gareth Knight).[3]

[365] *The hawk of which Castrars had great fear:* this is the only reference anywhere to Amangons's son, Castrars, who is not otherwise known. While there are many tales about hawks, none seems resonant with our story.

[370–73] *Story of the Great Lamentation:* there are many incidents that could stand here. Lancelot's loss of valor in the *Prose Lancelot* happens at a tournament that Guinevere calls. In the *Queste del San Graal,* he falls into a trance for twenty-four hours, while in *Lanzelet,* he enters into the enchanter Mabuz's "Schâtel le mort" (Deathly Castle), in which everyone loses their valor. In terms of the Grail legend, Lancelot's worst defeats come when he is bested by his son, and when he attempts to assist in the Grail Chapel in *Queste del San Graal.* His own abduction by a faery woman is described both in the *Prose Lancelot* and in *Lanzelet,* where his mother is called "a queen of great sorrow." Possibly this is a reference to Chrétien's own story, *The Knight of the Cart,* since here too he loses face by hesitating before mounting the cart used to transport criminals in order to rescue Guinevere.

[379] *Adventure of the Shield:* nearly every Arthurian legend seems to have a Shield story but the one intended here must be the White Shield with the Red Cross, which appears in an incident from *Gerbert de Montreuil's Continuation.* In his wanderings, Perceval comes to a castle where a mounted maiden enters carrying this shield in which was embedded a piece of the Holy Cross. It had been made by "two Chaldeans" in such a way that no one would be able to find the Grail or the Bleeding Lance unless he was the first to remove it from the maiden's neck. Only in a state of grace could any man take it, says the inscription. Perceval, in helping her to dismount, takes it from her neck. Immediately the maiden casts herself to the ground in front of him, recognizing him as the rightful Grail winner. In the fifteenth-century *Morte d'Arthur* this story is transferred to Galahad who receives from the heathen king, Evelake, a white shield with a red cross upon it.

THE JOY

This adventure brought about
The Joy whereby the people multiplied
385   After the great destruction.
Through these [adventures] were
The court and the Graal truly found,
How the kingdom was repopulated,
So that the streams that had not flowed,

390   And the fountains that had sprang up—
395   On the day that the court was found,
      Where, throughout all the land,
      The forests became so great and so flowering,
      And so fine and well grown,
      That all marvelled at it
400   Who traveled through the land.

Expanation of The Joy
[lines 383–400]

The Joy: the Joy of the Court is an episode that happens in Chrétien's *Erec and Enid,* and refers to an oppressive incident where an evil custom is overturned. The Joy in *The Elucidation* refers specifically to the finding of the court of the Rich Fisher, which accesses the healing of the Grail, enabling the repopulation of the land and the reflux of the waters (see chapter 7).

[383] This adventure: The text says "this adventure brought about the joy," but doesn't specify which of the preceding seven adventures is meant. If it is merely the last one, as the text implies, then it would be that of the Shield.

THE RICH COMPANY

      Then there came in turn a people
      Full of great ill will,
      Who came forth from the wells
      But they were not known.
405   They built castles and cities,
      Towns, boroughs, and strongholds,
      And built for the damsels
      The rich Castle of Maidens;
      They made the Perilous Bridge too,
410   And the great Castle of Pride.
      For nobility and lordship,

They created an order for themselves
Of the Peers of the Rich Company,
In their great pride set up
415 Against the Table Round;
It was well known by everyone.

Therein each had his lady love;
Many thus led a fine life.
There were three hundred and sixty-six
420 Who maintained the castle,
And each one of these had
Twenty knights, whose leaders they were,
To the number no less than:
Seven thousand, six hundred,
425 Plus four times twenty and six.
To deny that these things happened,
Know this, through all the world,
That you won't find any such today.
They rode through this country
430 And made war on King Arthur.

From the court, the good knight
Set off to put them to the test;
I know that, once they captured one, [of Arthur's men]
That they held him captive without parole.
435 King Arthur wanted to go there,
To destroy and ravage the castle;
But all those who hated him
Attacked him at every point,
And kept him engaged in the wars,
440 So none could go on quest
When the warfare was so great,
That lasted more than four years,
As the stories tell us;
As does he who wrote this book.

Explanation of The Rich Company [lines 401–44]

[401] *The knights of the Rich Company:* these knights seem to come forth from the wells after the Finding of the Courts of Joy has healed the Wasteland. It would appear that the original service of the maidens is not reinstituted, but instead, all the greed and violence that caused their service to stop originally is somehow channeled into the Peers of the Rich Company who use the bounty of the land to create their own proud kingdom. Instead of the simple hospitality of the wells, this company make great cities and set themselves up against the Round Table knights.

[408] *The Castle of Maidens:* Castellum Puellarum is the location of one of Arthur's twelve battles, a name associated closely with Edinburgh. In the *Second Continuation,* the castle is inhabited by a lady and her hundred maidens who test those who go on quest. Perceval stops there but wakes on the bare hillside the next day. In the *Queste del San Graal,* the Castle of Maidens is the location where seven brothers have killed the castle's original owner, captured his daughter, and brought any passing maiden to be a sexual slave of the brothers. Galahad eventually overthrows them and ends this custom (see chapter 8).

[409] *The Perilous Bridge:* in the *Second Continuation,* this half-finished bridge leads to the Castle Orgueilleux. When Perceval attempts to cross it and reaches the other side, it immediately turns 180 degrees and keeps him riding over it. Also, in the *Vulgate Lancelot,* the Perilous Bridge leads to the realm of Gorre, a name sometimes applied to the otherworld, since Gorre is a corruption of the early French *voire,* or glass—as in "the Isle of Glass" or Glastonbury. The bridge Lancelot crosses over to reach Guinevere and rescue her in Chrétien's *Chevalier de la Charette* is known as the Sword Bridge.

[410] *The Castle of Pride:* in the *First Continuation,* 566 knights and their lady loves are bespelled within the Castle Orgueilleux. While Gawain attempts to release them, Perceval wanders about for four years until he comes upon a Good Friday procession.

[425] *The Peers of the Rich Company:* these total 7,686 persons.

[435] *King Arthur wanted to go there:* Arthur is often depicted in later medieval legend as a *roi fainéant,* or lackadaisical king, who stays at

home while his knights go on quest on his behalf, but in this story, he is simply too busy to do either, since the wars keep him occupied.

[439–40] *None could go on quest because of the wars:* the suspension of improving works of rescue, charity, or adventure all play second best to the onslaught of war.

[444] *As does he who wrote this book:* is the narrator merely confirming this point or speaking from another source of testimony?

THE FOUR YEARS WAR

445   And if I tell you one by one—
For he wishes to show each of you
In what way the Grail served—
For the services that it gave
Were revealed to him by a good master.

450   [This service] has been known but hidden.
The good that it served will openly
Be taught to all people.
Just as you have heard from me

455   About King Arthur, as I told you:
That he had four years of war
Against the people of his country;
But all that drew to an end,
There was not man or neighbor
Who did not do his will.

460   This known, by force or by agreement,
Thus, were truths proved;
But know that it was named
To the shame of them and the honor
Of the king, as most people know.

465   Then was in that day abandoned
The court, and the Rich Company
Went hunting in the forest,

Those who wanted to hawk
Following the good rivers.
470   Just so are the people of good upbringing:
Some paying court to the ladies,
Others preparing to do so.
And they took their ease there
Throughout winter until summer.

Explanation of The Four Years War [lines 445–74]

The earliest known information from any source about Arthur is that he fought twelve battles. Here the four years of war pay off and restore Arthur's authority once more.

[449] *Revealed by a good master:* the storyteller of *The Elucidation* once more asserts his intention to tell us all, because he himself has been well instructed by a good teacher. While this latter person is not named, two conclusions can be drawn: he either means the book that was given by Philip Count of Flanders, or else by Blihis.

[463–64] *To the shame of them:* those who did not submit willingly to Arthur are named and shamed.

[465] *The abandoned court:* it is not clear which court is abandoned; the story has three courts: that of the Rich Fisher or the Court of Joy; the court of Arthur; and the court of the Rich Company. The context seems to denote that of the Rich Company, who break off hostilities with Arthur and go off into the forest to overwinter in a careless way.

ENVOI

475   Now will Chrétien tell
This moral tale, that has been heard,
Which effort won't be wasted,
For Chrétien strove and labored
To put into verse the best story,
480   By order of the count,

That it will be told in royal courts.
Which is the story of the Graal,
The book of which he was given by the count.
Pray that he acquits himself well!

Explanation of Envoi [lines 475–84]

The words about Chrétien not wasting his labor are directly taken from the prologue of Chrétien's *Perceval:* "So, Chrétien will not be wasting his efforts as he labors and strives, on the count's orders, to tell in verse the best story ever told in a royal court, that is the story of the Graal, the book of which was given to him by the count. Hear how he acquits himself!"[4]

[475–76] Now will Chrétien tell: in the first two lines of the envoi, the tenses mix, saying that *we will* hear Chrétien tell the moral tale *that has been heard.* Of course, we must remember that *The Elucidation* is supposed to be a prequel to *Perceval.*

We now turn to the narrator of this text to look at the sources of the story and the narrator, Master Blihis and the seven guardians of the story, by whose quests and witness the Grail reveals itself.

3

THE STORYTELLER
AND SEVEN CLOAKS
OF THE STORY

*The storytellers such as Blihis are the wandering "voices
of the wells," for they tell the story of the Grail's secret—
neither in prose nor verse, as the text says, but in their
own lives. They are the true memory of the Grail, these
wanderers, telling no one its secrets but implanting the
seeds of the quest in the hearts of their hearers.*

CAITLÍN MATTHEWS, *THE VOICES OF THE WELLS*

THE NARRATOR OF *THE ELUCIDATION*

Throughout the realms of England, Wales, France, and the
Low Countries, in the twelfth century and before, the wandering storyteller plied his way between courts, reciting and
performing tales and story sequences. These stories were a mixture of
creative invention, of heroic *gestes,* and folktales, and the storyteller a
welcome visitor who regaled hearers through many a dark night. The
nature of storytellers' influence, in the estimation of *The Elucidation's*
narrator, was considerable.

> *For the seven guardians of the [Elucidation's] story
> will be*

> *Those who rule throughout the world*
> *All the good stories ever told.*[1]

The nearest we will get to seeing those who told this story can perhaps be seen on the opening page of the Mons manuscript of *The Elucidation,* which shows a faint rectangular miniature at the top of the page: on the left, a knight on horseback approaches a crowned figure, whom we must see as Arthur; beside him, to his left, are seven seated figures—the seven guardians of the story!

Some storytellers were fixtures at the courts of Europe, which is where the Grail legends were first written down, moving from oral recitation into written lore.[2] Chrétien was one of these with a kind patron who enabled him to sustain his impressive output of tales. In *The Elucidation* we find immediate traces of a conscious imitation of Chrétien. Not only is the verse form the same, but parts of *Perceval* have been lifted and reinserted at either end of the poem.

Because of this we are beguiled into asking, could the narrator possibly have been Chrétien himself? The last ten lines speak of him in the third person and the implication may seem that way, but we know that it cannot be Chrétien. Internal evidence of certain themes and narratives in *The Elucidation* show us that whoever the narrator was, he or she was aware of the *First Continuation* of the Perceval story, penned by someone who wrote *after* Chrétien's death.

Most strikingly, it is the description of the Wasteland, which only appears first in the *First Continuation* that settles this question. If we compare *The Elucidation*'s description of the Wasteland and its healing with that of the *First Continuation,* we can immediately see the resonances. Here the Wasteland is caused:

> *The kingdom was laid waste*
> *With no wells nor tree in leaf;*
> *The meadows and the flowers dried up*
> *And the brooks diminished.*[3]

And here is its healing:

> *The court and the Graal truly found,*
> *How the kingdom was repopulated*
> *So that the streams that had not flowed*
> *And the fountains that had sprang up*
> *But then had dried up*
> *Were now running through the meadows;*
> *Then were the fields lush with green*
> *And the woods once more leafy*
> *On the day that the court was found,*
> *Where throughout all the land*
> *The forests became so great and so flowering.*[4]

And now compare the *First Continuation*'s description of the Wasteland's healing:

> *Never have eyes beheld*
> *A land so richly flourishing*
> *In wood, water, and meadowland.*
> *In this way was the wasted land*
> *Which had been completely empty of all good things*
> *The night before, as God so willed,*
> *During that night—as was fitting—*
> *Had restored the rivers to their courses,*
> *And all the woods, to my best knowledge,*
> *Restored to greenness once again,*
> *And all because Gawain had asked*
> *About why the lance bled.*[5]

We can see that the waters flow once again, the trees are green with leaf, and the land is repopulated. So, since the *First Continuation* postdates Chrétien's death, it cannot be he who is the author.

The voice of the narrator telling us the story of *The Elucidation* is persuasively anonymous. But while the text leaves the storyteller's identity very loose indeed, there is another, a subnarrator, who is not only the source for a key part of the story, but is himself part of it: Blihos or Blihis Bleheris, the knight who is captured by Sir Gawain in the course of the story.

THE TALE OF MASTER BLEHERIS

Master Blihis, Blihos, or Blihis Bleheris, as he is called in full, is the source of *The Elucidation*'s alternative Grail myth, appearing as a character in his own story. After his capture by Gawain he relates a portion of the backstory that is as yet unknown to King Arthur's court. The Round Table knights, who hear the initial myth of the Maidens of the Wells, their hospitality, and their rape by Amangons, vow a vengeance quest and set out to look for the descendants of Amangons's men,

> *to destroy the lineage*
> *Of all who had done them [the Maidens] harm.*[6]

And by their

> *courtliness and honor,*
> *And by prowess and strength*
> *Swore to recover by force*
> *The wells . . .*[7]

After many skirmishes on this quest, the Round Table knights come across a party of knights protecting the maidens who travel with them, in the middle of the forest. The first knight is captured by Gawain and sent to surrender himself to King Arthur—a trusting, chivalric self-surrender that is found throughout the Arthurian legends whereby the captured or defeated knight gives his parole to return to the court of his capturer and there to submit to the overlord.

Only when this first captive knight, Blihis, tells his story does understanding finally shatter the illusion of any possible vengeance on the part of the Round Table knights. Blihis relates that his fellow knights and sister maidens are *all* descended from King Amangons and his men, certainly, but—and here we draw in our breath—they are *equally descended* from the Maidens of the Wells! The Round Table knights' oath of vengeance falls hollow—for to kill Amangons's lineage is also to kill the descendents of the maidens who once gave the hospitality of the wells!

Blihis finally tells the Round Table knights that he and his brothers and sisters are fated to wander about the land, in the wild places, until God allows them to find

> *the court from which joy will come,*
> *By which the country will be resplendent.*[8]

Behind this statement lies an eternity of generations uncounted: the time scale between Amangons's violation and the time of Arthur is not specified. As in many a folk story, Blihis and his relatives have nowhere to lay their heads, ever moving on, unsettling in their wanderings until this ultimate quest is achieved. We will speak further of this court in chapter 8, but let us consider for a moment: how long has this Court of Joy been sought? Why is it that Blihis and his company cannot find it?

Just as if they were people from the past, sprung out of an ancient and ancestral story, Blihis and his kind cannot find what they seek: they need the help of the Round Table knights to open the way. Blihis is the ancestral myth's ambassador: unable to find the court himself, he is still able to tell the story that paves the way to a finding, as the central section of *The Elucidation* relates in lines 213–338.

Stories open up blocked entrances to lost places and conditions, stirring the imagination so that those who do have the power to go there—maybe even those from later generations—can find the stamina and the method from their own deeper resources. The Arthurian court cannot get enough of Blihis's stories, as the text tells us: not only can no one become tired of hearing them, but they keep pestering him to tell them more, with some knights even staying up all night to feast on the promise of the quest that lies within his words.[9]

The sons and daughters of perpetrators and victims, down how many generations we don't know, cannot always retrace the steps that lead to healing or restoration: they are impossibly conflicted and generationally entangled with what has taken place. They seek unceasingly, unable to settle or make homes for themselves, but keep moving on to the next place, in the hope that something will break the bonds, cancel the shame, and make everything well again. We see this legacy today in the aftermath of traumatic tales of war, genocide, and vengeance that have afflicted the world, where even the grandchildren and great-grandchildren of perpetrators and victims are unable to move on or find healing. Their personal and emotional resources have often been depleted to such an extent that they need the help of others to find the way.[10]

Almost as soon as Blihis halts his telling, the Round Table knights get together and make a fresh oath that they will seek for the court of the Rich Fisher, which Blihis and his company have themselves been unable to discover. The story has done its work and now the finding of the court is in other hands.

BLEHERIS AND HIS ORIGINS

Who is Blihis Bleheris and where does he come from? Echoes of his name appear elsewhere as Sir Bliobleheris in Chrétien's *Erec and Enide* who sits next to "Tristan who never laughed" in a lineup of Arthur's knights, while in the *Suite du Merlin* a knight called Blios is the jealous lover of the lady Seneheut. But these have a different character to the Blihis of this story.

In the *First Continuation,* at the great tournament, a knight called Bleheris is felled by Perceval, but we hear no more of him. Since the *First Continuation* seems to have been the major influence upon *The Elucidation* we might look no further than here for our source, perhaps? The jousting is a conventional knockout tournament, with the odd melée, but it is actually part of the siege of the Proud Castle, held by the mysterious Rich Company (see chapter 8).

Thomas D'Angleterre in his *Roman de Tristan* tells us that the source of his book is none other than Bleheris or Breri,

> *Who knew the deeds and the tales*
> *Of all the kings, of all the counts,*
> *Who had been in Britain.*[11]

The *Second Continuation* tells us that Bleheris,

> *Was born and conceived*
> *In Wales, whose story I tell,*
> *And who told it to the Count*
> *Of Poitiers who loved the story.*[12]

Looking outside the Arthurian legends we find another possible reference to him in the irrepressible roaming cleric Gerald of Wales (1145–1223) who in his *Description of Wales,* based on a journey he undertook in 1188, tells a silly story. Having discussed how Welsh fishermen carry their coracles on their backs when they get out of the water, he goes on to talk about Bledri or Bledhericus, a well-known storyteller, "who lived before our time"; Gerald amusingly describes, "There are men among us who, when they go hunting, carry their horse upon their backs until they approach their quarry. When they have done, they lift their horses back onto their shoulders and carry them home again."[13]

The fact that Gerald describes Bledri or Bleddri as a storyteller from a time prior to his own suggests that to Gerald, Blihis or Bledri was already a known figure. Since we can absolutely pinpoint the *Description of Wales* to 1188, around the date that *Perceval* was written, it is a promising lead from an independent and non-Arthurian source.

Another coincidence is worth considering. *The Elucidation* was bound together in the Mons manuscript with another prologue to Perceval, which tells of his father, in the text of *Bliocadrin*. This short text reveals the backstory to Perceval's birth, the unfortunate death of his father, and the resultant retirement of his mother to a forest fastness where he is brought up. Since Bliocadrin has died during a somewhat manly and gung-ho tournament in a friendly passage of arms, Perceval's mother subsequently becomes steadfastly opposed to all forms of chivalry. Shutting herself and Perceval away from all such influences, she warns her son that if he should ever see mounted men dressed in iron, he should shun them as demons. But though the name Bliocadrin shares a prefix with Blihis, the two figures are in no wise similar.[14]

What are the origins of the name? We might think immediately of the Scottish expression "blether" or "blather" for talking rubbish, which comes into the language from Old Norse *blathr,* or nonsense, which is certainly the sense in which Gerald of Wales uses it above, for a teller of nonsense. Jessie Weston derives *blio* from the Breton for "hairy." *Blehuc,* Old Breton, *bleuak,* Cornish, and *bleuog/blewog,* Welsh, all have the same hairy meaning.[15]

What does any of this prove? The name suggests a kind of *gruagach,* or hairy man, a wild man of the woods, or a churl or carl, such as Gawain encounters in the late medieval story of *The Carl of Carlisle,* a rustic figure deriving from an earlier time.[16] The prior existence of a legendary figure who is a source of the figure in *The Elucidation* may be posited: a kind of male Mother Goose, who is the source of all folk stories. We find many such ancient storytelling figures in Irish legend, like Tuan mac Carill, who lives through many animal transmogrifications from the first settling of Ireland to the time, many generations on, when he is evoked to remember all that ever happened.[17] Is Blihis merely a convenient remembrancer who lives through time, able to give us prior chapter and original verse?

Medieval manuscripts are littered with what might be called "literary coat hooks"—supposed learned sources—fabricated "old books," and legendary storytellers, all giving the writer his literary justification. Master Bleheris may well prove to be one such coat hook, though there is a sufficiently large amount of evidence to posit otherwise.[18]

Another possibility arises. Chrétien's *Erec and Enide* speaks of the wedding guests who arrive including,

> *The leader of the dwarfs came next,*
> *Bilis, the king of the Antipodes.*
> *This king of whom I speak was a dwarf,*
> *The shortest of all dwarfs*
> *And Brien, his brother,*
> *Was half a foot taller*
> *Than most of the knights in the realm.*[19]

Bilis/Blihis as a dwarf, of a race apart from humans and faeries, is another version of our storyteller, who is himself a man of two races, the descendant of Amangons's race and of the race of the maidens. The Antipodes from whence Bilis and his brother come are not the lands of Australasia but rather, in the understanding of the Middle Ages, the realms beneath the earth. In *Le Draco Normand* by Étienne de Rouen we have an account of Arthur's passing that tells us how the underworld realm was seen:

> *The grievously wounded Arthur requested healing herbs*
>   *from his sister:*
> *These were kept in the sacred isle of Avalon.*
> *Here the eternal nymph, Morgan, helped her brother.*
> *Healing, nourishing, and reviving him, making him*
>   *immortal.*
> *The Antipodes were put under his rule. As one of Faery,*
> *He stands without armor, but fearing no fray.*
> *So he rules from the underworld, bright in battle,*
> *Where the other half of the world is his.*[20]

We will have more to say about Bilis later in chapter 5, since this precedes our exposition of the realms of Faery to which Bilis Bleheris properly belongs.

Or could Bleheris be something more prosaic? Might he be a known storyteller who moved through the courts of western Europe, a Welshman who spoke French, one related to or attached to the household of those who became the hearers of the tales enshrined in writing by Chrétien and others, as the one who originally told the stories? Arthurian scholars such as Constance Bullock-Davies and Sharon Kinoshita have both explored the cross-border influences that created the permeable courts of Europe at this time, finding many possibilities, but no named person as the composer of this most mysterious of texts.[21]

The second continuator of Chrétien de Troyes's *Conte du Graal* says that his literary authority is a certain Bleheris who was born and reared in Wales and that he told it to the Count of Poitiers, who loved the story so much that he held it more than any other firmly in memory. Many attempts have been made to date this character by establishing just which count of Poitiers was intended. It has been proved that the earliest French references to Tristan occur in the works of Cercamon and Bernard de Ventadour, both attached to the court of Poitiers in the 1150s. This evidence may lead us to suppose that Bleheris did visit the court at Poitiers or briefly enjoyed the patronage of the count and that he had a command of Norman French.[22]

Corin Corley in his study of the *Second Continuation* cautiously thinks so: "I am inclined to believe that the reference to Bleheris may be authentic and that to the count of Poitiers certainly is."[23] If this was so, then the inclusion of Bleheris in *The Elucidation* could have been seen as a kind of in-joke that anyone at the court of the counts of Poitiers would have enjoyed. Some scholars have associated Bleheris with the Welsh Bledri ap Cadifor, who was a Latimer, or translator, for the Normans: the only dates we have for his existence stem from a gift he made to Saint John's Priory in Carmarthen around 1113 to 1135.[24]

Bleheris as a literary device is one thing, but as the source of the Grail story, he takes on a different stature. His name is certainly associated with the most folkloric version of the Grail story, and its deep connections to the realm of Faery will become even more interesting as we will see in chapter 5. However we view him, Bleheris nevertheless stands as the reciter of this part of *The Elucidation*. But the text continuously tells us that it is not a story that can just be told any way or in any order. Let us explore what the narrator has to tell us, because he acts as a gatekeeper to the revelation: if we sip too quickly from his cup, we lose something precious.

THE MAGIC TABLECLOTH

The tone of *The Elucidation* narrative keeps promising full clarity and revelation, but it also warns us not to open up this story cache all at once, or too quickly, lest we miss something. We may not,

> *Tell the secret or even sing of it;*
> *For that would reveal the story*
> *Before all was said,*
> *That some might be sorry for*
> *Who had not been at fault.*[25]

Here the text is not unlike the magic tablecloth from the Scottish folk story of the *Battle of the Birds,* where the hero is given a bundle and told not to untie the bundle until he is in the place where he would most wish to dwell. Unfortunately the bundle grows very heavy and the hero decides to peer inside. "But when he loosed the bundle he was astonished. In a twinkling he saw the very grandest place he ever saw. A great castle, and an orchard about the castle, in which was every kind of fruit and herb. He stood full of wonder and regret for having loosed the bundle—for it was not in his power to put it back again."[26]

At the outset, the storyteller of *The Elucidation* warns us that revealing the story before all is said might make the innocent suffer. This loaded statement is telling us two things: that there is a certain order to the revelation of the text that has to march with our understanding, and that we shouldn't, like many a desultory book browser, just sneak a look at the last page to see how it all works out. This dilemma about the balance of innocence and knowing revolves around how we understand things in a specific order. When a particular component isn't yet revealed we cannot fully comprehend the story. By looking ahead or anticipating the story we foster a false knowledge that may lead astray.

This is probably why the Grail quest is achieved first by Perceval who, of all the Grail seekers, is the most innocent and unpracticed. His mind is a tabula rasa, devoid of prior knowledge. He first finds the court of the Rich Fisher, but fails to ask all the questions that would reveal the central core of the mystery: he asks whom the Grail serves, but not about the Bleeding Lance, nor the about the broken sword's two halves, or about the corpse on the bier, or anything about the great vanishing that he witnesses. That is six questions in total, or seven, if we count the silver cross that preceded these things. Again, we come back to the magical seven that is intrinsic to this text.

The driving narrative throughout *The Elucidation* is to explain, show, and tell, but it is continually held back by the tension of this caution. This is not entirely about being secretive or reticent to reveal, but more about the ability of the hearer to heed and absorb the revelations as they arise. We are also given the promise that "all people" will know or be told:

> *And if I tell you one by one—*
> *For he wishes to show each of you*
> *In what way the Grail served—*
> *For the services that it gave*
> *Were revealed to him by a good master.*
> *[This service] has been known but hidden,*
> *The good that it served will openly*
> *Be taught to all people.*[27]

This remarkable statement reveals that the Grail's function was originally revealed to the narrator by "a good master." Are we then to understand that Bleheris himself is meant here, or some other? What the Grail does and how it does it has been "known but hidden" before this point, but its benefits will be openly taught to all people, bespeaking a prior tradition. This is in diametrical contrast to the later, but inferior, text of *The Elucidation* that informs us:

> *He who tells it shall have great woe,*
> *For of the Grail it is the sign*
> *That he is pain, and ills will pine*
> *Who reveals its secrets to any man.*[28]

Punitive strictures and open revelations seem to jockey for place here. And the warning given to Perceval by the Maiden of the White Mule in the *Second Continuation* makes it clear that only well-qualified, celibate knights or clergy might speak of these mysteries:

> *She said, "Sire, it cannot be*
> *That I may tell this mystery,*
> *If a hundred times you ask*
> *I may not speak more of my task,*
> *For this would be too bold,*
> *It is too secret to be told.*
> *No lady, girl, or maid may say it*
> *Nor may any man betray it*
> *Who is wedded to a wife.*
> *Only a man of holy life*
> *Or a priest of this may tell*
> *Revealing all its wondrous spell*
> *Which no one can ever hear*
> *Without turning pale with fear,*
> *Trembling, becoming a wretched sight,*
> *A man stricken by utter fright."*[29]

Secrecy for its own sake, as we noted in the introduction, is not what the mystery tradition is about; however, in this mysterious Grail text the mystery is not thrown wide, but is rather an open secret that is discoverable by the sheer act of going on quest. If the desire to quest for it isn't present, of course it will remain a mystery. The Grail mystery is a parcel that we must each unwrap for ourselves, but it is not an exclusive one only meant for the élite initiate. We are clearly told that the benefits will be openly taught. In such a way, we hope this present book fulfills this purpose, opening the paths of the quest in ways that make it possible for anyone to follow.

There are many mysteries to unfold, but there is another stricture on the storytelling that halts us in our tracks:

> *Then came the great marvel*
> *For which none could prepare.*
> *But I cannot now speak of it*
> *For Perceval himself must tell it*
> *Further on in the middle of the tale.*
> *It is a great villainy and shame*
> *To dismember such a good story*
> *Before it has run its road.*[30]

The storyteller has just opened another dialog box—one in which the characters within the story themselves *become the narrators:* only they can tell their own story; they are the seven guardians of the seven branches of the story.

THE SEVEN GUARDIANS

As we saw, at the head of the physical manuscript of *The Elucidation* the allusive illustration above the text shows eight figures seated at a table, including a king, while from the left-hand end approaches a knight.[31] It is tempting to see the seated figures as the seven guardians with the Rich Fisher, with a quest knight approaching, but these anonymous figures remain unidentified, much as they do within the text.

In the search for the court of the Rich Fisher (see chapter 7 for more about him) we are told that the court itself was found seven times.

Each discovery helps create one of the seven branches of the story. The narrator sees our puzzlement and says to us:

> *But you do not know what this means!*
> *Know that the seven branches*
> *Are really the seven guardians;*
> *Each one of the guardians will tell*
> *The place where the court was found;*
> *Before, it was not allowed to be told*
> *Now I reveal it in this writing*
> *And name the seven guardians;*
> *And will omit nothing from it,*
> *Thus they will be well named and described*
> *All in order, from beginning to end.*[32]

Not only are there seven branches of the Grail myth, these story branches are actually represented by the seven guardians, each of whom has his own take on this quest. These knights have been on their quests but—like reporters on a secret mission who cannot file reports until they are safely back—their adventures couldn't be written about. Indeed, the narrator ensures that all we will know about them are their names, despite his assertion to reveal all, because it is up to the knights in question to speak about their own experiences. But he doesn't even name all their names!

The listing of the seven branches of the story, dealt with in reverse order, is very frustrating. We would like to know a lot more about these stories and how they were shaped. We have to see the word *branch* in a literary way, as a bough upon a larger tree of the story. Each of the branches can also be seen as representative of one of the guardians of the whole Grail myth.

The Grail cannot be known from just one perspective but needs a full spectrum of witnesses in order to reveal itself.

Let us track the guardians alluded to within lines 339–82, attempting to follow them as best we can, since some of these stories are neither told within *The Elucidation,* nor are they found in any other place: some are lost, while others can at least be partially reconstructed.

Branch 7: The Story of Longinus

> *The seventh branch that pleases best,*
> *It is all about the lance*
> *With which Longinus struck the side*
> *Of the King of Holy Majesty.*[33]

This seventh branch takes us directly into the midst of the legends surrounding the Passion of Christ. The lance that drips blood is one of the central hallows or holy objects within the Grail procession (see chapter 9). While Chrétien makes the finding of this hallow part of Gawain's own quest, it is not until the *First Continuation* that we first hear explicitly about Longinus and his spear, which becomes a relic of the Passion and later a major feature of the Grail procession. Longinus is not referenced much elsewhere in the Grail corpus, save in the mid-fifteenth-century text of the *Suite du Merlin,* although the spear is often described; its catastrophic effect upon the fertility of the land we shall explore further in chapter 8.

The Roman soldier who pierces the side of Christ on the cross is unnamed in the gospels, but is called Longinus in the apocryphal fourth-century Gospel of Nicodemus, which is appended to the Acts of Pilate. Further legends abound, especially the fourth-century pseudo-epigraphical *Letter of Herod to Pilate,* which describe how Longinus had to suffer a Promethean punishment for his temerity in piercing the side of Christ, by being mauled by a lion by night and healing back by day, in an unending cycle till doomsday.

Also of interest is the tradition found in *Cursor Mundi,* an anonymous religious poem of 1300 that divides the history of the world into seven ages. The poem, given here in Middle English and translation, tells how the blind Longinus was told to strike with his spear, not knowing it was a man he was striking until he realized what he'd done, and how, after Christ's blood ran down his spear onto his hand, he wiped his eyes and so regained his sight.

With a spere in hand	With a spear in hand
And til his hert hit sett,	Right to his heart he set,
Ther-with he therled his hert,	Therewith he pierced his heart,
Bothe blode & water oute let	Both blood and water outlet
By the spere til his hand	From the spear to his hand
Ran doun of his blode.	Ran down his blade.
He wipped is eyen ther-with	He wiped his eyes with it
And silt he hade ful gode.	And since he had benefit:
"Mercy," he cried, "oure lord!"	"Mercy," he cried, "Our Lord!"
And gart cristen him I-wis	And became a Christian, I believe,
Sithen for his luf was slayn.	Who for his love was slain.[34]

From this popular medieval legend we immediately understand how the constantly streaming blood of the lance in the Grail legends would have been perceived as a salvific relic of miraculous power. This premise of the healing blood is seen in the *Lancelot-Grail* where Galahad touches the Bleeding Lance and then anoints the Wounded King with its blood, resulting in his immediate healing.

In *l'Histoire du Graal,* which deals with the backstory of Joseph of Arimathea's descendants, Josephus, Joseph's grandson and an earlier Wounded King in the lineage of the Grail company, receives his wound from an angel with the spear; the tip of the spear remained within the wound and no one had been able to remove it since that time. The angel took the lance and came

> straight toward Josephus and struck him with tipless lance in the very same spot where he had struck him before . . . and when he pulled the lance out, everyone saw that the tip had come out with the lance.[35]

It is usually the Grail question that heals the Wounded King, but here it is the holy blood itself that brings healing.

Of all the hallows or holy objects sought throughout the Grail myths, it is the lance that has the longest, most unchanging appearance. In *Perceval* it appears in the hand of a squire, with a bead of blood running down the shaft unceasingly. The action of the Roman soldier who pierces the side of Christ with his pilum furnishes us with a clear connection between the Passion and the quest. The blood and water that run out from Christ's side, and are collected by Joseph of Arimathea in the Glastonbury legend, have both a Eucharistic and baptismal resonance. The redeeming blood of atonement and the Eucharistic cup set up another whole scenario for the Grail itself, while the water, which baptizes and cleanses sin, also echoes the waters that are released to heal the Wasteland of the Grail legends in the *Lancelot-Grail.*

The legend of Joseph of Arimathea and the cruets is found in the *Cronica Sive Antiquitates Glastoniensis Ecclesie,* or Chronicles or Antiquities of the Glastonbury Church of John of Glastonbury (fl. 1340). In this later tradition, which is topical to Glastonbury, John drew upon everything he could find to put together a hodgepodge of material suggesting Glastonbury's connection with the Grail. He quoted the famous prophecy of the Bard Melkin, a figure who appears in few other sources—notably in John Hardyng's *Chronicle* of the mid-fifteenth century, and in the reports of John Leland, who had the unfortunate task of cataloging the libraries of the abbeys ripe for Reformation and dissolution for Henry VIII. Leland speaks of Melkin as a well-regarded bard who was largely forgotten after the Saxon invasion, who wrote a *Historia de Rebus Britannicis,* a prophetic text, among other lost titles and who flourished before Merlin.[36] Despite this, it is most likely that Melkin was based on the figure of the Arthurian enchanter.

The Melkin prophecy has been the center of much debate, discussion, and wild surmise:

> *Amid these, Joseph in marble*
> *Of Arimathea by name*
> *Hath found perpetual sleep;*
> *And he lies on a two-forked line*

Next the south corner of an oratory
Fashioned of wattles,
For the adoring of a mighty Virgin
In his sarcophagus
Two cruets, white and silver
Filled with blood and sweat
Of the Prophet Jesus.
When his sarcophagus
Shall be found entire, intact
In time to come, it shall be seen
And shall be open unto all the world
Thenceforth nor water nor the dew of heaven
Shall fail the dwellers in that ancient isle
For a long while before
The day of judgment in Josaphat
Open shall these things be
And declared to living men.[37]

We note that Christ is referred to here as "the prophet Jesus," a terminology more often associated with Islam. A possible Middle Eastern source for the Grail was further suggested by Wolfram von Eschenbach in his *Parzival,* for whom he provided a source narrator called Kyot of Provence who had learned of the legend from a certain Flegitanis, descendant of Solomon.[38]

The two cruets of blood and water that Joseph collects from the act of Longinus gives us another echo of *The Elucidation.* In the Orthodox Troparion for Holy Saturday, the choir sings of Joseph, who provided the tomb for Christ,

Give me that Stranger
That I may bury him in a tomb,
Who being a stranger has no place
Whereon to lay his head.[39]

This Troparion aptly recalls the circumstances of Christ's birth: just as he has to "borrow" the body of Mary in order to enter humanity, so too he has to "borrow" a place to be born and a place to die.[40] The strangers who have no place to lay their head in *The Elucidation* are, of course, the offspring of Amangons and the Maidens of the Wells, the knights and maidens who wander with Bleheris.

The Bleeding Lance in *The Elucidation* is accompanied by a collection vessel where the blood runs down through a silver pipe or tube into a vase:

> *And the stream of blood ran*
> *From a vase where the lance was*
> *Through the rich silver tube.*[41]

This seems to be a feature unique to the lance in this text, dealing rather practically with the mess that one might imagine would need continual mopping up. What is done with the contents of the collection vase is not revealed in *The Elucidation,* but in the *First Continuation* we hear that it passes through a pipe of green emerald into a channel of gold and thence out of the hall.[42] This is in line with all the descriptions of the Grail Chapel, which suggest that it is a type of the Earthly Paradise, as we are told explicitly within the *Gerbert de Montreuil Continuation* where, in his Grail Castle visitation, "Perceval has seen quite openly the earthly Paradise,"[43] through the little wicket gate.

In *Perceval* it is Gawain who swears to go in search of the Bleeding Lance, though it is not until the *First Continuation* that he finds it (see chapter 8). Gawain is accused by the knight Guigambresil of killing his lord and charged with treason, at which Gawain promises to make satisfaction. The quest for the lance is then set on Gawain by a wise vassal of the king of Escavalon, as a proper means of satisfying Guigambresil and healing the bad blood between them: Gawain promises to postpone going to battle against him and to deliver the lance to Guigambresil, or else to surrender himself to captivity by the end of a year. But the wise vassal of the king of Escavalon then speaks of a prophecy:

It is written that the time will come when the whole kingdom of Logres, which was once the land of the ogres, will be destroyed by that lance.[44]

Despite this devastating preknowledge of its destructive powers, Gawain duly swears to go for the lance, rather than live in shame. On reaching the Grail Castle, Gawain asks its king about the Bleeding Lance and is told that it has bled continuously since the day of the Passion and that it will not leave the castle until doomsday. Then he adds that, unless someone can unite the broken sword lying upon the dead body in the Grail procession, the task of healing is incomplete. Gawain fails at this task and is unable to stay awake during the telling of this tale; he falls asleep, only to wake by the sea on a towering cliff. Berating himself, he resolves to try again. Meanwhile, overnight the Wasteland is restored to fertility because of his question, and it could have also been repopulated, we are told, had Gawain not neglected to ask any more. So, while many people bless him for his efforts as he rides home, others berate him for bringing them only partial success.

However, the lance remains in the Grail Castle and Logres is saved from this prophecy, which doesn't make its reappearance in any of the subsequent *Continuation* texts. Of all the Grail writers, only Wolfram von Eschenbach took up this theme and made it central to the Dolorous Blow in his *Parzival*. We will explore the circumstances of the Dolorous Blow fully in chapter 7.

Although this seventh branch story is about the Spear of Longinus, it is largely Gawain who is the knight active in its finding. This has led commentators like Jessie Weston to posit that Gawain's quest has equal importance to that of Perceval (see chapter 8). She suggests that in an early, now lost, cycle Gawain may have been the Grail winner.[45] One scholar has even projected two preexisting Grail stories—those of Perceval and Gawain—suggesting that Chrétien merely spliced these together, but this does not seem likely from the internal evidences of Chrétien's language.[46]

Branch seven immediately immerses us into the myths of the

Passion, creating a linkage between the native European Grail stories and mystical Christianity.

Branch 6: The Great Strife of the Toil

> *And the sixth, without fail, is*
> *About the great strife of the toil.*[47]

The two bare lines that introduce branch six tell us very little. This branch is difficult to place with certitude, but there are many possibilities. The sixth story, since it follows that of the Lance of Longinus, might merely continue the theme. If the Lance speaks of the blood, does the "great strife of the toil" refer to the Passion itself? After all, in some legends, the cruets of Joseph of Arimathea contain the blood and the sweat of Christ.

Relics of the Passion were highly valued in the Middle Ages and became increasingly more varied in Europe as the Crusades wore on. The most famous relic of the Holy Sweat is the *sudarium,* or Cloth of Saint Veronica, who held her veil to Christ's face on his way to the Cross. A relic called the *Vindicta Salvatoris* was housed in Rome and reportedly seen by both Gerald of Wales and Gervase of Tilbury in the late twelfth century, though it seems to have disappeared by the seventeenth century. Many painters made depictions of the careworn face upon the veil of Veronica, or Vernicle, as it is sometimes known. In the *First Continuation* the Wounded King tells how Nicodemus, friend of Joseph of Arimathea, painted an image of the Crucified on the cross: this image is found at Lucca, as the *Volto Santo.*[48]

Another possibility suggests itself that would change the whole way we look at the Grail legends in the context of Arthur. All British accounts of the Battle of Camlann describe it as a *gueith,* or strife/toil, the British name for a civil war. All of Arthur's twelve battles, as accounted for in Nennius, are against the invading Saxons and Angles and described as battles, with only Badon being described as an *obsession,* or a siege.[49] Camlann alone among them is known as a civil strife, becoming in Welsh legend and poetry a byword for futility and mayhem. The *Annales Cambriae* give us one of the earliest references to Arthur:

537: The battle of Camlann in which Arthur and Medraut perished, and there was death in England and Ireland.[50]

It is of course at Camlann that Arthur receives his unhealing wound from which, later legends tell, he is taken into Avalon, there to be cured. This is one of the few instances we come across in Arthurian literature of a realization that the mortal wound that Arthur receives at this battle puts him into the category of a Wounded King who exists in an otherworldly enclave awaiting healing! But at no point does the Battle of Camlann enter into any account of the Grail legends. While Arthur carries a cross or the image of the Blessed Virgin upon his shield at the siege of Badon, there his spiritual duties cease.

But how would this branch fit in the context of *The Elucidation*? Can such a theory be upheld in the rest of the Grail legends? As we shall see in chapter 8, Arthur is kept busy in the wars against the Rich Company, so busy that there is no chance of anyone going on quest during that time. Throughout the wider legends, Arthur is described as one on whom the responsibilities of kingship or leadership weigh heavily, from the earliest poems about him onward, as here where he leads the harrowing of the underworld of Annwfyn in the ninth-century British poem *Preiddeu Annwfyn,*

> *When we went with Arthur on arduous visit;*
> *Except seven none rose up from Caer Fandwy.*[51]

This poem reveals Arthur as an active quester for the cauldron of the underworld, the cauldron that only feeds the hero and not the coward; this story of the quest of the cauldron of Diwrnach or Pen Annwfyn, the Lord of the Underworld, is undoubtedly one of the sources of the later Grail legends, as we shall see in chapter 4. It reveals an active king, not the *roi fainéant,* or inactive king, of the later legends.

The "toil" in the context of *The Elucidation* and the Grail legends as a whole is the quest itself, whereby the Wasteland is healed. In the words of filmmaker John Boorman's *Excalibur,* "The land and the king are one."

The ancient Celtic myth of the wounded king tells us that what blights the land, wounds the king; when the king is wounded, the land becomes infertile. The symbiosis of land with king creates an enduring theme that subsequent myths play with and build upon, as we shall see in chapter 7.

That this Wounded King may once have been Arthur is a possibility not previously confirmed, though his nonparticipation in the quest is usually put down to his kingship, whereby knights go on quest on his behalf. An obscure text, written not long after the *Conte del Graal* in the Spanish-speaking area of the Balearic Islands, casts further light on this. *La Faula* (the Tale), written by the Mallorcan Guillem Torroella in 1360 to 1370, is a magnificent mélange of surreal adventures, including the voyage by the hero/author on the back of a whale, to the island of Morgan la Fay. There Guillem encounters Arthur, lying on his bed of pain, his wounds yet unhealing, his life preserved by a yearly visit from the Grail! This hitherto unnoticed account makes it clear that Arthur was at one time perceived as a type of the Wounded King—perhaps as a Grail King—but this appears to have been a storyline that was not developed beyond this time.[52]

Another possibility is presented from a wider reading of the Grail legends. In *Perceval,* where his uncle begins to instruct him properly in arms, Perceval asks, "Do you think my toil will be worthwhile, if I keep on trying?"[53] In the *Continuations* of the Grail the "great toil" that is many times instanced there is that of Perceval himself. In both *Gerbert's Continuation* and the *Third Continuation* Perceval's quest is acknowledged in the following words, firstly by the Fisher King who greets Perceval's successful rejoining of the broken sword with, "All your toil is well rewarded,"[54] and then in the *Third Continuation* where he relates to the hermit all the toil and hardship he's suffered in the quest for the Grail. "The toil" might be used here to indicate Perceval's quest itself.

It is true that the achievement of the Grail is made up of many episodes whose repetitive attempts often prove to be mere distractions from the quest, resulting in failure or a period of toilsome persistence. Many times the knights find themselves back where they started, having to find fresh inspiration to continue.

So, can we assign this unknown sixth branch of the story to the wars that Arthur fights after the Wasteland is healed against the Rich Company? We will have to reserve judgment until we see the evidences in chapter 8.

Branch 5: Huden

> *The fifth I will tell you in turn*
> *The anger and loss of Huden.*[55]

Another elusive two lines introduce the fifth branch story. If this story ever featured in any proto-Grail legend, then this is the only source for it, for it appears nowhere else. Huden is known as Tristan's dog, sometimes also called Houdenc or Housdenc. But a dog as a Grail guardian, we hear you say? How is that possible?

The Tristan stories stand in parallel to the Arthurian ones, sometimes merging, but they are not majorly part of the Grail legends. The only character within Tristan's saga to actually partake in the Grail quest is the Saracen knight Palomides, who chases the Questing Beast and who later, during the Grail quest, converts to Christianity, but then only at the later end of the Arthurian textual history, notably in Malory's *Morte d'Arthur*.[56]

It is true that, in the *Second Continuation*, Perceval is lent the dog of the Lady of the Chessboard Castle with which to hunt the White Stag, and to which he becomes quite attached. This dog is stolen by a black knight but finally rediscovered by Perceval who uses it also to help him find the court of the Fisher King.[57] While the dog is indeed lost for a while, it is finally regained.

In the *First Continuation*, on the journey to rescue the knight Girflet from the Castle Orgueilleux, as Arthur and men enter the castle of Bran de Lis, a snow-white brachet (a hunting dog) runs into the hall. Kay, the seneschal of Arthur, runs after its trailing lead and claims it to be the companion of his other dog, Huden.[58] No sooner has Kay spoken this than the brachet flees with the leash trailing behind it. Kay attempts to catch it, as the dog moves rapidly from chamber to chamber. It leads him out into a garden where, amid the olive and pine trees, are assembled a huge multitude:

> They were playing at diverse games, and making such joy and festivity as 'twere overlong to recount, for that day they were keeping the feast of a saint of that land.[59]

Under a laurel tree in an orchard a knight is disarming, with the help of the best people in the assembly. The brachet runs to him, taking shelter between his legs and barking loudly at Kay. The knight in question is Bran de Lis, the owner of the castle. He immediately comes into the castle and seeks out Gawain there to combat with him.

Bran de Lis is the keeper of an otherworldly, moated castle and Gawain has a liaison with his sister. Bran de Lis is also potentially on the Rich Company, as we will see (in chapter 8). The story is part of Gawain's history and the incident with the dog merely leads to his combat with Bran de Lis, whom he has promised to fight. In itself, this isn't very plausible and doesn't fulfill the criterion of the fifth branch, for the brachet isn't Huden but another dog, and we are not told of its anger or loss. All that we can concede is that the dog does lead to a reverse "joy of the court" in that it acclaims Bran de Lis and not the healing of the Grail.

A similar incident from the *First Continuation* gives us a parallel reversal. Just as Kay is the fall guy for the brachet incident, so too he plays the fool here. We pick up the story as King Arthur sets out to rescue his dear friend Girflet, son of Do, from Castle Orgueilleux where he was imprisoned for three years. Arthur, weary and hungry, is directed to the castle of Meliolant, who amuses himself with his hawks. Kay goes in ahead his master to requisition board and lodging for his king, and finds a dwarf roasting a peacock, over which they squabble. Then Meliolant enters, with his greyhound on a green leash, demanding to know why Kay is injuring his servant, and courteously offering to share the peacock with him. During their struggle, Kay seizes the peacock, splitting the roasted bird in two so that the hot gravy runs down and burns his hands, leaving him with the marks forever afterward.[60]

The knights besiege Castle Orgueilleux, on whose walls are 3,000 shields and gonfalons. Many jousts ensue between both sides and Gawain meets the lord of the castle who is called the Rich Soldier (from the French *Riche Soudoier,* or mercenary), with whom he jousts and finally overcomes. The Rich Soldier agrees to submit to Arthur if his *amie,* or lover, is spared the news of his submission: Gawain agrees to make it look as if he himself has been captured. The Round Table knights, including Girflet, are released from the dungeons.

In this bathetic echo of the Bleeding Lance, Kay receives roast peacock juices on his hands and, like Pecorins in the third branch of *The Elucidation,* is marked for life by the scalds he receives. But again, in this incident, Meliolant's dog is neither offered nor given, nor does it play any further part. We will explore this incident of the besieging of Castle Orgueilleux further in chapter 8.

But what if, as in the fourth branch story, we have a scribal error? It has been suggested that the fifth branch is based on an episode at the end of *Lancelot* where Gawain's brother Gaheriet fights against a knight called Guidan. Could *Guidan* be the same as *Huden,* since in that story he is indeed both angry and eventually perishes?

Lancelot is part of the *Lancelot-Grail,* previously known as the *Vulgate Cycle,* which was composed between 1215 and 1235. In the incident we are examining, Gaheriet has agreed to champion a maiden whose brother-in-law, Guidan, has taken her lands and placed his own followers upon them. Guidan is summoned to the court of the Lady of Roestoc, there to combat with Gaheriet. He arrives with an entourage of richly dressed knights; before the holy relics, Guidan swears that the lands are rightly his, given by the maiden's father, while Gaheriet refutes him, calling him a liar. Their combat takes place on a little island in the middle of a river where they fight together. Covered with wounds, and after a rest at midday, they both resume combat; Gaheriet is about to draw his sword to give the death blow when his sword breaks off at the hilt leaving only the pommel in his hand. They struggle and Gaheriet manages to grab Guidan's sword. Guidan, realizing that he is going to die, suffers such a proud revulsion at being in the power of another that he dashes to the water and drowns himself rather than having to submit.

This incident seems to have nothing whatever to do with *The Elucidation* and its subject matter, at first view, but Gaheriet is the brother of Guerrehet, respectively the younger brothers of Gawain. It is Guerrehet who appears to be the hero of the fourth branch.

The guardian of the fifth branch is hard to uncover indeed. The incident with the broken sword is familiar enough within the Grail legends, but here, rather than being associated with Perceval, it is Gawain's brother Gaheriet who has this difficulty.

The frustratingly sparse information of this fifth branch leaves us with no certain hero or storyteller, but the incident with the dog leads us into the morass of tales that presage the besieging of the Rich Castle, and it is possible that this branch speaks of that in a way we cannot now clearly reconstruct. Fortunately, the fourth branch is more promising.

Branch 4: The Stories of the Swan

> *The Stories of the Swan are the fourth,*
> *For he was no coward*
> *The dead knight in the skiff*
> *Who first came to Glamorgan.*[61]

Line 361 of *The Elucidation* reads in Old French, *Li Contes del Ciel est li quars* or "the stories of heaven are the fourth." The text is very unclear and may be a scribal error for *li contes cil ki* or "the stories that make up the fourth." But there is a possible alternative, as several scholars before us have noted. If *ciel,* or heaven, should have been written *cigne,* or swan, the translation makes much better sense since we can readily cite the story of the dead knight in the skiff.

If we are right, then "the stories of the swan" clearly refers to an incident from the *First Continuation* in which a sleepless Arthur sees a skiff brought to shore by a swan who draws it on a silver chain. In it lies a dead knight with a broken lance sticking from his body and an illumined candle. A letter with the body says that the embalmed corpse is a king and should remain in an open tomb for a year and a day. If no one is able to pull out the lance by that time, he may be finally buried. But if any knight is so able, then he must avenge the death of the king by striking the murderer *in the same place* as the corpse was hit. The letter further says that whoever draws out the lance would be as dishonored as was Guerrehet in the garden. Arthur doesn't understand this last reference and orders this mysterious discovery to be hidden. On the shore below, the swan that has pulled the skiff now departs wailing for its master and, with a beating of wings, draws the skiff away by the silver chain, which causes the bright candle to be extinguished.

Elsewhere, in the meantime, Guerrehet, who is searching for his brother Gawain, finds a deserted castle and comes into its garden where in a pavilion sits a maiden nursing a wounded knight. This knight is angry at the intrusion, but a page tells his master not to worry for soon the intruder will meet the Little Knight who will shame him. Immediately a dwarf knight appears and challenges Guerrehet who is indeed defeated by his diminutive opponent. Guerrehet has to promise to return and fight again in a year's time, or else to serve the wounded knight as a weaver, as do other prisoners who are menially indentured to serve him. Guerrehet chooses the combat option. However, on returning to what was previously a deserted castle, he finds it full of people who taunt him about his shameful defeat and promise to advertise his disgrace. On leaving the castle he is even pelted with rubbish by the townspeople.

At Arthur's court, the king discreetly asks Guerrehet about his "shame in the garden" but the knight pretends to be ignorant of this. However, when Guerrehet stands by the body and lays his hand on the protruding broken lance, he receives a splinter of it in his finger, and immediately the lance head slips easily from the body. He takes it away, affixing it to one of his own lances. Arthur finally raises the sensitive matter of the letter again, and Guerrehet tells him the true story and then leaves to fulfill his promise.

Guerrehet kills the Little Knight, but now the wounded knight in the tent also challenges him. The wounded knight is struck in the chest with the same lance head that Guerrehet took from the corpse in Arthur's hall, in the very same place that the wounded knight killed the corpse. A maiden comes and tells Guerrehet that his duty is fulfilled. He is received into the castle with great rejoicing and goes to sleep there, but on awaking, finds himself with the maiden in a swan-drawn skiff at the shore by Arthur's court. While Guerrehet sleeps, the maiden tells Arthur that the corpse in his hall is that of King Brangemor, the son of a mortal father and a faery mother. She prophesies that when the corpse leaves his court, Arthur will view a great marvel. The corpse is brought to the skiff and the whole court sees its departure, guided only by the swan and by no human agency. This incident takes place at either Carlion or Glamorgan, according to variant texts, and we are in no doubt that here we have the missing fourth branch story.[62]

Immediately we see parallels between *The Elucidation* and the underlying story of the Grail legends. Guerrehet's "shame in the garden" where he is overcome by a knight his inferior in stature, is a clear reference to the loss of paradise, while his following success in overcoming the dwarfish Little Knight, which is accorded the greatest joy, is a clear vindication of his earlier failure. The broken lance that cannot be removed from the corpse—apart from its resonance with the drawing forth of the Sword in the Stone—parallels the lance that gives the Dolorous Blow, becoming the instrument by which the Wounded King is both hurt and healed in the *Lancelot-Grail*. Here the lance is easily drawn out by Guerrehet and, now mounted on a new shaft, it is the instrument by which the wounded knight is killed.

We learn that the corpse in the swan-boat story is King Brangemor, the son of a human father and a faery mother, paralleling the half-human, half-faery status of Bleheris's company.

There are many "Bran" names in the Grail legend, all of which seem to stem from the undying nature of the British god, Bran the Blessed, who in the second branch of *The Mabinogion* commands his warriors to take his head and bear it to the White Tower, after receiving an unhealing wound. Bran is the first of the Wounded Kings, about whom we will speak more in chapter 6. The half-mortal, half-faery status of

Brangemor and his avenging by Guerrehet seem to make the identity of this fourth branch part of the wider Grail legends, something we will explore further in chapter 4.

The Little Knight or Little King is a character appearing in a multitude of Arthurian legends: in Chrétien's *Erec* he defends a fountain.[63] The appearance of dwarfs in Arthurian legend frequently signals the operation of otherworldly rules. They are a byword for discourtesy and disruption and, as here, a challenge to the ordered state of things: we shall discover more about them in chapter 4.

Again, this fourth branch of the story deals with a shameful death where the unburied and undecaying corpse remains until it is properly avenged. On Guerrehet's successful return to the scene of his first shame he is able to bring about the end of the matter, and the corpse of King Brangemor is returned to Faeryland. As we will see further in chapter 5, this incident forms part of the avenging of Faeryland in which the Round Table knights are instrumental.

Branch 3: The Hawk

> *The next is the third, of the hawk*
> *Of which Castrars had great fear;*
> *Pecorins the son of Amangons*
> *Carried all his days the wound on his forehead.*
> *Now I have named for you the third.*[64]

This wonderfully allusive branch is a stand-alone incident in Arthurian literature, for there is no known parallel anywhere else. In an age where themes were continually being retold or recycled by other storytellers of less creative mind, this one has not survived.

This remains also the only known reference anywhere to Amangons's son, Pecorins, who is not otherwise named. It suggests a Harry Potterish incident whereby Pecorins is scarred for life. While there are many tales about hawks, none of them seems particularly resonant with our story. The notable sparrowhawk contest in Chrétien's *Erec and Enide* seems promising at first glance, because it is a story eventually leading to the

Joy of the Court, which we will discuss fully in chapter 8, but there the sparrowhawk in question is merely the prize in a tournament.

We read above, in the fifth branch, about how Kay becomes scarred for life during his struggle with a roast peacock, in a bathetic echo of the Bleeding Lance, and of his tussle with Meliolant, the great falconer, but that doesn't help us much here either. Is the guardian of this branch really a hawk or something else?

There is a way in which we can read this branch if the hawk is not a bird but a knight. Gawain's British name was originally Gwalchmai, or "Hawk of May." In the Grail legends, Gawain is equally as much a Grail winner as Perceval, as *The Elucidation* tells us: though Perceval finds it first, the text says,

> *Sir Gawain found it [the court]*
> *In the time that Arthur reigned,*
> *And was at the court, in truth.*
> *This will be told later on,*
> *The joy that he found there*
> *By which all the kingdoms were restored.*[65]

The Grail scholar Jessie Weston, in her *The Legend of Perceval*, argued strongly for a prior tale, *The Geste of Syr Gawain*, in which Gawain was the primal Grail winner.[66] Her reasons for this supposition are borne out from even a superficial reading of the Grail texts: Gawain is as active as Perceval and has equal success in the early texts. As the Grail continuations and proliferations extend into later centuries, Gawain falls behind, becoming the reverse of his originally courteous and professional self, ending as a boorish and unsuccessful quester. John Matthews has explored the true nature of Gawain in his *Sir Gawain: Knight of the Goddess*.[67]

Gawain is the most active quester within the *First Continuation*, being its main character. It is this text that seems to pervade *The Elucidation* most strongly, as we shall see in chapter 4. It is Gawain who, after the raising of the siege of the Proud Castle, experiences the

Perilous Chapel that lies nearby and then onward to the Grail Castle where he achieves partial success and where the Wasteland is healed though not repopulated. In the German text of *Diu Cröne* Gawain is the successful Grail winner.[68]

Two things immediately strike us about this third branch, first that the name of Amangons's son, Pecorins, is suggestive of sinfulness, bestiality, and destruction: if we scan quickly through the linguistic possibilities, we have the Old French *pecier,* "to smash in pieces"; *pecora* is Italian for "sheep," from the Latin *pecus,* a "sheep" or "cow"; while *pécore* is French for "peasant." The Latin for "I am sinning" is *peccor.* These are suggestive, but we shouldn't be too attached to any of them, since there is no other name like Pecorins in the whole Arthurian legend.

But the second thing we note is that a mark on the forehead is definitely associated with the first man to do murder, Cain, who is marked after killing his brother Abel, as we are told in Genesis 4:

Then the Lord asked Cain, "Where is your brother Abel?" He answered, "I do not know. Am I my brother's keeper?" The Lord then said: "What have you done! Listen: your brother's blood cries out to me from the soil! Therefore you shall be banned from the soil that opened its mouth to receive your brother's blood from your hand. If you till the soil, it shall no longer give you its produce. You shall become a restless wanderer on the earth."

Cain said to the Lord: "My punishment is too great to bear. Since you have now banished me from the soil, and I must avoid your presence and become a restless wanderer on the earth, anyone may kill me at sight." "Not so!" the Lord said to him. "If anyone kills Cain, Cain shall be avenged sevenfold." So the Lord put a mark on Cain, lest anyone should kill him at sight.

Cain then left the Lord's presence and settled in the land of Nod, east of Eden. Cain had relations with his wife, and she conceived and bore Enoch. Cain also became the founder of a city, which he named after his son Enoch.[69]

We see that Cain's mark is given him to protect him from random revenge, but we also note that Cain is not able to farm the land because the earth will no longer yield for him—a striking echo of the Wasteland theme. Cain becomes a wanderer who founds a city and no longer tends the land, becoming an urban dweller like the Rich Company.

Within the Grail legends a lingering trace of gnostic ideas is present. According to the gnostic thought, there were three kinds of people in the world, each of whom was generated by the Anthropos, the heavenly Adam or Adamas. This being is not the earthly Adam, but the "Adam above," the Primordial Man. The Mandaeans called him "the Secret Adam," and he comes into Kabbalistic lore as Adam Kadmon, the heavenly template for all humanity.[70] These three kinds of human being were thought of by the gnostics as:

Hylics: hedonist materialists
Psychics: people who sought for spiritual connections
Gnostics: people who were in a state of understanding (literally, "knowers")[71]

The "knowing" of the gnostics was not of the intellectual kind so much as a state of consciousness in which the world of appearances and the world of spirit were viewed as one: this way of mystical understanding is still one of the goals of most religious faiths.

These three different conditions were exemplified by the three sons of Adam: Cain, Abel, and Seth. Not only were each of them associated with different lineages of humanity, but also with three different kinds of human being: Cain provides the prototype of the unenlightened *hylics;* Abel, as the innocent tender of the earth, is a representative of the *psychics;* while Seth, who discovers intelligent solutions, is representative of the *gnostics.*

We can identify three kinds of main protagonists in *Elucidation* who echo these groupings: the rapacious men of Amangons's are a type of Cain; the wandering relatives of Bleheris who cannot find the Court of Joy are a type of Abel, still seeking for a place to rest; while the

Knights of the Round Table who quest for solutions and healing are a type of Seth. We also note here that the Hebrew for Cain, *qayin*, means "spear"—a fact that seems to relate squarely to the Dolorous Blow.

In these three prototypes of Cain, Abel, and Seth we have the full complement of a lineage that gives us the Grail opponents, those who suffer at their hands and the Grail family, about whom we will read more in chapter 7.

COMPARISON OF THE THREE KINDS OF MEN IN GRAIL LEGENDS AND GNOSTICISM

Protagonists from the Eludication	Sons of Adam	Men in Gnostic Thought
Amangons	Cain	Hylics or Materialists
Bleheris & Co.	Abel	Psychics or Seekers
Round Table Knights	Seth	Gnostics or Knowers

In our search for the hawk that marked Pecorins, son of Amangons, our clearest candidate is Gawain. Such a conclusion rests entirely upon the supposition that Gawain's British name, Gwalchmai, was known by the author of *The Elucidation:* an intelligence that we cannot definitively establish. There is only one mention of a son of a King Margons (variant name for Amangons) in the *Third Continuation,* but his name is Quagrilo and his end a very different one. We will examine this further in chapter 8.

Branch 2: Story of the Great Lamentation

> *The second is not found*
> *In the testimony of good storytellers;*
> *It is the Story of the Great Lamentation,*
> *How Lancelot of the Lake came*
> *To the point where he lost his strength.*[72]

The second branch leads us back onto firmer soil. The text gives us a clue that the second branch is somehow missing from what the author calls "the testimony of good storytellers." Is this simply a typical ploy of the type found in many other texts, where the author decries the previous storytellers for leaving out the best part, which he, of course, knows? (We see a similar down-putting in Wolfram von Eschenbach's *Parzival* where he takes Chrétien to task for getting the story wrong!)

The only Lancelot text by Chrétien that would have been well known in Europe was *Le Chevalier de la Charette:* this is the earliest non-Grail text that establishes Lancelot as the knight who serves the queen as a lover. Though Lancelot was in all probability a creation of Chrétien's, he is absent from the Grail quest at this point—although he appears among the lists of knights taking part in various tournaments in the *Continuations*. In the *Lancelot-Grail* cycle, which is dated after the *Continuations,* Lancelot is one of the questers, though he fails to achieve the Grail because of his secret love for Guinevere, which we are repeatedly told is greater than his love for God. Lancelot is known as the strongest of Arthur's knights, the best and most worthy, but it is his secret love for Guinevere that causes that strength to finally fail—that and enchantment. His loss of valor in the *Lancelot-Grail* happens at a tournament that Guinevere calls. His inability to refuse Guinevere's love ultimately results in a loss of strength that eliminates him from the final reaches of the Grail quest.

Curiously, although Chrétien is credited with "inventing" Lancelot (though the name possibly relates to older Celtic heroes) he calls him "of the Lake" though he did not include the story of how Lancelot came by this title in his own work: that fell to the pen of Ulrich von Zatzikhoven who wrote *Lanzelet,* which tells how Lancelot's mother has no sooner given birth to him than their castle catches fire and her husband dies. From a safe distance by the nearby lake, she temporarily puts her newborn baby on the ground to look back at the burning castle, whereupon Lancelot is abducted by a faery woman. She gives him an upbringing in Faery, including a knightly education.[73]

But perhaps we should look for the story of the Great Lamentation not in any of the later romances but in Chrétien's own work, specifically in *Le Chevalier de la Charette* (Knight of the Cart). The story revolves around the abduction of Guinevere by Meleagant, who is known elsewhere as Melwas, king of the Summer Country, or in Chrétien's account as the ruler of the otherworldly land of Gore (the Glass Isle, sometimes identified with Glastonbury).

The oldest version of this story appears in the eleventh-century *Vita Gildae* where it is used as an exemplar of the strength of the Church against that of King Arthur, who is unable to retrieve his wife from captivity until Bishop Gildas himself intervenes. Another version of the story is possibly to be found in the carving above the arch of the Porta della Pescheria (Gate of the Fish) at Modena Cathedral in Italy, completed by 1126. We see on this arch how a woman named Winlogee (Guinevere) is held prisoner in a tower by two men, named Mardoc and Burmaltus; the tower is besieged by Artus de Bretania (Arthur) and Isdernus (Ider), while another knight identified as Carrado (Caradoc) is battling three knights labeled as Galvaginus (Gawain), Galvariun, and Che (Kay). Mardoc and Burmaltus are almost certainly Melwas and his father Bagdamagus.[74]

Chrétien took this story and elaborated on it to form a complex courtly tale in which he introduced us to the knight Lancelot, who is represented as holding an impossible and secret love for Queen Guinevere. When Meleagant tricks Arthur into allowing the queen to ride out accompanied by Kay the seneschal, which results in her capture, Lancelot is one of the first of the knights to ride out in search of her. In doing so he kills several horses under him and is forced to ride in a cart of the kind that was usually used to convey prisoners to execution. The deep shame evinced in Lancelot, who is pelted with rotten food and mocked by villagers through whose streets they pass, is such that he is, for a time, paralyzed. At one point, Chrétien tells us,

> The Knight of the Cart was . . . a man with no strength or defense against love, which torments him. His thoughts were so deep he forgot who he was; he was uncertain whether or not he truly existed; he was unable to recall his own name; he did not know if he were armed or not, nor where he was going or nor whence he came."[75]

Lancelot is dogged by sorrow over his means of transportation, which goes against every aspect of courtly chivalry, throughout the work; his shame is deepened when Guinevere finds out that he hesitated for two steps before getting into the cart. This she regards as the deepest betrayal of their love, and as punishment demands that Lancelot fight as poorly as he can in a tournament she has organized. As a slave of love the knight must obey and is repeatedly beaten by lesser men. Only when Guinevere learns of his actions does she soften and give him permission to respond. He does so, and of course wins every battle in the tournament. But in the process, he is wounded and weakened, allowing Meleagant to capture and imprison him also.

Meleagant now agrees to free the queen provided that Lancelot agree to single combat, knowing of course that he has the knight imprisoned in a tower that has no door, which he has had made for just this purpose, and that he will therefore be unable to meet him. Arthur agrees and Guinevere is released. Lancelot, still languishing in the tower, despairs and longs for death. Meleagant's sister, who is deeply upset by her brother's treacherous behavior, decides to seek out the lost knight. She makes her way to the tower and hears him lamenting:

> Feebly, in a low and trembling voice he lamented: "Ah Fortune, how cruelly your wheel has not turned for me! Once I was at the top, but now I've been thrown down to the bottom; once I had everything, now I have nothing; once you wept to see me, now you laugh at me. . . . Ah, Holy Cross, Holy Spirit! I am lost! I am damned! How totally destroyed I am!"[76]

Freed at last, with the help and encouragement of the maiden, Lancelot casts off his despair, regains his strength, and returns to Camelot in time to fight and kill Meleagant, thus earning back both Guinevere and Arthur's praise.

This is certainly a great lamentation from the greatest of Arthur's knights who is brought low by the wiles of Meleagant and the torments of love, equally. It is also, perhaps, another kind of lament—that of the author of *The Elucidation* for the fact that the great knight created by his fellow storyteller, Chrétien de Troyes, is not yet part of the Grail story. He would, one imagines, have been very glad to see the great knight appear center stage as the greatest of the Round Table fellowship, until displaced by his own son, Galahad, the ultimate Grail winner of the later legends.

In the *Queste del San Graal,* where Galahad becomes the Grail winner, Lancelot who is also on quest, falls into a trance for twenty-four hours, while in the Middle Dutch *Lanzelet,* he enters into the enchanter Mabuz's Schâtel le Mort (Castle of Death) in which everyone loses their valor. But in terms of the Grail legend, Lancelot's worst defeats come when his son, Galahad, bests him, and again when he attempts to assist the priest celebrating mass in the Grail Chapel in the *Queste del San Graal.* Seeing the priest at the point of the elevation of the host holding up the body of a crucified man, Lancelot rushes into the chapel to help, but is driven out immediately by an angel with a flaming sword, who bans him from the quest and blinds him temporarily.

It is also possible that the narrator of *The Elucidation* is referring in this second branch story to the lamentation of the people of the Wasteland, following Perceval's failure to ask the question, or indeed to another text, the *Sone de Nansay,* where a group of ancients is found perpetually lamenting,[77] but the reference to Lancelot is quite explicit here.

We read in the *Merlin* of the *Lancelot-Grail* that because of his love of Guinevere, Lancelot is given the strength of three knights, by which he becomes the best knight in the world and the savior of Arthur's kingdom in many incidents. But while Lancelot's adulterous love of the queen is presented there as an ennobling thing, generally speaking, the failure of a knight's strength upon the quest is seen as a lamentable occurrence, meriting the title of "the Story of the Great Lamentation."

The major lamentation that actually takes place within *The Elucidation* happens when the bier is processed with the Grail hallows:

> *There was therein such lamentation*
> *That no man would be so hardy*
> *Not to be frightened when he heard it.*[78]

With no early story of Lancelot as a Grail seeker, we are left with either the absence of a story or a link to a hidden story. Did the narrator of *The Elucidation* plan a *Lancelot-Grail* story of his own, or did he regard the rescue of Guinevere in *Le Chevalier de la Charette* as a lost part of this sequence?

The otherworldly upbringing of Lancelot by the Ladies of the Lake does make a much stronger warrant for Lancelot's inclusion in this elusive Grail text: a statement that will make a lot more sense when we reach chapter 4 where we explore the nature of Faery in the Arthurian legends as a whole.

Branch 1: Adventure of the Shield

> *And finally there is the last story;*
> *Since I have started this with great effort,*
> *I have to tell you all of it*
> *You'll not hear me extenuate.*
> *It is the Adventure of the Shield,*
> *There was never a better.*[79]

The first branch promises us the kind of chivalric adventure that is common to general Arthurian legend, where nearly every story seems to have its own shield-winning episode, usually as part of a quest or joust. The shield intended here is likely to be the White Shield with the Red Cross that appears in an incident from *Gerbert de Montreuil's Continuation*, which follows the *Second Continuation* and precedes the *Third Continuation*.

As mentioned earlier (p. 53) in *Gerbert's Continuation* we discovered how the wandering Perceval comes upon a castle where a mounted maiden enters carrying this shield in which was embedded a piece of the Holy Cross. It had been made by "two Chaldeans" in such a way that no one would be able to find the Grail or the Bleeding Lance unless he was the first to remove it from the maiden's neck. The inscription says that only someone in a state of grace could take it. While Perceval is helping the maiden to dismount from her horse, he takes the shield from her neck. Immediately the maiden casts herself to the ground in front of him, recognizing him as the rightful Grail winner. In *Morte d'Arthur,* written in the fifteenth century, this story is transferred to Galahad who receives a white shield with a red cross upon it from the pagan king, Evelake.

This same shield is the cause of another disappointment for Perceval who, in the same *Continuation,* distractedly forgets to ask this maiden about the origins of his shield, nor does he remember, when he has opportunity, to ask the Hermit King if he knew anything more about it.

There are also two more shields of significance in the Grail story: the Shield of Judas Maccabaeus in *Perlesvaus* and the Shield of Joseph of Arimathea, which becomes the shield of Evelake or Evelach. Both are white and painted with a red cross. Superficially they represent the blood of Christ, as well as the protection of the shield of faith, but they are more than this in the world of Arthurian adventure.

Judas Maccabeus, a Jewish hero who led a revolt against the Syrians in circa 175 BCE and reclaimed Palestine for the Jews, possessed a shield that in *Perlesvaus* was won by Gawain. In the *First Continuation* Gawain also wins Judas's sword, now called the Sword with the Strange Hangings, which later came into the hands of the ultimate Grail winner Galahad. It is possible that this is the shield that *The Elucidation* author is referring to, though it is impossible to be certain.

But it is in the *Queste del Saint Graal,* part of the *Lancelot-Grail* cycle, that we find the backstory of this particular shield. Evelake, who some have identified with the Celtic Avalloc, otherworldly Lord of Avalon, was a Saracen king converted to Christianity either by Joseph of Arimathea himself or his son Josephus, according to which version one follows, who gave him a shield on which was a likeness of Christ. The power of the shield enabled Evelake, newly baptized as Mordrains, to win a battle against his former Saracens, after which the shield became plain white.

On his deathbed, Josephus painted a cross on the shield with his own blood and urged Evelake/Mordrains to give it into the keeping of his brother-in-law Naciens to be kept safe until the coming of Galahad. Later Mordrains tried to look into the Grail and was blinded. He prayed to be allowed to see Galahad and lived though the many centuries until the time of Arthur, apparently ruling over the City of Sarras, to which Galahad, Perceval, and Bors would eventually bring the Grail. Galahad did indeed claim the shield and at that time Evelake/Mordrains regained his sight, after which he died a holy death.[80]

The shield of branch one may be either of these, or some other of which we no longer have the story, but its importance lies in the fact that it is part of the hero's regalia, setting him apart from the rest of his peers, showing him to have been selected for a special task.

Much later, in the fifteenth-century *Chronicle* of John Hardyng, Joseph of Arimathea leaves both shield and sword in Glastonbury for Galahad to collect when he needs them, but this is arguably too late to be considered and is the only source for this story. Galahad's inclusion in the later *Lancelot-Grail* sequence effectively knocks Perceval from his position as the chief Grail winner.

It is worth considering what the winning of the shield signifies in the context of the Grail quest. All knights bore their own armorial achievement on their shield, helping heralds to identify heavily armored individuals in joust and battle and, while sometimes in the Arthurian legends knights covered their shields or took up a plain shield to hide their identities in a joust, knights are not usually given a new shield. The gaining of the shield by Perceval's quest would therefore signify his entering into a kind of spiritual kinship with the shield's earlier bearer.

We note that this first branch seems to provide yet another, only partially successful quest. Since it seems to be a shield entirely intended for the Grail winner, it seems safe to assign it to Perceval who, at the time of *The Elucidation,* is still the primary quester to achieve it. In the last analysis, we see that Perceval is more concerned with a broken sword than with any shield. It is not a story that is elucidated any further by our text.

AN UNFINISHED STORY

The Seven Guardians and their Seven Branches cannot be authoritatively restored in their entirety, but we can see certain major trends within them. They comprise a kaleidoscope of incidents that form part of the major story. Like the seven pillars of Wisdom's temple, they each hold up part of the roof. In a few lines, they each allusively refer to parts of the whole legend, for it seems that the narrator regarded *the whole of the Grail legends* as somehow included within the seven branches of the story.

The Seven Guardians, tentatively restored, can be seen as

1. Perceval and his shield
2. Lancelot and his loss of strength
3. The Hawk (Gawain as Gwlachmai?) who frightened Castrars and scarred Pecorins
4. Guerrehes and the Swan boat
5. Huden's anger and loss (unascribed)
6. Arthur and his unhealing wound
7. Gawain and the Lance of Longinus

If we are to remain with these suggestions, then we note that Perceval and Gawain both appear twice in these exploits. So what are we to make of these stories, which are described as

> the seven genuine stories
> Which proceed from the Graal.[81]

If we look at them in total, we note that, apart from Perceval and the shield, which has its own disappointments, these are all stories that result in loss, failure, wounding, or death. Two of the guardians seem to be animals—a hawk and a dog—unless, as we have suggested, these are nicknames or references to knights? In what way then, can they be seen as witnesses and how will, or can, they tell their stories? We are left here with the seven branches hanging, unfruited or not yet blossoming, like seven characters in search of an author. How do we make these taciturn guardians speak so that we can hear them?

If we turn to the tradition of a different lineup of characters that inspired the Middle Ages, we can see a vast discrepancy. In 1312, Jacques de Longuyon wrote a *Chanson de Geste,* called *Les Voeux du Paon* (The Vows of the Peacock) for the Bishop of Liège. In this work, he presented *les Neufs Preux* or the Nine Worthies, heroes who represented the best of chivalry.[82] De Longuyon grouped these nine into three categories:

The heroes of the Old Law of the Jews: Joshua; King David; and Judas Maccabaeus
The heroes of the Pagan Law: Hector; Alexander; Julius Caesar
The heroes of the New Law of Christendom: Arthur; Charlemagne; Godfrey de Bouillion, King of Jerusalem

These heroes provided the Middle Ages with a template for courage in adversity, for persistence in the quest for justice, and victory in the face of evil for the whole of Europe. They were depicted on tapestries and other places as living exhortations to chivalric sovereignty, appearing in poems and exhortations to greater chivalry.

How utterly different are our collective, the seven guardians of *The Elucidation*'s story! While we are led to believe that our seven might represent the seven branches of the Grail legend as brave knights upon quest, we discover that they are much more like seven storytellers who aren't speaking clearly enough, and whose deeds result in a raft of failures rather than a series of victories.

Although we are possessed of a rich story trove, within the Arthurian legend there are still many more lost stories. Some of them have frustratingly survived only as story titles, while others, like the lost text by Robert de Boron, *Le Conte du Brait* (The Story of Merlin's Cry) we can reconstruct because a continuator used the story elsewhere; part of this lost incident remains embedded in the *Didot Perceval,* a prose work of 1190 to 1230, in which Gawain hears the cry of the imprisoned Merlin.[83]

In the seven branches of *The Elucidation*'s story, might we be looking at a wider series of stories about which we don't have the full information? Here are some possible titles of the seven branch stories, as they might be restored:

1. The Quest of Perceval to Achieve the Grail Winner's Shield
2. The Lamentable Loss of Lancelot's Strength
3. The Wounding of Amangons's Son by Gawain
4. The Avenging of Faeryland by Guerrehes
5. The Besieging of Castle Orgueilleux
6. The Unhealing Wound of Logres and the Battles of Arthur
7. The Quest of Gawain for the Bleeding Lance

Branches one, two, and seven are tales that we possess with certainty, for they appear in known texts. Branches three and six are speculations on our part, based upon reasonable supposition that we will explore in chapter 8. Branches four and five we will look at in more detail in chapters 4 and 8 respectively, where we examine the wider background of the breaking of an accord between the Faery realms and Arthur's Logres, and how the Rich Company are finally brought down. Throughout the rest of the book the evidence to justify some of these possible reconstructions will be presented, whereby the main lines of story can be more clearly seen.

The unfinished and sometimes fragmentary tellings of the Grail myth stand in contrast to the many attempts at continuity given us by several writers. The many versions that perpetuate, contradict, and open up new narratives for different audiences are confusing in their multiplicity and often serve to obscure the truth. Like "the ongoing voyages of the Starship Enterprise" whose sequels and prequels we referenced at the beginning, so the Grail myth is an unending narrative.

Something that the narrator of *The Elucidation* well understood is that it is by the very unfinished nature of the legends themselves that we are enabled, living in any time or place, to become participants in this story. This is a story that continues within each of us and has many phases of growth, including failure, defeat, and persistent new attempts. Nor can we unfold the story all at once: it is only as we step upon the path of quest that parts of these stories begin to make sense to us, and the frustrating gaps become filled.

We have examined the surface evidences for the seven guardians and begun to look more closely at the nature of the Grail's sacred effect, but let us turn now to the underside of the legends. What of the Maidens of the Wells and their world? And are there other, earlier guardians who are also seven in number?

4

THE MAIDENS OF THE
WELLS AND THE
FAERY ACCORD

*In the fées [faeries] who come forth from their wells we
certainly have the vestiges of a prehistory of the Grail.*

PIERRE GALLAIS, *PERCEVAL ET L'INITIATION*

(TRANS. CM)

THE FAERY WORLD

In medieval literature, and especially within the Arthurian legends, the gap between our world and the realms of Faery has always been narrow. That the folk traditions of the early Middle Ages comprehended the faery race is ably demonstrated in many ways within the Arthurian legend. Arthur himself is raised by the faery queen, Argante, according to the English priest Layamon who, in 1204, based his *Brut* on that of the French Wace's *Roman de Brut* of 1151, while in Ulrich von Zatzikhoven's *Lanzalet* of 1194, Lancelot is himself fostered in Faery.[1] At the end of his story, Arthur departs back into Faery, for the realm of Avalon is an otherworldly or faery location, not known to the realms of mortals, part of the mysterious Blessed Islands that lie somewhere in the western ocean.

Our sense of faeries and the realm of Faery has altered so radically since medieval times that we have to stretch our awareness to encompass what the writer of *The Elucidation* would have understood more clearly. This is why in this book, we are using the spelling *faery* in a deliberate way, to signal that we are talking about a parallel race of beings who inhabit the otherworld, and in order to distance ourselves from the modern and degraded definition of a fairy as "a diminutive, wish-bestowing being," which is not what we mean at all. When we use it capitalized as Faery, we are talking about the realm where faeries live.

The diminishment of the faery races to a set of sentimentalized and vapid beings suitable only for children's tales has been ably traced elsewhere and is not an argument that we need to rehearse again here.[2] We need to be aware that the prevailing folk culture of Europe in the Middle Ages was a long-established and ordinary understanding among agrarian people, who had a different relationship with the land than we do in the twenty-first century, having become distanced from the land and its ancient inhabitants. The beings who dwelt in the woods and waters, under hills and mountains, who blessed or cursed, who had neighborly relationships with humans and human communities are attested by folk custom throughout Europe.[3] The history of the faery races is long and complex and beyond the scope of this book, but a few words must be said concerning them if we are to understand how they fit into the story of *The Elucidation*.

Most people, if asked, would probably describe faeries as tiny, winged creatures with the power to change shape and grant wishes. But this is mostly a Victorian view, and there is a great deal more to them than that. The idea of faeries as tiny, fragile, and winged became hugely popular and still influences the way we see them today.[4] True faeries, from before this mistaken notion took root, were seldom small and rarely friendly. They could carry off human children and replace them with their own as changelings, pale and wizened like weathered apples; or if they caught human beings trying to steal their fabulous riches, or sometimes even just watching them, they responded with severe punishments—blindness, seizures, or an inability to stop dancing.[5]

It was never safe to go into Faeryland. If you were unfortunate enough to stray into their world you had to be careful. If you ate or drank their food or water, you could find yourself stuck there for a thousand years—during which time you would grow no older. But if and when you found your way back into this world, you would very likely turn to dust the moment your feet touched the earth because time had accelerated since your departure. These cautionary stories stem from the fracture of an important premise, as we shall see.

Faeries were completely real to medieval writers—as to many others since then. In the twelfth century, well before *The Elucidation* was composed, two chroniclers of the time, Ralph of Coggeshall and William of Newburgh, recorded a curious story apparently dating from the reign of King Stephen (1135–1154) that offered a glimpse into the realm of Faery itself. In this the villagers of Woolpit in Suffolk discovered two children with green skin who spoke an unknown language. Taken to the home of the local lord, they refused to eat for several days until they found some raw beans, which they consumed eagerly. The children gradually adapted to normal food and in time lost their green tinge. The boy, who appeared to be the younger of the two, became sickly and died shortly after he and his sister were baptized.[6]

In time, the surviving girl, named Agnes, learned to speak English and described how she and her brother came from a land where the sun never shone, and that was forever twilit and green. They had been herding their father's cattle when they heard a loud noise, said to be church bells, and suddenly found themselves outside in the human world. William of Newburgh says that Agnes eventually married a man from King's Lynn, where she was still living shortly before he wrote.

The faery *glamour*, which originally meant "a spell cast upon a mortal so that they were irresistibly drawn to a faery like a moth to a flame" was to be feared. However, at the same time, faeries were seen by country people to be their neighbors, with whom humans observed the standard rules of courtesy: borrowing and returning items, keeping agreements and promises, putting out offerings of your manufacture, including gifts from the dairy or kitchen.

Even the Plantagenet dynasty derives its origins from faery forebears, according the French legend of Melusine, whose descendants also included the crusader kings of Jerusalem.[7]

Again and again in medieval literature, especially in the Arthurian legends, wandering knights encounter faery women and fall hopelessly in love with them. Thus, in the *Lai of Lanval* by Marie de France, the titular knight encounters a group of women who offer him refreshment in a manner exactly comparable with the Maidens of the Wells.[8] Soon he is in love with one of the women, who are very clearly faery in origin, and discovers the dangers attendant on such a liaison. Similarly, in the Scottish folk story of *Tam Lin*, a young man called True Thomas falls in love with the queen of Faery and becomes her slave, unable to escape for many years until a mortal girl who loves him wins him back by undergoing terrible tests in which she must hold on to him as he changes from human to animal, fish, and finally, red-hot iron.

Opinions differ hugely as to the true nature and origins of the faery people. Some insist they are ancient pagan gods, diminished as other beliefs overcame them, who lost their original power and were remembered less and less as time passed. It was almost certainly as a result of this that stories were told of them living under the earth, in the "hollow hills," from which they issued forth only rarely, and most often at night. Others claimed they were fallen angels, cast out of heaven for rebelling against God or for dancing on a Sunday (see chapter 5).

THE REALMS OF FAERY IN TIME AND SPACE

Within the Arthurian legends, the realms of Faery are contiguous and overlapping with the realm of Logres. It is not so easy to disentangle one realm from the other as the locations and their inhabitants intermingle. According to *The Elucidation* the kingdom of Logres ruled over by Arthur is also the realm of Logres ruled over by the Rich Fisher. These are not rival kingdoms but rather descriptions of human and faery life that meet within the kingdom of Logres, living nested within each other. Let us define these locations a little more.

The Court, held at Carlion, or the other seats where Arthur holds sway, are part of the everyday world, the place where government and ruling happens. But the Grail Castle is not an ordinary location, resembling rather an earthly paradise: a place that cannot be easily found and, no matter how many times the questing knights discover it, they lose it again immediately by their failure to pose the right question. Just as in the traditions of Faery where human visitors wake up to find themselves back in the human realm, sometimes a hundred years or more astray from their own time, so the questing knights find themselves on the bare hillside with the otherworldly castle vanished away.

The many castles, woods, chapels, hermitages, and places discovered on the quest inhabit zones existing in a liminal space between the Court and the Grail Castle. These are rightly called the Lands Adventurous wherein wounds are got in single combat and bound up again; where wronged maidens seek redress from willing knights; where wars and injustices work themselves out; where relics, signs, dreams, and wonders instruct or confuse the questers. The Grail legends, too, are full of wounded knights and nameless maidens who, to some degree or the other, are existent in the zone between Arthur's court and the realms of Faery.

Many time zones are at work in the liminal realms of the quest. While the Court is always "now," in general, time within the quest zone shifts and changes. Within the Grail Castle and in the Castle of Maidens, long periods of time are either stretched beyond reckoning or else compressed into visionary moments where the quest becomes achievable, but that the questers miss time and again because they are still trying to apply the rules of ordinary time to timelessness. It is only by entering into timelessness that the quest is gained.

The further we travel through these legends in historical time, the more we discover that "faery" is often confused or confounded with "devil," becoming an uneasy mix of deep enchantment and Christian sinfulness. We find this exemplified in the person of Merlin, the child of a human mother and an unknown father of a supernatural race. In

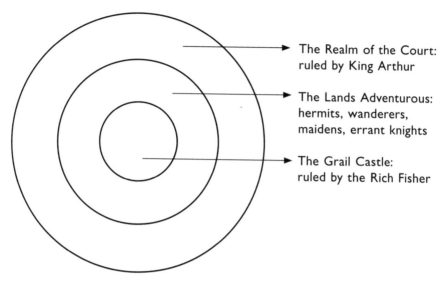

The Realm of the Court:
ruled by King Arthur

The Lands Adventurous:
hermits, wanderers,
maidens, errant knights

The Grail Castle:
ruled by the Rich Fisher

Fig. 4.2. The Realms within Logres: The everyday world of Arthur's Court is constantly impinged upon by the Lands Adventurous and affected by the deeper zone where the Grail Castle is found.

the context of Celtic myth, someone like Merlin would be thought of as a person who is half faery, half human; by the time we gain the later reaches of Arthurian legend, he has become a half-human demidevil, one whose demonic inheritance is harnessed by his Christian baptism to the service of Logres. This same elision from faery being to demon besets many figures within Arthurian literature, where some of the originally faery characters become merely evil human beings, as we can see is the case with Morgain le Fée who changes from the faery queen of an otherworldly island to a human enchantress in a matter of three centuries.[9]

The perceived devilish trickiness of faeries becomes more and more pronounced in the Grail legends until, by the time we come to the *Third Continuation,* Perceval is drawn to a tree full of lights. Later, this experience is explained to him by a hermit like this:

This is the tree of enchantment around which the faeries gather. The candle-like lights seen from afar are the faeries who will lead all astray. . . . As you rode up to the tree, you chased away the faery women, and no one will ever hear of them again.[10]

The demonizing process at work on the otherworldly characters in the Arthurian legends results here in the diminishment of faeries as deceiving little tricksters.

As for the Maidens of the Wells who offer their hospitality at the beginning of *The Elucidation*'s story, it is clear that they are not human women, but rather what the French understood as *fées,* faery women, and it is as such that we have to consider them if this alternative Grail story is to have any sense. The maidens do not behave as humans, and the hospitality that they offer is too rich and various to be considered as the kind service offered to wayfarers by monastic foundations or castles. Their otherworldly role was still to be later developed by Thomas Malory in his *Morte d'Arthur* as "the ladies of the lake," but at this point they remain anonymous faery women. Interestingly, the English *Merlin,* which predates Malory, develops the faery women theme even further, perhaps because of the powerful folk memory still persisting within medieval England.[11]

Within *The Elucidation*'s own time line, the story moves from a time of peaceful accord wherein humans and faeries enjoy good, neighborly relations, to a time of Wasteland when no faeries can be seen, and where a state of distrust exists between the two races. Beyond that time, we are not told how many generations might have ensued: Arthur's Round Table knights swear to punish the lineage of the perpetrators who first broke the accord. The story has strange starts and sudden extensions forward in time, but somehow the Wasteland is healed. If only the court of the Rich Fisher can be found, everything looks as if it can be made well, but what emerges instead is a rival Rich Company who do battle with Arthur: we shall explore this further in chapters 7 and 8.

How does Faery enter into this story? In this chapter, we will attempt to see the themes more clearly and see how, under and through the tapestry woven by the miraculous relics of the Passion, there shines another story.

THE FAERY ACCORD AND ITS BREAKING

The hospitable custom of the Maidens of the Wells who offer all travelers food and drink is universal in *The Elucidation:* the maidens do not discriminate but offer refreshment to any traveler who applies:

> *No one who wandered the by-ways,*
> *Be it in evening or morning,*
> *Whether to drink or to eat*
> *Would need to change his route*
> *Save he who turned towards the wells.*
> *He could request nothing*
> *By way of fine food that pleased him*
> *That would not be given to him,*
> *Provided he asked reasonably*
> *Then would arise, as I understand,*
> *A maiden from out of the well.*
>
> *He could not have asked for one more beautiful.*
> *Carrying a golden cup in her hand*
> *With meats, pies, and bread.*
> *Another maiden bringing in turn*
> *A white napkin and dish*
> *Of gold and silver in which was*
> *The meal that had been asked for,*
> *By whoever had come for the meal.*
> *At the well, many were well received;*
> *And if the meal did not please him,*
> *Many others were brought him*
> *[lacuna] . . . all as desired*[12]

This hospitality seems completely unconditional, suggestive of an ancient accord upheld by both faery and human races. To understand this accord in a wider sense, we turn to stories of the theft of the faery horn, a theme common throughout much of Europe. Here is an English example from *Otia Imperalia* by Gervase of Tilbury of 1211, a text that is near contemporary with *The Elucidation*. It is called *De Cornu et Etiam Pincerna* (Of the Horn and Its Butler):

There is in the county of Gloucester, a forest abounding in boars, stags, and every species of game that England produces. In a green grove of this forest, there is a little mount, rising in a point to the height of a man, on which knights and other hunters are used to ascend when fatigued with heat and thirst, to seek some relief for their wants. The nature of the places, and other business, is, however, such that whoever ascends the mount must leave his companions, and go quite alone.

When alone, he was to say, as if speaking to some other person, "I thirst," and immediately there would appear a cup bearer in an elegant dress, with a cheerful countenance, bearing in his stretched-out hand a large horn, adorned with gold and gems, as was the custom among the most ancient English. In the cup nectar of an unknown but most delicious flavor was presented, and when it was drunk, all heat and weariness fled from the glowing body, so that one would be thought ready to undertake toil instead of having toiled. Moreover, when the nectar was taken, the servant presented a towel to the drinker, to wipe his mouth with, and then having performed his office, he waited neither for a recompense for his services, nor for questions and enquiry.

This frequent and daily action had for a very long period of old times taken place among the ancient people, till one day a knight of that city, when out hunting, went thither, and having called for a drink and gotten the horn, did not, as was the custom, and as in good manners he should have done, return it to the cupbearer, but kept it for his own use. But the illustrious Earl of Gloucester, when he learned the truth of the matter, condemned the robber to death, and presented the horn to the most excellent King Henry the Elder, lest he should be thought to have approved of such wickedness, if he had added the rapine of another to the store of his private property.[13]

This story is so like that of *The Elucidation* that we cannot help but wonder if our author had heard or read it. Though the cupbearer here is male rather than female, the story is remarkably similar. One of the oldest versions of the same story concerns the Oldenburg Horn. It tells how count Otto of Oldenburg, who succeeded his father Ulrich in 967, was hunting in the wood of Bernefeuer and fervently wished for a cool drink.

No sooner had the count spoken the word than the Osenberg opened, and out of the cleft there came a beautiful maiden, fairly adorned and handsomely dressed, and with her beautiful hair divided on her shoulders, and a garland on her head. And she had a rich silver vessel, that was gilded and shaped like a hunter's horn . . . and it was full, and she gave it into the hand of the count, and prayed that the count would drink out of it to refresh himself therewith. When the count had received and taken this gilded silver horn from the maiden, and had opened it and looked into it, the drink, or whatever it was that was in it, when he shook it, did not please him, and he therefore refused to drink for the maiden. Whereupon the maiden said, "My dear lord, drink of it upon my faith, for it will do you no harm, but will be of advantage"; adding further, that if the count would drink out of it, it would go well with him, Count Otto and his, and also with the whole house of Oldenburg after him, and that the whole country would improve and flourish. But if the count would place no faith in her, and would not drink of it, then for the future, in the succeeding family of Oldenburg, there would remain no unity.

But when the count gave no heed to what she said, but, as was not without reason, considered with himself a long time whether he should drink or not, he held the silver gilded horn in his hand and swung it behind him, and poured it out, and some of its contents sprinkled the white horse, and where it fell and wetted the hair, it all came off. When the maiden saw this, she desired to have her horn back again, but the count made speed down the hill with the horn, which he held in his hand, and when he looked round he observed that the maiden was gone into the hill again. And when terror seized on the count on account of this, he laid spurs to his horse, and at full speed hasted to join his attendants, and informed them of what had befallen him. He moreover showed them the silver gilded horn, and took it with him to Oldenburg, and the same horn, as it was obtained in so wonderful a manner, was preserved as a costly jewel by him, and by all the succeeding reigning princes of the house of Oldenburg.[14]

Here, the trust of the drinker in the hospitality offered is less than perfect: but we note that his lack of faith will have consequences to the successive rulers of the country where "there would remain no unity." In both these folktales we note that the cupbearers issue from a mound or cleft in the earth, and we are forced to reconsider whether the maidens in *The Elucidation* come forth from wells or from hills. In general, the faery mound, or *sheehan* as it is anglicized from the Irish *sí*, is where the faeries live. It doesn't help that the Old French words for "well" and "hill" are virtually identical: wells are referred to as *puis,* while a hill is *pui.* Perhaps we can understand this confusion better by examining the story of the *Vessel of Badurn.* This otherworldly cup is one of the famous "Irish Ordeals," one of many objects that have capacity to discern truth and falsehood.

Badurn was a king. His wife went to the well and there saw two women *coming out of the faery-mounds,* and between them stretched a chain of bronze. When they saw Badurn's wife coming toward them they went under the well. So, she followed after, going *under the well* and in the faery mound saw a marvelous ordeal, a vessel made of crystal. If anyone should utter three lying words under it, it would divide into three pieces in his hand. If anyone should utter three true words under it, it would reunite. Badurn's wife begged to be given that vessel from the folk of the sheehan, and so it was. This was the vessel that Badurn kept for distinguishing lies and truth.[15]

Taking this story as an example we can see how the wells of *The Elucidation*'s maidens can easily be both cleft in the ground that has a spring within it, and also a sheehan or faery hill that rises over the well. However, it is the context that clinches the argument since, in *The Elucidation,* the immediate result of Amangons's violation is Wasteland, a state where no waters irrigate the soil. Both the service of hospitality and the waters that fructify the land are withdrawn, while the court of the Rich Fisher, which purveys all kinds of resources to Logres, becomes unfindable. Let us remain with the wells.

The theft of the faery horn of hospitality has particular features that we should note. In Gervase's story, the mound is one that only a lone traveler can climb, the horn gives a drink of sweet flavor; it is stolen away for personal use by the thief. In the Oldenburg Horn story, the proffered horn comes with the promise of good fortune but, because Otto doesn't trust the maiden and pours out the drink upon his horse's back, the drink becomes poisonous and strips the hair from its hide. He also takes the horn. Both stories either relate or imply that unity and harmony result from this courteous act of hospitality until the custom is violated:

This frequent and daily action had for a very long period of old times taken place among the ancient people, till one day a knight of that city went out hunting, went thither, and having called for a drink and gotten the horn, did not, as was the custom, and as in good manners he should have done, return it to the cupbearer, but kept it for his own use.[16]

Since the act of theft breaks the accord between humans *and* faeries within *The Elucidation*, we precisely understand what Amangons has perpetrated: an act that will resonate through time. Between our world and the realms of Faery there have been many permeable boundaries as faeries visit mortal realms and humans visit faery hills: the point of exchange is the giving and receiving of hospitality. When what we may call "the Faery Accord" is broken, human beings can no longer have clear and untroubled relations with Faery. The result of this fracture is catastrophic for our world.

The nature of this Faery Accord is demonstrated in the *Book of Fermoy* of 1391, in a story known as the "Fosterage in the House of the Two Pails." While the story has a clear Christian bias and attempts to demonstrate how, from the faery side of things, the worlds of men and faeries are parted, it is helpful to see how things work from the viewpoint of the realm of Faery. The story is set on the eve of the coming of Saint Patrick and the conversion to Christianity of the Irish. Knowing this, Manannán mac Lír, god of the otherworldly Land of Promise and chief among the Tuatha de Danann people, decides to assign some special support to the faery race. He made

> a special dwelling to each noble and made for the warriors the Feth Fiadha, the Feast of Goibniu and Manannán's Swine: that is, the princes could not be seen through the Feth Fiadha, the monarchs escaped age and decay by the feast of Goibniu, and Manannán's Swine could be killed by the warriors but it come alive again.[17]

Manannán makes the *sí* mounds or faery hills for his race, creating the *fé fiadha,* or faery mist, which creates a cordon between our world and that of the faery realms, preserving faeries from prying eyes. The faeries likewise escape death and aging by attending the feast of Goibniu, the smith, at which the pigs of Manannán are cooked but, as long as no bones are broken, the very next day are alive again and ready to be cooked once more.

The story concerns a young human girl, Eithne, who lives in Faery as the much-loved foster sister to Curcog, Manannán's faery daughter. After being insulted by a visiting lord, Eithne goes into a deep decline and finds herself unable to eat the foods of Faery, except for the milk of a Dun Cow milked into a golden cup: both cup and cow have come "from an (unspecified) holy land," beyond Faery. Manannán is saddened to hear of it and, since he had the ability to diagnose and cure any illness, he has food of every flavor prepared to tempt her to eat, but to no avail. He finally diagnoses that the cause of her decline is the insult given to her and—remembering that this is a highly Christianized text—that "her guardian demon (spirit) left her heart and an angel came in his place."

Eithne cannot be nourished any longer by the food of Faery, only by the milk of the cow, which is from a "righteous" (non-Faery) land. The cup gives her nourishment now because, although she has never been exposed to Christianity, the Trinity have mysteriously become the gods of her heart. We may speculate that it is the insult offered to her by the visiting lord that has made her vulnerable both to hurt and to new influences, just as the rapine of Amangons changed the condition of the maidens forever.

Eithne and Curcog then go swimming in the river Boyne when, suddenly, Eithne loses the protection of the *fé fiadha* and can no longer see her companions. She swims to the opposite bank, finding herself upon a shore of Christian people. A cleric who views her arrival says to her, "Your coming to us is welcome . . . though not to you." She is given welcome by the cleric while, meantime on the other side of the river, her Tuatha de Danann kindred search for her: she herself can still faintly discern them through the *fé fiadha* and they are aware of her, but the cleric himself is unaware of any such land. Eithne finally accepts baptism and is lost to the Land of Promise forever, stepping outside the faery cordon of protection.

This story gives us a faery mist or cordon and a perpetual, life-preserving feast, very like that of the Grail Castle, which is so hard to find. Eithne herself begins by being totally at home in Faery but, after the wounding insult, is unable to eat the food of her foster family. In one stroke, she has become wholly human and only able to eat the food of Christians, which is why she passes out of the timelessness of Faery into the time-bound world of her own people once again. As this sad little tale informs us, once the accord between humans and faeries is broken, it would take a miracle to repair it.

On what is the Faery Accord based? The standard contract can easily be recovered from reading any of a multitude of faery stories that tell us, over and over, the exact clauses and the small print entailed in any relations between faeries and humans: speak kindly, never strike, respect mutual boundaries, never show greed, do not steal, keep your word. As soon as one of these is fractured, it breaks the accord and from this point friendly relations cease. As we see from the horn stories, the theft of the cup causes the fracture of the accord, while in the story of Eithne, her ability to be at one with the faery realms is shattered by her being struck by insults. These are deep violations.

The original mission of the Faery Accord is very simple: the act of sharing food or drink renders taker and giver into friends by the act of hospitality. Those who are used to reading about the Holy Grail as a sacramental vessel are invited here to consider this Faery Grail in a similar light. For the faery cup is a vessel that joins people of different dispositions into a state of accord and unity. Its withdrawal from our world marks the sad loss of an accord that bridges differences and breaks long-held trust between the human and faery worlds: a fracture whose environmental consequences can be easily appreciated, for the faery kind uphold the world of nature.

In the light of this we may consider the oft-repeated warning from faery stories to not eat while in Faery, which is at such variance with what we have seen as the primary hospitality mode of the faery hills and wells. It would seem that this traditional warning arises *in the aftermath of the accord's fracture,* when there is no longer trust between humans and faeries.

Instead of partaking in a simple and trusting act of hospitality, Amangons's act forthrightly closes down the Faery Accord as several of the clauses above are broken and all neighborly relations henceforth cease. The violation and abduction of the maidens and the theft of the vessel of hospitality—cup or horn—ensures the cessation of all hospitality to travelers and a resultant loss of fertility in both land and people. Wasteland and depopulation are the outcome. We will further explore the violation of hospitality again in chapter 7.

From these faery legends of Gervase and the Oldenburg Horn, we see that the cup that is proffered to the visitor by the faery maiden is a drinking horn, not a graal, Grail, or chalice. Fortunately, the Arthurian legends supply us with another incident or two in which a horn is brought from Faery, although in an utterly different manner.

The brief but significant Breton lay, *Le Lai du Cor,* penned by Robert Biket between 1170 and 1180, may hold a key to the mystery of the wells and the breaking of the Faery Accord. *The Lay of the Horn* tells how a young page brings to the court of Arthur at Carlion an ivory horn decorated with jewels and hung with musically chiming bells. The page has brought the horn from his king, Mangons the Blond of Moraine, as a gift, but it has been made by a faery of a particularly spiteful kind. It can be drained only by someone who has a faithful lover. Unfortunately, Arthur tries it and is covered with wine from head to toe. Guinevere makes some plausible excuses for this upset, and then Arthur, not to be the only one shamed at court, makes the other kings and knights attempt this marvel. Of them all, only Caradoc dares drink with impunity, with his loyal wife quietly confident that he will succeed. Crying, "Wassail," Caradoc drains the horn without accident, thus proving the constancy of his relationship.[18]

This lay, with its "yard of ale" test, stands in the tradition of "chastity or faithfulness tests" where objects are brought to Arthur's court, only to radically change things, depending on who is testing them. This horn test is largely one for men, just as the one for women is a testing mantle. In the thirteenth-century lay, *Lai du Mantel,* a magical mantle is brought to Arthur's court that, when placed about the shoulders of a faithful woman will entirely cover her, but when placed about an unchaste woman will suddenly and embarrassingly shrink up above her loins.[19]

In our inquiries, we are most interested in the horn, who sent it, who made it, and why it was brought. *The Lay of the Horn* dates from before *The Elucidation* was composed, and this incident is also retold in the *First Continuation,* so it is squarely part of the Grail cycle. The king who sends the horn to Arthur is significantly called Mangounz or Mangons, in the original Norman French. The only further information we have about him is that he is blond haired and that he lives in Moraine. Now, the Old French *moraine* means "pestilence," from *mourir,* "to die." (The same root gives us the English word *murrain,* now used specifically as "a disease among livestock.") Is this our own Amangons, the first of the known anti-Grail Kings, whose castle is death? (See chapter 6.)

In this lay, the horn is neither the generous vessel of the Maidens of the Wells, nor is its purpose innocent. Its provenance is totally different: instead of an evil Amangons and innocent maidens, the *Lai du Cor*'s horn is made by a spiteful faery into a testing vessel that will not give drink without public embarrassment, except for a very few drinkers who have faithful partners.

Let us consider, for a moment, the reason *why* the horn is sent. If we keep the Faery Accord and its fracture foremost in our minds for a moment, we can focus more exactly upon the motivation of this horn's mission. The original accord between the two races is based upon hospitality, which is afterward withdrawn when the contract is broken. In the horn test, the horn is brought from a liminal realm, made by faery manufacture, to the court of Arthur, there to test the faithfulness of his people: Arthur is the first to be personally embarrassed, followed in turn by nearly every other person in his court. It would seem that the result of drinking from the horn is completely the reverse of its original offering in the folktales of the hospitable vessels and in the story of *The Elucidation.* Rather than refreshing thirst and putting the drinker at ease, this horn makes the drinker embarrassed and shows him up to be living a lie because his sweetheart is faithless to her vows of love. It is a horn that underscores the human penchant for betrayal.

Mangons primarily seems to send the horn to embarrass Arthur. The messenger who brings the cup makes plain the nature of the gift and the condition that is upon it: "The brave and courtly King Mangons, sends this horn to you, taken from his treasury with a certain condition. Attend to his wishes, without either being grateful to him or wishing him any harm."[20] In other words, the condition is that Arthur shall neither express gratitude for the gift nor wish harm upon the sender: a complete suspension of the usual reception of so rich a gift, which is made of ivory, inlaid with silver and jewel, and with hundreds of golden bells. Knowing full well what the horn's action brings about, Mangons purposely set this "certain condition" to remove any obligation or blame, so that no human from Arthur's court will seek redress of Faery. The clauses of this "certain condition" are carefully worded in a way that smacks of the devious nature of faery small print: a caution that prevents Arthur from taking any revenge.

The text tells us that the vengeful, unnamed faery woman who bespelled the horn ensures that "no one however wise or foolish, cuckolded or jealous, or having a wife who has lewd thoughts about another man than himself," will ever be able to drink from it without embarrassment. It is a horn that shames men and women alike, like the common medieval "cuckold's horns" that are said to grow upon the husband whom a woman cuckolds. Much though he would like to, Arthur cannot even call upon any kinsman or neighbor to make war on Mangons, because he has sworn not to harm him as a consequence of accepting this dubious gift: "To go back upon my word would be to perjure myself. I do not like forsworn kings."[21]

Guinevere attempts to dissuade Arthur from passing the horn into the hands of another nobleman, lest he be similarly embarrassed, but the king makes every other man try it, "Since I will not be the only one to be covered with shame!"[22] It is clear that a certain amount of *schadenfreude* is enjoyed by Arthur at the discomfiture of his fellow kings and knights, as they each slop wine over themselves. The Round Table company is only saved from total humiliation by the couple Caradoc and his unnamed lady who bids her husband drink without fear. The horn is charged with a measure of wine (about six pints) and Caradoc drains it without spillage, thus proving his own relationship constant. The story ends with the departure of the feasters who all "took their wives back and loved them all the more."[23]

In terms of the Faery Accord, the *Lai du Cor* seems to be a story that postdates the breaking of the accord that we find in *The Elucidation*. The mocking gift that is sent back into human realms is one that brings harm to both men and women, a testing gift designed to highlight what the faery regard as the most despicable of human vices: inconstancy and the breaking of promises—the very point upon which the hospitality of the wells rests. Mangons gets off scot-free, without either thanks or blame resting at his door, and all that is left is the nagging, vengeful spell of the undrinkable horn, the very reverse of the Maidens of the Wells' refreshment. The episode of the *Lai du Cor* is actually repeated, in brief, within the *First Continuation*, and we will further explore its placement and significance in chapter 8.

We read of a similar vessel to this horn, this time a precious and magical tankard, or lidded stein, brought to Arthur's court in *Diu Cröne* (the Crown) by Heinrich von dem Türlin, written between 1210 and 1240 in a Bavarian-Austrian dialect.[24] The vessel performs a similar accident upon the unwary drinker with a false sweetheart, like the ivory horn of the *Lai du Cor;* it is a vessel once more embarrassing to most of the court. This lidded cup is made by a Toledan craftsman with knowledge of necromancy (magic). Whoever owns it will never be robbed of it wherever he goes, and it will always appear at his demand.

The cup's messenger informs the court that should any person be able to drink from it without spillage, then the successful drinker will ensure that the testing cup comes into Arthur's possession forever. But, if no one is so able, then the messenger will personally joust with anyone there and, if defeated, will give the cup to the victor. Soon each member of the court is covered with wine and also falling down into a drunken stupor, until only Keii (Kay) and the messenger are left standing.

The story is largely the same as *Lai du Cor,* but there are details that arrest us suddenly. In *Diu Cröne,* the vessel has been sent to Arthur by a King Priure from overseas, and his messenger is King Bilis the Dwarf, a being no taller than a six-year-old child, with a hooded cloak of gray silk. His appearance is strange, with his skin hidden by scales, his wide mouth, large icy-gray eyes the size of ostrich eggs, and his hair like fish fins. Such a being seems to emanate from an otherworldly or undersea realm.

Suddenly we are all attention on two counts: first because someone called Bilis (Blihis?) is associated once again with a vessel, and secondly because the name Priure leads us into one of the main sources of the

Grail legend. *Priure,* when pronounced aloud (PRI-urry), has the resonance of a much earlier character from Welsh legend, Pryderi (Prud-ER-y). Let us follow the clues.

THE VESSEL OF THE UNDERWORLD

For the Celtic peoples, realms overseas were liminal, otherworldly places. In Ireland, the Blessed Islands of the West are typified by the Land of Promise, ruled over by Manannán mac Lír, god of the otherworld: this same divinity is known as Manawyddan across the water in Britain, where the underworld was a realm reachable by water or ocean-going voyages. The realm beneath, Annwfyn, was the "not world," or the inverse to our own.

In the Welsh tradition, Pryderi, whose name so closely parallels King Priure, is the child of Pwyll of Dyfed and Rhiannon, a faery woman from the otherworld. Both Pwyll and his son Pryderi are famous for their sojourns in the realm of Annwyfn (modern Welsh, Annwn), or the In-World, which lies beneath our own. Pwyll, as ruler of Dyfed, spends a significant time in Annwyfn as the guest of its king, Arawn: between the earthly ruler and the underworldly king a faery accord is agreed. Pwyll spends some time, while in the form of Arawn, in Annwyfn, while Arawn spends an equal time in the realm of Dyfed, in the likeness of Pwyll. This reciprocal arrangement leads to Arawn gifting Pwyll with pigs—a species of beasts never previously seen in Britain, we are told.

Pwyll goes on to become the husband of Rhiannon, finding her upon the Hill of Wonders: a hill that only one man can climb at a time, just as in the Oldenburg Horn story, and to whom it is promised that he will meet either blows or wonders. Rhiannon appears on horseback and no matter how quickly Pwyll attempts to follow her, she is always ahead of him, until he asks her to stop. His attempts to marry her are serially interrupted by Rhiannon's faery suitor, Gwawl, until finally, with Rhiannon's wise help, Pwyll captures and beats Gwawl, causing him to relinquish his attempts to stop their marriage by violence.

However the couple's troubles are not finished. After giving birth to a boy, Rhiannon wakes to find her baby missing: a mysterious hand has come down the chimney and removed it. The midwives, in an attempt to cover themselves from accusations of neglect, kill a puppy and strew its bones suggestively about Rhiannon, who is then unjustly accused of eating her own child. The child, spirited away by a mysterious hand, turns up in another part of Wales where he is brought up kindly by foster parents. Rhiannon's punishment, to bear guests into the hall on her own back and relate her misdeeds to any stranger, comes to an end only when the child's foster parents realize that the boy must indeed be Rhiannon's. On hearing her child is found, she pronounces, "At last my troubles are over." And it is from this, *pryder,* or anxiety, that Pryderi gets his name.[25]

The story of Pwyll's accord with Arawn, the gift of pigs, and his marriage with Rhiannon in *Pwyll, Prince of Dyfed,* precedes the story of how his son becomes lost a second time, related in *Manawyddan, son of Llyr.* In this later story, Pwyll has died and Rhiannon has married the wily Manawyddan. No sooner has Pryderi attempted to come into his inheritance than a magic mist and an enchantment descends upon his home; his castle vanishes and he, his wife, his mother, and his stepfather are bereft from their own land, so that they have to resort to living off the place where they find themselves, the realm of Logres.

While following a white boar on a hunt, Pryderi finds a gold bowl hanging from chains in an otherworldly castle. He grasps the golden bowl, becoming ludicrously and physically stuck to it. His mother, Rhiannon, in attempting to rescue him, clutches Pryderi and becomes likewise stuck to the bowl. The castle vanishes with them both in it. Mother and son enter into a form of otherworldly slavery, until rescued by Rhiannon's second husband, Manawyddan, who draws out the culprit, Llwyd, by magical means. Llwyd turns out to have acted due to his family relationship with Rhiannon's ex-suitor Gwawl, his cousin, and caused the golden bowl test to spirit them away. We learn that, during their sojourn in the otherworld, Pryderi has had the door knockers of the otherworldly palace about his neck, while Rhiannon has had the collars of asses about her neck.

So, both Pwyll and Pryderi are travelers in the realms of the faery hills. Pwyll's accord with Arawn brings the gift of pigs to Dyfed, but his marriage with the faery woman, Rhiannon, lays up troubles that keep recurring: not only does Rhiannon have to behave like a horse in bearing guests into the hall on her back but she also has the collars of asses put about her neck. Pryderi is led inexorably back to the otherworld, from whence came his father's pigs, by a white boar; he becomes stuck to the golden bowl that draws him and his mother back to her own faery people. To conclude everything, Pryderi has to wear the door knockers of the otherworldly gates about his neck, symbolically and actually becoming a door warden of that realm. Both mother and son are drawn back to faery realms, and it is only by the cunning of Manawyddan that they are rescued.

In the ancient memory of the British, Pwyll and Pryderi are remembered as heroes who entered into the perilous place of the Lord of the Underworld, Pen Annwfyn, whose cauldron provides us with one of the earliest prototypes of the Grail. In British tradition, this is a cauldron that, like the testing horn and tankard above, is itself a test: it will not boil the food of a coward, and thus the result can only be achieved by a hero. It abides in the otherworld and is finally sought by Arthur himself who goes with three shiploads of men through the seven caers, or castles, of the underworld to bring it back, as we hear in the tenth-century British poem, *Preiddeu Annwfyn*. The cauldron is found in many different ways. The poem tells us that both Pryderi and his father, Pwyll, know about the captivity of the otherworldly place where the cauldron dwells, and speaks of their likeness to Gweir, an even earlier hero who came to seek it and who was caught in the gyrations of the turning tower of Caer Sidi (the Faery Tower), from which is he known as the Great Prisoner:

> *Gweir's captivity in Caer Sidi was resonant*
> *With the tale of Pwyll and Pryderi.*
> *None before him was sent into it,*

Into the heavy blue chain that bound the faithful youth.
Because of the raid upon Annwfyn he sorely sang.
Until the world's ending our poet's prayer shall sound:
Three ship-burdens of Prydwen entered within
Except seven, none rose up from Caer Sidi.[26]

The sevenfold nature of the cauldron's discovery is unsurprising to us, having read *The Elucidation* and knowing that its precious vessel is guarded by seven mysterious branches and guardians. So, if the sense of walking downstairs and finding another stair we didn't expect grips us, then we should not be surprised: we have merely gone down a mythic level, even deeper into the far memory of the Grail myths.

Pwyll's reciprocal sojourn in the underworld is the result of a faery accord, amicably and mutually entered into, but the captivity of Pryderi in the underworld is rather a result of Rhiannon's marriage to Pwyll, which sets aside Rhiannon's former suitor Gwawl and does violence to him: Gwawl is beaten black and blue—thus violating one of the major clauses of the primary Faery Accord, that faeries should never be struck. In these two *Mabinogi,** we find the template for the Faery Accord and its breaking: human Pwyll and underworldly Arawn change forms and places, building trust to such an extent that Pwyll ends up marrying a faery woman. Rhiannon's disinterest in her faery suitor, Gwawl, and Pwyll's action of striking Gwawl, stores up trouble for Rhiannon and Pwyll's later relationship; finally, this affects their son, Pryderi, against whom great malice is rolled out.

If we take into account the Celtic tradition of the descent to the underworld, we also have another level of our quest: the Great Prisoner. As in the labyrinthine journey of the Grail quest, the hero who enters into the faery fortress of Caer Sidi to gain the cauldron is indentured to continue in its service until he is released. He becomes "the Great Prisoner." His sojourn is full of lamentation because the faery cordon,

---

*The *Mabinogi* are four connected narratives, or branches, of Welsh legend. Together with additional tales, they form the text called *The Mabinogion.*

the "heavy blue chain" of ocean, keeps him islanded, unable to return to ordinary life. His state is like that of the Fisher King who is bound to remain in suffering until the right moment. In the tenth-century Grail quest poem, *Preiddeu Annwfyn* (the Raid on the Underworld), it is Arthur himself who wins the cauldron, penetrating the seven caers to find it. The implication of his quest is that the Great Prisoner is released, just as Manawyddan rescues Pryderi and his mother. We will follow this theme further in chapter 8.

In the *Defence of the Chair,* a poem attributed to the sixth-century bard Taliesin, both Manawyddan and Pryderi, stepfather and stepson, are paired together, as the poet proclaims:

> *My chair is in Caer Sidi,*
> *where no one is afflicted with age or illness.*
> *Manawyd and Pryderi have known it well.*[27]

The location of the cauldron within the seven caers of Annwfyn is not an earthly or human one. It is a place wherein age and illness do not strike: it is the realm of Faery.

Translating these early Celtic traditions back into medieval Grail quest terms, the wondrous vessel cannot be accessed by just anyone. The first entrant into the quest after the Faery Accord's fracture becomes stuck there in timelessness, just as the Fisher King does with the endlessly repeating Grail procession. The toil of the Grail seekers is to serially endure the spiraling of the quest as they find the Grail Castle, neglecting to ask the right questions, and then losing the location time and again. In more than one of the Grail texts, including *Diu Cröne,* the castle of the Fisher King revolves, requiring the seeker to take a leap of faith, to enter at the right moment as the door whirls past.

The purpose of the original faery vessel is primarily the provision of hospitality. It is a cauldron from which all may feast, as an early medieval list of the Thirteen *Thlysau,* or Treasures, of Britain reveals:

the cauldron of Diwrnach the Giant; if you placed meat to boil for a coward, it would never boil; but if you put the meat of a brave man into it, the meat would boil quickly and so distinguish the brave from the cowardly.[28]

Although the cauldron is assigned to the ownership of Diwrnach the Giant in this source, it is clearly the same as the cauldron of the underworld, owned by Pen Annwfyn. In the same text, we hear about "the Horn of Bran the Miser from the North; it provided the drink that the drinker most desired."[29]

We will speak more of Bran in chapters 6 and 7, but we note that the two vessels from the Thirteen Treasures list provide precisely the same services as the golden cups of the Maidens of the Wells, and also of the Grail. While the shape of the vessel may change, the cup of accord remains one of hospitality: it satisfies hunger and thirst in appropriate ways, to the diner's taste, as well as being a symbol of the accord between humans and faeries, or between the living and the dead, since the cauldron of Annwfyn is in the custodianship of Pen Annwfyn, Lord of the Otherworldly Feast of the ancestral dead.

The testing horn of the *Lai du Cor,* like the golden cauldron to which Pryderi and his mother become attached, is a vessel of embarrassment: the horn is sent to test the virtue of the courtiers, while the sticky golden cauldron prefaces Pryderi's servitude and suffering. It is with this understanding that we need to consider the tankard that is sent to Arthur's court in *Diu Cröne,* a cup sent by King Priure (Pryderi) and delivered by Bilis the dwarf. It is sent as a further proffer of the original vessel of accord and hospitality: if there are but one or two who pass the test, then restoration may be possible.

The fact that we have someone called Bilis as the cup's messenger in *Diu Cröne* just underscores what we have already understood about Blihis Bleheris: a man who is the half-human descendant of Amangons, but also the half-faery offspring of a Maiden of the Wells. Bleheris and his kindred are unable to rediscover the court of the Rich Fisher for themselves, but they need other seekers to come in search of it—only then can they cease from their wanderings and the Court of Joy be found:

> *[we] must wander so*
> *Until God allows them to find*
> *The court from which joy will come,*
> *By which the country will be resplendent.*[30]

That joy can only be the original accord that was once between humans and faeries, where everyone is restored to a shared vision of the world when harmony and concord are maintained.

5

IN THE LAND
OF WOMEN

*The green-backed wave brought them over the calm sea to
an island, with a mound and fortress full of folk.
Beautiful maidens dwelt therein, as they could see; the
bath they tended was filled with the brightest water.*

"VOYAGE OF MAELDUIN" (TRANS. CM)

OTHERWORLDLY ISLANDS

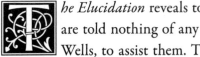he *Elucidation* reveals to us the Maidens of the Wells, but we are told nothing of any male counterparts, no Squires of the Wells, to assist them. This fact alone tells us one thing: that we are looking at an antique tradition of female guardians of otherworldly resources, wisdom, and hospitality, a tradition that is well established in the mythology of the northwest Atlantic coast of Europe.[1]

The early medieval nature of Faery in the Arthurian legend was strongly influenced by the British and Irish traditions, which frequently located the realms of Faery in a place divided from mortal realms by water. In the ancient Irish tradition, the Island of Women is one such location, as found in the Irish eighth-century text of *Immram Brain* (the Voyage of Bran). The warrior Bran mac Febal is invited by an otherwordly woman to come to her island; he voyages thither with a band of men and finds this realm. When finally persuaded by his homesick followers to leave this paradisal island, they sail home but, as they approach the shores of Ireland, they dialogue with some shepherds on the shore, only to discover that hundreds of years have passed since their embarkation and that all their family and friends are now long buried. For the living, Bran's outward voyage has become just an ancient story. Rather than lose their lives by stepping ashore, when time may reassert its power, or risk a return to a land from whence all their kindred have departed, Bran and his companions sail onward.

The Land of Women, or *Tír na Mna,* is part of an Atlantic coastal myth that is shared from France up to Scotland and Ireland and was already ancient when the first Classical scholars wrote of it. An island of just women may seem fantastic but Pomponius Mela reported that

> the island of Sein, near the Ossimiens, is known as the oracle of a Gaulish God. The priestesses of that God number nine, and they are called "Senes" by the Gauls. Possessed by the God's spirit, they believe that they can create storms in the air and at sea by their spells; that they can shapeshift into any sort of animal, cure grave illnesses, and know and divine the future, but only to those sailors who voyage over the ocean to visit them.[2]

The oracular Senes live on an island that can be visited only by invitation but other priestesses are recorded by the first-century CE Greek geographer Strabo, who reports a similar regime.

> Not far from the mouth of the Loire lies a small island in the ocean; it is inhabited by the women of the Samnitae, who are possessed by Dionysius, propitiating the god with initiations and other sacred rites; and no man may land on the island, though the women themselves sail out from it and have intercourse with men, returning afterward.[3]

The women discussed by Strabo and Pomponius Mela may well be human priestesses, but the Land of Women reported in Irish legend enters mythology as but one of many islands that lie somewhere off the western seaboard of Europe. The Land of Women serves as an enclave of wisdom, healing, mystery, and sexual joy. Like Odysseus and Bran before him, the Irish hero Maelduin and his followers are bespelled by the delights of the Island of Women.

They came to a large island with a massive interior plain, covered with grass. A great fortress stood near the sea, a beautifully appointed house with soft beds. Seventeen nubile maidens were preparing a bath. As the crew landed and made their way to the fort's entrance, Maelduin remarked, "That bath is being prepared for us." They saw a richly dressed horsewoman coming toward them, who entered the fort. One of the maidens came and said, "The queen welcomes you, enter here." Maelduin sat with the queen and his men with each of the maidens while they feasted. The queen bade each man take the maiden next to him and retire to the canopied cubicles where the beds waited, while Maelduin slept with the queen. They slept till dawn. The queen said, "Remain with us and you will not grow older. You shall have immortality and enjoy what you enjoyed last night. Be no longer wanderers of the wave."

When Maelduin asked how she came here, she replied, "I was married to the king of this island to whom I bore these seventeen girls. He died and left no successor, so I ruled in his place and every day I go out to judge the community and guide its affairs." "Why do you need to leave us today?" Maelduin asked. "Because, unless I judge the people, you will not enjoy the delights you had last night."

They stayed for the three winter months and it seemed more like three years. The crew grew restless and wanted to return home. "We shall never find the like of this at home," said Maelduin. "Stay here and enjoy your woman, then, but we are going home," they said. Maelduin reluctantly accompanied them. But as they left, the queen threw a sticky clew of thread at Maelduin and drew him back. They stayed thrice three months and resolved once more to leave. "If the thread strikes Maelduin, we will be brought back to this place." "Then let some other catch it," said Maelduin. Again, they embarked and the queen threw her sticky thread. One of the crew caught the ball and his hand was severed by Diuran, so that they might escape. At that, the queen began to wail and cry, and that was how they escaped.[4]

In the eleventh-century Irish text, *Immram Maelduin,* from which this incident comes, Maelduin's stay in the Island of Women is of short duration, but he becomes, in effect, the consort of its queen who is also a judge. This combination of roles reveals that she is a faery queen, independently ruler in her own realm, the sovereign judge of all who live under her care. Throughout European folktale, we find similar stories of the youth or young man who encounters the faery queen or a faery woman who brings him into her own realm, for her own purposes. By so doing he becomes virtually immortal, as long as he remains within its confines.

Behind *The Elucidation* lies the French tradition of the *fées,* as well as the Irish tradition of the Island of Women, and the Romano-Celtic triple goddesses who hospitably bear cornucopias, bread, and fruit upon their laps; these and many elements fuse together to create the Arthurian faery tradition.[5] Taken together, these traditions give us the ladies of the lake, and a superabundance of faery women who come to invite, initiate, exhort, and irritate the Round Table knights.

Within the pages of the early French *lais* and stories, lone knights go on adventures that lead them ultimately into regions so dangerous that none before have returned to tell of them. The ultimate prize of some of these adventures is to overcome a guardian knight who, like the slave devoted to Arician Diana in the Roman Forest of Nemi, is but the latest champion appointed to defend and protect an otherworldly maiden against all comers. We find such a story in *The Lady of the Fountain,* the Welsh parallel to Chrétien's *Yvain,* where Owain comes to a clearly liminal place guarded by a black knight, who is the champion of the Lady of the Fountain.[6] By defeating and killing the champion, Owain automatically becomes the lady's new champion, just like the Roman Rex Nemorensis, the King of Wood who defended the shrine of Diana.[7]

Over and over, individual Round Table knights enter into situations

Fig. 5.1. *The Lady of the Fountain* by Chesca Potter

wherein they are brought into the realms of a powerful, otherworldly woman, to become her consort and to create a faery-human partnership, as we shall see again below. The Island of Women and the encounter with the faery queen takes a different kind of turn within the Grail legends but, since it is not an immediate or obvious connection, we need to bear the Land of Women in mind as we explore the unfolding themes presented by the Castle of Maidens.

Within *The Elucidation* we are told that the coming of the Rich Company brings forth a wave of building:

> *They built castles and cities*
> *Towns, boroughs, and strongholds,*
> *And built for the damsels*
> *The rich Castle of Maidens;*
> *They made the Perilous Bridge too*
> *And the great Castle of Pride.*[8]

These two castles, the Castle Orgueilleux or Proud Castle, and the Castle au Pucèlles or Castle of Maidens are both dangerous zones for the Round Table knights who venture there. The Proud Castle holds Girflet and other knights as prisoners without parole, as we saw above, while at the Castle of Maidens there are some tricky tests to negotiate, like the Perilous Bed, about which more below. Are we to understand that the Castle of Maidens is built by the Rich Company *for* the Maidens of the Wells? If so, then we have to rearrange our understanding of the Island of Women, for the Castle of Maidens seems to be the inverse ratio of the Island of Women. Instead of a land where faery women are in charge of their own affairs, we have instead a castle wherein the men of Amangons's kindred keep their imprisoned paramours locked up. We will look more closely at the Proud Castle and the Rich Company in chapters 7 and 8, but here we must examine the Castle of Maidens and learn exactly what kind of place it is.

The Castle of Maidens has a long history within the Arthurian tradition as a mysterious location in its own right, one with which Arthur himself has one of the oldest connections, which we will explore further in chapter 8, where we see *Castellum Puellarum* as the locus for a famous siege. *The Elucidation* reveals to us a very different Castle of Maidens, one created by the Rich Company putting a different spin on our understanding, which will be explored further in chapters 7 and 8. But let us first learn more about the Castle of Maidens as it appears in the Grail legends, starting with a summary of it from toward the end of Chrétien's *Perceval,* where it is part of Gawain's adventures.

GAWAIN AND THE CASTLE OF MAIDENS

Bearing in mind the Island of Women scenarios of earlier times, we can see how Gawain's own quest brings him to make a similar visit. In the following incident from *Perceval,* Gawain encounters a very proud maiden, as well as a collection of ladies whose antecedents prove to be most impressive.

Gawain is proceeding upon his quest for the Bleeding Spear when he comes upon a maiden grieving over a wounded knight who advises him to proceed no farther as he is on the border of Galvoie (Galloway), which no knight has ever crossed nor ever returned from. The wounded knight says he himself is the only one to have done so, but that he has been bested by a fearsome opponent stronger than any he has met.

Gawain pursues his quest, coming to a city girdled by a river that flows into the sea that borders one side of its castle. Here he encounters a pale maiden looking into a mirror who asks him to get her palfrey (a walking horse) from a nearby garden. She speaks haughtily and insultingly to him. Gawain is about to lay hand upon the palfrey's bridle when another knight tells him that if he takes it, he'll find even worse challenges elsewhere, for no one has taken the palfrey and escaped beheading. Nevertheless, Gawain brings the palfrey to the Maiden with the Mirror who refuses his help but agrees to follow him.

Gawain returns to the wounded knight whom he left at the border with herbs to heal him. He asks Gawain to give him the means to find confession and communion before he dies and asks to be given the packhorse of an approaching squire. So ugly is this squire that Gawain says he would rather bring him a better mount. The squire irascibly refuses Gawain who strikes him to the ground. The wounded knight asks Gawain to help his companion mount her horse and while he does so, the not-so-wounded knight steals Gawain's own horse, Gringalet, for this stranger is none other than Greoreas whom Gawain, in the past, had bound, making him eat with the dogs for a month as punishment for abducting a maiden and raping her. Gawain expostulates with Greoreas, who is clearly a cad: "You know full well that in King Arthur's land girls are protected; the king has given them a safeguard, and watches over them and ensures their safe conduct."[9] But Greoreas is intent on his revenge by stealing Gringalet, leaving the miserable pack horse to Gawain. The Maiden with the Mirror rejoices in Gawain's humiliation.

Gawain and the insulting maiden ride on until they come to a castle bounded by a wide river. From its five hundred windows peer down girls and ladies in beautiful clothes. The Maiden with the Mirror tells Gawain to get quickly into the ferry to come to the castle, but he turns aside to fight off Greoreas's nephew, whom he defeats roundly. But on turning toward the river he finds no trace of the boat or his packhorse.

A pilot in a skiff now approaches and demands the defeated knight's horse as his perquisite in return for taking Gawain over the river. The pilot also tells him that the Maiden with the Mirror who led him to the castle has previously caused many knights to be beheaded through her provoking behavior. The next day Gawain inquires about the castle and its lord, but the pilot says he doesn't know who it is, only that the castle is defended by many weapons, with crossbows that shoot ceaselessly. There is, however, a queen of the castle who came to live in the land with a great treasure, and who brought thither her daughter and granddaughter, which is how Gawain learns about a three-generational line of ladies.

The pilot tells how the hall is defended by magic, arranged by a clerk versed in astronomy and in service to the queen. No knight can enter the castle if he is full of lust, vice, greed, or lies. No coward or traitor can survive there, nor any disloyal or perjured man. This reads like the usual constraint placed upon any entrant into the realms of Faery.

Within the castle are five hundred squires from many lands serving a training in arms: a hundred beardless squires, a hundred whose beards are just begun, a hundred who shave once a week, a hundred whose hair is gray, and a hundred whose hair is snowy white. There are old women without husbands who have been disinherited, as well as orphaned girls, all of whom live in the castle yearning for a knight to come and support them, who will restore the ladies to their positions, give husbands to the orphans, and make the squires into knights. If such a knight without stain of vice might come hither, he would be lord of the castle and bring an end to the deadly wars.

Sir Gawain is shown to the room furnished by the Perilous Bed. This richly appointed bed is hung with swags of samite and its cordage hung with bells and is mounted on carven dogs with casters on their legs, so that the whole thing can move about. The pilot nervously tells Gawain to go home rather than stay the night, since no one has so far left the bed alive. But Gawain is determined to try the adventure. As soon as he sits on the bed, the bells on the overhead cords all ring, windows within the enclosed bed open up, and crossbow bolts start flying:

fortunately, Gawain has his trusty shield. After wiping off the blood from the bolts that have grazed him, Gawain then has to deal with a marauding lion that starts attacking him. He deals the beast such a blow that he cuts off its head. He is then congratulated on lifting an enchantment that has been troubling the castle for a long time, and a bevy of squires comes to serve him. Gawain has withstood this test and overcome the enchantment. A beautiful maiden sends the queen's greetings and brings him royal clothes to put on.

Gawain them climbs up a tower to survey the land around the castle and expresses a longing to go and hunt in the abundant, game-stocked forest, but the pilot tells him that whoever gets to be lord and protector of the castle will never be able to leave it again. The maiden goes to tell the queen of Gawain's change of mood and the queen bids him to dinner.

The queen yields the castle to his protection and elicits from him that he is one of the Round Table knights. She then asks him how many sons King Lot had by his wife; Gawain replies: "Gawain, Engrevain (Agravaine), Gaheriet (Gareth), and Guerrehet (Gaheris)." She also asks about how King Arthur and Guinevere are faring, and Gawain tells her. The next day Gawain is looking out of the window and sees the Maiden with the Mirror coming toward the castle, accompanied by a knight with a quartered shield. Despite being importuned to the contrary, and with the wailing and lamentation of the women of the castle, Gawain goes down and speaks with the Maiden with the Mirror; he fights the knight and goes off with the Maiden at her behest.

As they ride, they encounter a most handsome knight who is none other than Gawain's old foe, Guiromelant. In an incident that works because neither knight knows who the other is due to their enveloping armor, he and Gawain promise to exchange information. From him, Gawain learns that the Maiden with the Mirror is known as the Proud Maiden of Nogres and that the name of the knight with the quartered shield, whom Gawain defeated, was her love, the Proud Knight of the Narrow Passage who guards the border of Galvoie (Galloway). The castle from which Gawain has lifted the enchantment is called the Rock of Canguin, and its white-haired queen is none other than Ygerne,* King Arthur's mother. The other lady accompanying Ygerne is none other than the wife of King Lot and Gawain's own mother.

Here Gawain, still preserving his anonymity, astoundedly tells Guiromelant that, "Gawain has had no mother for over twenty years" (the context gives us to believe that she has previously died), but his enemy asserts it is indeed she, and that King Lot's wife also had a daughter whom he loves above all—Clarrisant, Gawain's own sister. Guiromelant bids Gawain take a ring to present to her. He then finally elicits that it is Gawain himself who he has been talking to all this time. Enraged by this revelation, since they are at enmity, Guiromelant demands that they contend by the fifth day of Pentecost at Orkney, where Arthur is going to hold court.[10]

In this synopsis, we recognize some important features that speak of the Castle of Maidens' likeness to the Land of Women: First, that Gawain, despite extreme provocation, never slights or strikes the irritating Maiden with the Mirror, thus proving himself to be a man of honor. Second, that no coward, traitor, nor man of dishonor can enter the Castle of Maidens, a fact proven by Gawain's forthright encounter with the Perilous Bed, which seems to be based loosely upon the visit to the Land of Women. Third, that the castle has no lord, only a queen, and that it is under an enchantment by which disinherited women and orphaned girls are unable to enjoy their possessions nor receive husbands, and where squires of all ages remain unknighted and so unable to advance their careers. The castle is stuck in a time warp that somehow needs mortal action to make time run forward again. Last, that Gawain's success in overcoming the enchantment—if he chose to take up the lordship of the Castle of Maidens—would undoubtedly result in his being unable ever to leave it.

Add to this the extraordinary coup de théâtre moment of Gawain encountering the apparently long-departed mother of King Arthur, his own mother, and his own previously unknown sister, and we have a

---

*Arthur's mother is also known variously as Igraine, Arnive, Igern, and Igerna.

potent triplicity of Arthurian women to head up the Castle of Maidens, for such this is. Here Gawain has proven himself to be the worthy lord of the Castle of Maidens, standing in a long line of heroes who have gone into Faery and been made the consort of the faery queen of the Island of Women, yet he refuses this honor, choosing instead to pass onward to the quest for the Bleeding Lance.

We should note that, while the Land of Women scenario usually results in a union between the hero and the queen, neither Ygerne, as his aunt, nor his own mother or sister would be suitable for this role, and that Gawain's ability to become de facto lord of the castle would require a younger woman who is not a relative! This may explain why he goes so willingly with the proud Maiden of the Mirror whom he met on his way to the Castle of Maidens. Her name, Orgueilleuse de Nogres, or the Proud One of Nogres, is one that resonates with the Proud Company, with the land of Logres, and with the insulting faery of the faery horn, whom we met in the last chapter. She is actually the one responsible for cajoling him out of his hard-won guardianship of the Castle of Maidens. Her character is utterly at odds with the others within the castle: she is independent and free to come or go, setting store by neither *courtoisie* nor chivalry, yet it is with her that he continues his journey. She finally admits to him that Guiromelant, Gawain's adversary, loved her and caused her to hate him utterly after he killed her own knight. Gawain returns her to the Castle of Maidens where she is kindly received for his sake, but not for her own proud nature.

These will not be Gawain's last dealings with damsels, distressed or insulting, nor with the Castle of Maidens. His quest will take him from the Castle of Maidens on to the Proud Castle, and eventually the Grail Castle, but we will follow his adventures further in chapter 8, for they have a bearing on some of the understories that tie *The Elucidation* to the main body of the Arthurian legends.

Having related the main story, which speaks of Gawain in the Land of Women, we now turn to some other important denizens of the between zones of the realms of wonder, discovering Gawain in another more Gaelic guise and learning that the otherworldly women have other agents who ply between the worlds.

DWARFS, BLIHIS, AND THE ONES BETWEEN

No one can read far into Arthurian legends without stumbling over a dwarf or two. These diminutive beings seem to arrive from various Celtic sources, through the wandering storytellers and *conteurs* of medieval times, to be enthusiastically taken up and included in the world of chivalry and quest.

It is interesting to note that in the Romano-Celtic tradition figures like the triple *genii cucullati* (hooded spirits) often appear as diminutive cloaked and hooded beings who accompany the triple Matronae or triple Goddess-Mothers of Celtic tradition. Since these hooded dwarfs appear with erect phalli or with eggs, it is usually assumed from their

Fig. 5.2. Genii Cucullati from Housesteads Fort,
Hadrian's Wall, photo by CM.

priapic, or suggestive, appearance that they are concerned with the generation and protection of children, as well as guardians of mothers. In this respect, they appear to have the same profile as the Egyptian dwarf god, Bes, who protected households and children.

In Irish legend, we find dwarfs like Cnu Dheireoil and Senbecc existing at the margins between this world and the other, as masters of music and irony.[11] Within the world of Arthurian legend, it is hard to find any dwarf who is either obliging or peaceable, yet dwarfs nevertheless play an important guardian role in the Grail legends; neither convenient nor accommodating, they remind humans that pride comes before a fall, while protecting the boundaries to the otherworld with ironic wit and feats of arms.

In the Welsh Grail story, *Peredur,* we hear about the insult to Gwenhwyfar (Guinevere), an episode that reminds us of the theft of the golden cups and the rape of the Maidens of the Wells:

> The knight . . . went into the hall where the page was serving Gwenhwyfar with a golden goblet. Then he dashed the liquor upon her face and upon her gown, and gave her a violent blow on the face, saying, "If anyone has the courage to dispute this goblet with me, and to avenge the insult to Gwenhwyfar, let him follow me to the meadow where I will await him."[12]

Just at this moment Peredur (Perceval) enters the court to be recognized by Arthur. Peredur inquires of Cai (Kay), the king's steward, what is going on, announcing that he has come to be knighted by Arthur. Cai and the court distain Peredur for being meanly equipped and unworthy of such an honor; they start throw sticks at him, but one of the dwarfs who has been at Arthur's court for a whole year but never previously spoken, suddenly pipes up, "The welcome of heaven upon you, good Peredur ap Efrawc, chief of warriors and flower of knighthood."[13]

Now Peredur doesn't look anything like any kind of knight, being just a rustic Welshman attired in canvas overalls and a deerskin tunic.

Thoroughly irritated by this greeting, considering how long the dwarfs have remained silent, Cai boxes the male dwarf's ear until he falls unconscious to the ground. Then the female dwarf exclaims, "Good Peredur, son of Efrawc, heaven's welcome be to you, flower of knights and light of chivalry!"[14] Cai, now irritated beyond measure, kicks her till she falls senseless. In the light of this dwarfish sagacity, and despite the cruel distain of Cai and the courtiers, Peredur strikes the insulting knight a mortal blow and gets a knighthood for defending the queen's honor. Later on, it is clear that the dwarfs' greeting has been prophetic and that Peredur is a warrior to be reckoned with. His unlikely championship in putting down the insulting Cai who struck the dwarfs, and his defense of Queen Gwenhwyfar, reveals him to be a champion of Faery.

Dwarfs notice things that taller people do not notice, or else they show up as messengers or even as assailants in the Grail legends. As we have already seen, in the fourth branch of *The Elucidation,* the Little Knight—a dwarf warrior whose stature belies his skill with arms— engages the highly skilled Guerrehes in combat. Guerrehes, brother of Gawain, believes he will easily overcome so tiny an opponent, but is himself vanquished in a manner that gets shamefully talked about everywhere, until he is forced to stage a return match.

In the last chapter, we met a similar dwarf, King Bilis, the king of the Antipodes who, in *Diu Cröne,* comes from King Priure bearing the deceiving cup that embarrasses Arthur and his court. Apart from acting as a messenger, he is also shown to be a formidable opponent in the ensuing tournament.

In one extraordinary source text, both Gawain and Bilis, in the form of a warrior called Bile, have an encounter that brings together the many strands of the Faery Grail story. The Scots Gaelic song *Am Bròn Binn,* or "The Sweet Sorrow," collected in different versions by several hands between the eighteenth and nineteenth centuries, is a rare survival of an Arthurian story, which might be considered as "the Lost Lay of the Outer Hebrides," where it is also known as *Aisling Rìgh Bhreatainn,* or "The Dream of the British King."

Despite the lateness of its survival, it clearly carries themes and characters from a much earlier period. Linda Gowans, who assembled many of the extant versions of the ballad, traces its origin to the early Middle Ages, taking it well within the scope of influence of *The Elucidation* and other early Arthurian romances.[15]

In one version, Gawain is treacherously overcome and beheaded with the connivance of the woman who acts like "La Belle Dame Sans Merci." In another version, he has to hide from a giant and finally manages to get the giant's sword before beheading him, thus winning the woman. But in the version that interests us, on his arrival at the castle, he is immediately challenged by a young warrior with gold and silver spurs. They fight furiously and Gawain begs a truce, asking the warrior his name. His opponent answers, *"S mi Bile Buadhach nan rath,"* or "I am the victorious, fortunate Bile."

Bile then boasts that it is he himself who will possess the woman and her castle; it is he who will win the horse, hound, and ship that Gawain has brought with him. He boasts that he has already killed two of the sons of the king of Greece, while the two brothers have killed their third brother themselves. The woman then requests a grave be dug for these combatants if Bile is intending to take her away. A grave is dug and the woman leaps into it and dies. The singer of the song then laments that he didn't have a leech, or doctor, to bring her back to life.

In the following longer version, newly translated for this book, Gawain—who in Gaelic is known as *Fios Falaich,* or "Cache of Wisdom"—goes to find the mysterious harping faery who appears to Arthur in a dream. In this classic *immrama,* or otherworldly voyage, Gawain sails across the ocean until he comes to a fortress in the sea, replete with horns and cups. By means of a black chain, he climbs into the fort and there sees the maiden, who warns him of the lord of the place whom Gawain is keen to combat. However, although they make a pact to overcome him, Gawain is not the best knight of the two and, during a truce, Bile boasts that he will overcome Gawain, just as he has overcome other combatants for the woman's hand.

The ballad, which is divided up between several narrators, begins in a neutral narrative tense and then the maiden and Gawain dialogue, after which the neutral narrative disappears. After Bile's boasts (verses 17–21), Gawain interjects that, rather than killing the Greek king's sons, he would have checked and reasoned with them. The maiden, who seems inured to being abducted, begs for a grave to be dug for them, but then leaps into it herself and expires. The latter half of the song is narrated by Gawain, by way of explanation to Arthur as to why the maiden is not brought back. It is clear from the context that Gawain himself has fallen in love with her. Below, from verse 9 onward, we have given the titles of the dramatis personae to indicate who is singing.

1   *One day went Arthur of the Hosts,*
To the hill of victory, there to hunt;
He saw coming over the plain,
The fairest maiden under the sun.

2   *A harp there was within her hand—*
Her sweetest kiss and brightest face—
And sweetly though she played on it,
Sweeter the voice with which she sang.

3   *The harp strings sang so very sweet,*
That the king fell into gentle sleep;
When he awoke, his sword he sought,
But the maiden was no longer seen.

4   *Sir Gawain said unto the king,*
"I'll go and fetch her back to you;
Myself, my boy and my hound,
We three will seek your dream woman."

5   *Seven long months he was at sea,*
In his fair vessel sailing,
Before firm earth he found again,
Where he could bring his ship to land.

6   *He saw though the brightness of the sea,*
Some stately stones with greenest cress,
Glass windows in its high gables,
Plenteous were the cups and horns.

7   *Sir Gawain stood at its base,*
A black chain hanging from above.
A chain which did not quiver,
And brought him upwards at a run.

8   *The tender maiden there he saw,*
On a chair of gold within there.
A silken carpet under foot,
The hero hailed her gentle face.

9   Maiden: *"Has God so blessed you, my man?*
Deep love has sped you over sea;
If this castle's lord be in good health,
No pity he knows nor no mercy."

10   Gawain: *"If this castle's lord be in good health,*
Who knows not mercy nor pity,
I am on fire that he comes not,
For I will fight him speedily."

11   Maiden: *"But how can you be doing that,*
You're not the best knight under the sun?
No weapon will draw blood from that man,
Save his own bright and whitened blade."

12   Gawain: *"Then speak we now, set wrath aside,*
A trap we'll lay for this great man.
We'll steal the sword from off his side,
And so we will take off his head.

13   *"I saw newly come over the sea,*

An iron-wounded warrior,
With a gold spur on right foot,
In dress and form most elegant.

14   *"On his left foot another spur*
Of royal silver, gold inlaid.
I tried to seize one spurred foot—
A move that did not make good sense."

15   Narrator: *He seized his weapon in his hand,*
It was death to then be near him.
Gawain: *"A truce, a truce, great warrior,*
I am alive and my sword near."

16   Gawain: *"A truce, a truce, great warrior,*
I am alive and my sword near.
Come tell me true your own story,
Tell who you are and what your name?"

17   Bile: *"Bile the Victorious is my name,*
It's I who'll have the melodious house.
Is there much doubt I'll be its king?
I overcame the men of Greece.

18   *"It's I myself shall have the wife*
With fairest cheek and teeth so white.
It's I shall have the white-sailed ship,
That leaves the whitest wake behind.

19   *"It's I shall have the swiftest horse,*
That strikes its hoof upon the grass;
It's I myself shall have the hound
Which neither wrath nor arms confound.

20   *"Let's go to the house upon the rock,*
Where you can verify my tale;

And you shall learn how I rode my horse
Of swiftest pace over the sea.

21   *"When riding fiercely over the sea,*
Cantering there I soon did see,
A hound-loving troop of three,
About the woman they fought close."

22   Gawain: *"I would have stilled their fierce combat,*
I would have checked them by myself.
Those three brothers, my sad tale!
About the woman in grim combat."

23   Bile: *"I am the hero who knows no fear,*
The eldest son of the king of France;
By me two sons of the Greek king fell,
Themselves did kill their brother dear."

24   Maiden: *"If you desire to take me hence,*
For the Greek king's sons, a grave now dig.
Gawain: *"And that is why I dug the grave:*
A madman's task, on a woman's word.

25   *"I dug the grave, as the captive asked,*
The woman leapt into the pit,
The wise woman of fairest mien,
And from her body the soul sprang out.

26   *"Ochone! tonight is sorrowful,*
Had I a leech to heal her,
I would have brought her back to life,
My love I'd not leave in the grave.

27   *"On the path of Mount Righteousness,*
Where strength wins not over wretchedness,
On your right hand, O Son of God,

On doomsday may I gladly sit.

28   "*Ochone! tonight is sorrowful,*
     I would have brought her back to life.
     But that's the ending of my tale,
     And how the Sweet Sorrow is sung."[16]

This story, so like the *Dream of Macsen Wledig* and akin to the *aisling,* or dream genre of Gaelic story, was held in oral tradition until its collection in the nineteenth century; it represents an extraordinary, independent survival, not only of the *immram,* or voyage, of Gawain to the otherworld, but of the role of Bile as an opponent who defends or fights for the feminine. The many variants, including the version above, are very allusive and unclear. In some versions, we cannot tell whether it is Gawain or Bile who is the victor or the singer of the song. For our purposes, we immediately note that the seeker of the otherworldly woman is Gawain; that he searches on behalf of Arthur who is smitten with the woman; that the woman has many suitors who come to win her, only one of whom can become the king of the island; and that previous suitors have not only been killed but have also killed one of their own number in their attempt to win her. Primary of these points is that the remaining combatant when Gawain comes ashore is none other than Bile.

Bile's continual reappearance in these Grail and Arthurian stories has become more than ordinarily significant. The person of Blihis Bleheris whom we investigated in chapter 3 has now shown another facet of himself that is entirely part of the otherworld, not only of Chrétien's Antipodean kingdom in *Erec,* but also of the Land of Women in *Am Bròn Binn.*

The sixth-century glossarist Isidore of Seville, who wrote *the Etymologies,* one the best and earliest glossaries, wrote of the Antipodes as a race of people who were literally "opposite footed" because, as if from under the earth, "they make footprints upside down from ours."[17] This extraordinary notion was later borne out in another manner by

Rev. Robert Kirk who, in his *Secret Commonwealth of Elves and Faeries* in the 1690s, asserted that each person had a *co-imuimeadh,* or faery cowalker, who was their reflection or spirit double.[18] By the Middle Ages, "the Antipodean realm" was understood to be beneath the earth, the place, as we shall see, also assigned to the Faery realms.

We have already seen how it is Bilis who brings the testing cup from King Priure to Arthur's court in *Diu Cröne,* where he is a dwarf with a fishlike appearance. But can we really make connections between the victorious Bile from *Am Bròn Binn,* King Bilis from *Diu Cröne,* and Blihis Bleheris from *The Elucidation?*

While the three names carry a distinct family likeness, false etymology can be a trap that leads us inadvertently into boggy and unsubstantiated areas, so it is to the nature of each person that we need to look. Let us enumerate them, logging their chief characteristics.

- *Blihis Bleheris:* a warrior who, with his brothers, protects the wandering maidens and knights who are descended from the Maidens of the Wells and Amangons's men. A storyteller who holds the memory of the primary story. Exiled until the Rich Fisher's court is rediscovered. Of unknown appearance.
- *Bilis:* King of the Antipodes or under regions. A dwarf messenger of King Priure who sends the testing cup that spills wine over those with unfaithful partners. A jouster skilled in arms. He looks like a fish-being in appearance.
- *Bile:* Suitor to the woman of the island in the sea. Opponent of Gawain. Nicknamed "the victorious." A mighty warrior or giant.

Each man is a warrior, each stems from nonhuman realms, each is tricky and unobliging, except for the captured Blihis, but we can see that they each have more differences than similarities. It has been suggested that behind all these figures may lie an early British figure, that of Beli Fawr, a personage who has little history and who, in the Welsh genealogies, is identified as the father of Afallach, lord of Avalon.[19] Beli is thus a lord of otherworldly overseas realms, one whose offspring is king of Avalon, which is a realm under the governance of women. His name may even have been applied to Billingsgate fish market in London. There seems little doubt that behind the Grail figures of Bilis/Bile/Blihis is an otherworldly character, someone who is usually discovered in the Lands Adventurous, in the places between the deep realm of the Grail Castle and the everyday world of Arthur's court. This liminal realm is also where faery contact is most likely to happen: a realm we need to understand better.

THE ORIGIN OF THE FAERIES

The time has come to discover how the faeries themselves come into being, for they are the primary witnesses in this chapter. The myth that is related in the following account ties the faeries as "the ones between" into the rebellion of Lucifer. As early as the fourth century CE, Saint Augustine wrote that the devil "is proud and envious,"[20] while Saint Thomas Aquinas discussed the notion that "they who fell were of the lower grade of angels; yet in that order some of them remained good."[21]

The story told by the Scots Gaelic storyteller Roderick MacNeill to the collector J. F. Campbell in 1871 relates how the faery race came to earth:

The Proud Angel fomented a rebellion among the angels of heaven, where he had been a leading light. He declared that he would go and found a kingdom of his own. When going out at the door of heaven, the Proud Angel brought . . . prickly lightening and biting lightening out of the doorstep with his heels. Many angels followed him—so many that at last the Son called out, "Father! Father! the city is being emptied!" Whereupon the Father ordered that the gates of heaven and of hell should be closed. This was instantly done; and those who were in were in, and those who were out were out; while the hosts who had left heaven, and had not reached hell, flew into the holes of the earth . . . like the stormy petrels. These are the faery folks—ever since doomed to live under the ground and only permitted to emerge when and where the King permits.[22]

This faery origin story, couched in the context of the rebellion of Lucifer (the Proud Angel) gives us three groupings: some angels who are left on earth, some who are below the earth, and some who are in heaven. Those left between these regions, who wander on earth, become the faeries, long before Adam and Eve and their numerous offspring are created. As the race who preexist humanity, faeries are the first guardians of earth's hospitality: the keepers of the golden cup of the wells. But their kindred, the Proud Ones who follow Lucifer the Proud Angel, are also at work, as well as the Heavenly Company.

If we consider this origin myth of the faeries from Gaelic tradition and compare it with *The Elucidation,* we are immediately struck that it gives us three groups: the angels in heaven, the devils in hell, and the faeries on Earth. Let us set this story side by side with the evidences of the seven branches we posited in the last chapter, where we considered the possibility of three types of archetypal men, sons of Adam: the worthy Seth who resembles the virtuous Round Table knights; the unworthy Cain, who resembles Amangons and his company; and the innocent Abel, who resembles the company of Blihis. These archetypal sons of Adam provide us with a mythic template beneath the Holy Grail myth, but the mythic template for the Faery Grail seems to be provided by this Christian Gaelic story of the origins of the faeries.

Perhaps, in seeking to identify the protagonists of the Faery Grail myth, have we simultaneously discovered the partial identity of the Rich Company who lived in Proud Castle? The Rich Company behaved much more like aggrieved faeries or a more successful kind of demimortal than either Blihis and his company.

After the Faery Accord is broken by Amangons's rape of the Maidens of the Wells, the only ones who come forth from the wells are the Rich Company who build their perilous castles and bridges, behaving in an oppositional way to Arthur and his knights. In Scottish faery mythology, faeries fall into two categories: the *Seelie,* or blessed court, and the *Unseelie,* or unholy court. This is echoed in the use of the Gaelic *slaghmaith,* or good host, as a euphemism for the faery kind. The Rich Company seem to partake of the Unseelie court.

While the Seelie court maintain good relations with humans and largely do no harm, the Unseelie court tend to acts of malice or sorcery, as we have seen, with dubious gifts of testing vessels that cause upset and confusion. When humans like Amangons overset the primary hospitality of the Seelie court the Faery Accord is broken, and the Unseelie court alone remains to challenge.

The testing horn and cup are not the only instances of that challenge, nor are humans excluded from playing their part in the healing of the accord.

HEALING THE FAERY ACCORD

We have seen above how the tradition of the lone knight who wanders into Faeryland is played out over and over within the Arthurian tradition. It is also a central part of the Faery Grail tradition.

In the fourth branch of *The Elucidation* we heard about the adventures of Guerrehet and how he avenged the dead man in the skiff (see Stories of the Swan, page 87). This story provides us with a clue to the faery connections within the Grail story. In order to follow this, we need to discover the antecedents of the dead knight drawn in the swan boat to the shores of Arthur's realm. The *First Continuation* tells us that the corpse in the skiff is that of King Brangemor, king of the islands in the sea, where no mortal man dwells. His father is Guingamor, a mortal man, and his mother, Brangepart, the faery queen.[23] Let us examine his lineage more closely.

The *Lay of Guingamor* appears first as one of the early Breton *lais,* once attributed to the twelfth-century poet Marie de France, who may be the same as Marie, abbess of Shaftesbury (fl. 1181–1216), the illegitimate daughter of Geoffrey Plantagenet, and so a granddaughter of the Angevin King Henry II. However, since no certain proof is available, the lay remains anonymous.

In this lay, Guingamor is propositioned by the queen of Brittany to be her lover, but he spurns her. Stirring things up, the queen speaks publicly about the quest for a mysterious white boar of the forest and how no one is bold enough to pursue it. The king remarks how very dangerous it would be to pursue it, since he has already lost many knights to its ravages. Guingamor then takes up the challenge and goes forth, much to the king's distress, although the queen persuades the king to lend Guingamor his very own dogs for the purpose.

Guingamor comes first to a green marble palace with a tower of silver and doors of ivory,* but then hears his dog barking and resumes his quest. He finds a pool wherein a maiden is bathing. She promises to give him back his dog, which is lost, as well as the head of the fabled white boar to take home, if he will but remain three days with her. Among her company seem to be the knights who previously attempted the quest and who had not returned. When Guingamor asks to return, the faery maiden, for so she is, gives what she has promised and tells him to cross over the river to his home but to not eat anything there. He is immediately struck by the overgrowth of the forest and asks the directions to the king's castle of a woodman. The man says that such a king lived there three hundred years back. Forgetful of his instructions, Guingamor eats a wild apple and finds himself suddenly enfeebled and old. Two maidens ride by and lift him onto his horse and take him back over the river to Faeryland.[24]

We immediately recognize the classic theme of the enraptured youth who passes into Faery at the behest of a faery mistress, only to live with the woman whom we can identify as the faery queen and to become chief among the company of those who live on the Island of

---

*Virgil writes about the doors that lead into dreaming or vision:

> *Two gates the silent house of Sleep adorn;*
> *Of polish'd ivory this, that of transparent horn:*
> *True visions thro' transparent horn arise;*
> *Thro' polish'd ivory pass deluding lies.*[25]

The Greek for horn and ivory have a similarity with words that punningly suggest key words: κέρας, "horn," is similar to κραίνω, "fulfill," while ἐλέφας, "ivory," suggests ἐλεφαίρομαι, "deceive."

Women. This story is familiar to us from the Irish legend, found in the eleventh-century text of *Echtra Condla* (the Adventures of Connla). Here Connla is approached by a beautiful maiden who invites him to come to the lands of the living, where death and sin are unknown. She gives an apple to Connla, after which he refuses food and drink, but lives entirely on the apple, which is never diminished. At the end of that month, he sees the maiden again, bidding him sail in her boat of glass to the Plain of Delight where only women dwell. Connla leaps into the boat and is seen no more.[26]

In the *Lay of Guingamor* it is a white boar who leads the youth into the liminal forest wherein he finds the maiden. Again, a shimmering white, otherworldly animal opens the way between mortal and faery realms, as is common in much Celtic and Arthurian story. Guingamor is told not to eat on his return over the river: he clearly passes the faery cordon back into mortal realms and there eats an apple from mortal realms that enfeebles him, bringing down a harvest of years upon him. Conversely, in the *Echtra Condla,* Connla is given an otherworldly apple that sustains his life but that gives him a distaste for earthly food, and so he is gradually drawn back into Faery, from which he never returns.

Returning to the theme of *Guingamor* we learn in the *First Continuation* that the son of Guingamor and the faery queen Brangepart, the semihuman Brangemor, becomes a king of the Otherworldly Islands in the sea, where no men come. This mysterious role, which he seems to share with Rex Avallonis, the king of Avallon, is further underlined in Chrétien's *Erec* where among the guests who come to the wedding of Erec and Enide are Maheloas, lord of the Glass Isle—where no thunder sounds, where no lightning strikes, where no toads or snakes are found, and where the weather is always temperate—and a certain Guingomar (Guingamor), lord of the Isle of Avalon.[27]

Maheloas is almost certainly the same as Melwas of Glastonbury, king of the Summer Country, from the story found in the twelfth-century Welsh *Caradoc of Llancarfen,* which tells how Gwenhwyfar is abducted by Melwas.[28] This story is also the subject of the *Knight of the Cart* by Chrétien.[29] But Guingamor, like Connla, is a mortal man who has become king of the Overseas Island in the Land of Women. The realm in which the weather is always temperate and where no reptiles live is the same as that proposed by the faery woman who comes to Connla, a realm without sin or death known as the Ever-Living Lands, or Land of Promise—which are but two names for the otherworldly enclaves of Faery that Chrétien identifies as Avalon, realm of apples.

In the Fourth Branch of *The Elucidation,* as expanded in the *First Continuation,* the dead knight in the skiff conducted by the swan is thus none other than the son of this same Guingamor and of Queen Brangepart, his faery mistress. Their son's name, Brangemor, is an amicable fusion between his mortal father and his faery mother. When the swan boat returns with Guerrehet and a faery maiden, Arthur and the whole court hear that Guerrehet is responsible for the avenging of Brangemor and so, in a completely explicable way, he is the one who restores joy to the faery realms of Brangepart:

> *Rendés le cors à la roïne*
> *Lors ara sa joie entiérine.*[30]

These lines translate as "return the body to the queen so that her joy is complete," but the emphasis is not so much upon his avenging as upon his return. Helene Newstead has suggested that these lines might be understood as a request to "return the horn." This notion cannot be fully endorsed as the story makes clear that it is the body of Brangemor that is meant.[31]

However, within the original old French of the Grail legends, there is one word whose three-way meanings cause an interesting confusion: the words for court (*cort*), body (*cors*), and horn (also *cors*), all pronounced the same way, overlap to such a degree that the episode of Brangemor brings us into strange reverie.

Can it be that Guerrehet is responsible for not just the avenging of Brangemor but also for healing the Faery Accord? Here the Joy of the Court, so longed for by Blihis and his fellows in *The Elucidation,* is echoed by the joy of Brangepart and the whole court who, we are told, are expecting her consort home, and where a great wonder is also expected. The implication is that, like Guingamor who nearly died of sudden onset mortality, Brangemor will somehow be restored to life. Here too, the insult of the taunting horn that was brought to Arthur's court to mock his people—in converse mode to the hospitality of Faery Grail of the Wells—is overthrown, just as Guerrehet's shame and mockery is turned to rejoicing. Here too, the body of Brangemor is restored. Indeed, we see a coming together of body, court, and horn in a mysterious way.

The extreme importance of this episode is flagged by the anonymous author of the *First Continuation* whose words may seem familiar to us:

> *This story comes to an end*
> *And another branch begins*
> *Which you'll hear from me without delay,*
> *Each word by word, told and related.*
> *Each of you thinks you know*
> *How this story plays out,*
> *But, as God me guards, you really don't!*
> *All in order, with great care,*
> *Must the thing be uncovered;*
> *You will not hear me speak of it*
> *Except in the right order*
> *Exactly as the source presents.*[32]

This reminds us immediately of the many times in *The Elucidation* where we are told we will learn about the story in order and at the right time. The story that follows these words is that of the fourth branch, the Stories of the Swan (see page 87). Since the story of Guerrehet and the swan boat is also the closing episode of the *First Continuation*, it comes as the coda to Gawain's Grail quest. While Gawain has been able to ask about the Bleeding Lance, some part of the Holy Grail quest is concluded, but his brother Guerrehet is the one who, though initially shamed by the Little Knight, wins through and restores the consort of the faery queen to his rightful place. Strangely, Gawain and his brother Guerrehet have both been on quests dealing with a lance: respectively, the lance of the Holy Grail quest and the lance that killed Brangemor, whose death may have been at the hands of one of the Rich Company, making it central to the Faery Grail quest.

The implication of the lance head lodged in Brangemor's body is worth focusing on for it is spoken of in the text as *un fer,* "an iron" as well as "a lance." To remind us, let us read once more the letter—dictated by Brangemor before his death—that Arthur finds in the swan boat:

> King, from this corpse who lies here, before his death occurred, he requests that you will let him remain in your hall without disturbance until the lance is removed with which he was stricken and wounded. . . . May he who draws it forth have as evil and great a shame as Guerrehet had in the orchard if he does not strike the one who struck this knight, right through the body, and with this same lance head and in the exact same place. King, place him in an open coffin; he is so richly embalmed that the body may remain here a year or more without any odor. If the fragment is not withdrawn before the year is past, sire, bury this corpse at the end of the year without delay; you will never hear him spoken of again, nor will you ever be blamed. If he is avenged, your court will know well who this man, of what land and country, and how he met his death.[33]

The letter commands Arthur to keep the body unburied, in an open tomb for a folkloric "year and a day." Only the lance head struck in the very same place in the breast can kill Brangemor's killer. If no one comes to avenge him, then Arthur will give an honorable burial and is not to be blamed. While no one will hear the name of the corpse spoken of again—for in Faery no dead person is mentioned again—if he is avenged as described here, Arthur's court will be informed of who this is or, if he dies in the attempt, of what place he came.

Although several knights attempt to fulfill the drawing out of the lance head, it is only when Guerrehet comes near to the body of Brangemor that the splinter easily slides out. The lance blade looks perfectly polished and Guerrehet fits it onto his best spear shaft and returns to the castle to complete the avenging of Brangemor, as the letter in the swan boat instructs. It is only with the head of this lance that the perpetrator can be killed, in the very same place that he first struck his victim. The knight who killed Brangemor with the lance and who stole away Brangemor's sweetheart, was clearly wounded by his opponent, which is how Guerrehes first finds him, being tended by Brangemor's maiden, who has been abducted by him. After fighting with and killing the dwarf who first ignominiously shamed him, Guerrehes fights with the wounded knight, striking a mortal blow: as he kills the perpetrator, the lance breaks and the knight falls to the earth with lance head deeply embedded in his body.

Brangemor's faery sweetheart then comes forward, recognizing the iron, and asks if her dear love is yet buried. Guerrehet tells her that he has not so far been buried and goes to pull out the lance head of the body of his assailant, but Brangemor's sweetheart urgently forbids him: "If it's removed you'll be cut to pieces. The assailant cannot be avenged as long as it stays in his body." Guerrehet then cries, "Cursed be whoever takes it out, then!"[34]

Together he and the faery woman return to Arthur's court by the swan boat, where she goes straight to the coffin and mourns the corpse, telling him that the terms of the letter have been fulfilled. She then kneels to Arthur and begs him release the body into her keeping, saying that everyone in Brangemor's country will rejoice at his avenging. Then she tells him the history of the corpse, his parentage, and this curious detail:

It was necessary for King Brangemor to die outside; mortality was his from his father, but not from his mother. For this reason, his name was divided. . . . Brangemor was the name of the king; his people await him this very month. Sire, I have recounted the truth to you, and you may know assuredly that he was king of one of the islands where no mortal man may dwell. And when he departs from here, a wonder will occur in his court, but I am not permitted to tell of it.[35]

This extraordinary statement, of the necessity for Brangemor to be killed outside Faery, implies that Brangemor, like his father Guingamor before him who nearly succumbed to his mortality, is to be resurrected when his body returns over the seas to his mother Queen Brangepart. We catch our breath as we take in the implication for both Brangemor and the merest prophetic glimpse of Arthur's own fate, taken to Avalon.

The lance, or iron, as the blade is continually referred to here, like the iron blades that are inimical to Faery and cause the faery doors to stay open in many folktales, has been removed from Brangemor's body, which allows the possibility of his resurrection, whereas the body of his opponent remains wholly dead, with the lance head deeply broken off in his body.

This feature of a weapon that not only kills but also cures is one that is found as part of the Holy Grail quest in many texts, including the holy lance that Balin inadvertently wields to fend off the invisible knight, Garlon in Malory's *Morte d'Arthur,* thus wounding the Grail King, Pelles. Later, the same holy lance, when laid upon the site of the original injury, heals the lingering wound of Pelles. Garlon, like Amangons, is one of the anti-Grail Kings we will be exploring in chapter 6.

However, our concern in this chapter is with the Faery Grail quest. We can see from a number of Celtic sources that the reuse of a faery weapon has this effect: not of killing, but of resurrecting. This theme involves the first use of a weapon to bring death, while any secondary use of the weapon can actually revive the one so stricken. We see this played out in the story of *Pwyll, Prince of Dyfed,* where Pwyll makes a pact with Arawn, the Lord of the Underworld, to change places and swap appearances with each other for a year. Pwyll then enters the realm of Annwfyn where he is welcomed by the court as Arawn himself. As previously arranged, the mortal Pwyll fights Arawn's other-worldly enemy Hafgan, at the appointed time, striking him one blow but, despite Hafgan's entreaties "to finish his work," Pwyll refuses to accord him the second blow by which he would have revived.[36]

Fortunately, in the *First Continuation,* Guerrehet stays his hand and so enables the dead knight in the skiff to return. In thanks for Brangemor's return, the faery maiden, his sweetheart, says that Brangemor's mother, Brangepart the faery queen, will be so pleased about the return of her son that Arthur and his court may ask whatever favor they desire. Tears turn into joy as the swan boat returns with Brangemor and his sweetheart to the land of Faery. In Arthur's court, everyone celebrates the Feast of All Saints, at the suitably ancestral and faery time of Hallowe'en when the doors between the worlds stand open wide.

This episode that ends the *First Continuation,* and is only hinted at within *The Elucidation,* seems to reveal to us a possible way of healing the broken Faery Accord. Guerrehet's initially shameful showing in the garden and his successful return visit to the otherworldly castle, where he finally avenges Brangemor, seems to suggest an important healing of the accord between the realm of Faery and Arthur's Logres.

The twin appearances of the faery cup of hospitality *and* the testing horn within the Grail myths, are not there together by accident. They each represent different strata of tradition: a Faery Grail quest that the fourth branch of *The Elucidation* helps solve for us. Here loss, death, and sorrow are restored to rediscovery, life, and joy once again for the Faery realms.

Brangemor, the dead knight in the skiff himself is a representative of the two realms of Faery and Logres, just like Bleheris and his people. His seeming death is turned back to resurrection by the persistence of Guerrehet. Brangemor's return to his overseas Faery kingdom restores a faith and trust in the Arthurian realm. Just as Bleheris co-opts the Round Table knights to find for them the Courts of Joy, so that they might cease their wandering, just so, the human Guerrehet is lured deeper into restoring the demimortal, demifaery lord to healing, restoring to the Faery realms the Joy of the Court. So too, in the

Holy Grail story, will the Wounded King be healed by the agency of the Grail quest knights, and the Wasteland will flower.

Parallel quests are hidden deep within *The Elucidation:* the restoration of the Faery Accord, which involves Gawain and his family; as well as the Holy Grail quest, which is largely pursued by Perceval. Each is as important as the other.

Other events are unfolding in the world of *The Elucidation* that present an alternative story to the causes of the Wasteland. The hospitality of the Maidens of the Wells represents an ancient folk and faery tradition that should not be forgotten. Later on in the myth's development, this folk tradition was not considered sufficient or suitable to carry the myth alone: it had to be plugged into a newer current, and this is how this branch of the Arthurian tradition became part and parcel of the Passion narratives. We will explore that backstory in more detail in successive chapters, but now we turn to those who stand for the reverse of the Grail, the ones who cause the Wasteland, and who still ride, sword drawn, across the face of civilization and the environment, right into our own times, with depredation, rapine, and slaughter on their minds.

6
GRAIL KINGS AND ANTI-KINGS

Concerning this sorcerer, dark things are said. No one has seen him: he is known only by his power. That power is magic. The castle is his work, raised miraculously in what was previously a desolate place with only a hermit's hut upon it.

RICHARD WAGNER, 1865 PROSE DRAFT OF *PARSIFAL*

THE GRAIL FAMILY

he landscape of *The Elucidation* reveals many different zones in which we see different sets of forces in operation, often in opposition to each other: Amangons and his men, Arthur and his Round Table knights, the descendants of Amangons and the Maidens of the Wells, and Arthur set against the Peers of the Rich Company. Balancing all of these, and seeming to endure through all the time zones of the story, is the court of the Rich Fisher. *The Elucidation* gives us more descriptive lines about the Grail Castle than about anything else, revealing its central importance.

Although our text speaks little about the Grail Castle's inhabitants, almost from the beginning of the medieval Grail romances we find the idea of a family dedicated to the serving and protection of the sacred vessel. In time, these guardians became "kings," fitting easily into the hierarchical structure of the medieval world. There is also, as we shall see, a set of "anti-Grail" kings, of which Amangons is clearly a type. But before we examine these dark figures in detail, we need to look first at the guardians, and to uncover their relation to the mythic patterns they establish. This takes us immediately into the regions of the Holy Grail's Christian antecedents.

Our main sources for the Grail family are three texts that date from within the same period as *The Elucidation* and the *Continuations*. These are the *Joseph d'Arimathie* and the *Didot Perceval*, the first definitely by Robert de Boron, and the second sometimes attributed to him. De Boron, whose exact dates are unknown but who lived in the late twelfth and early thirteenth centuries, was a knight of Burgundy who, by all accounts, was a religious man. It is to him that we owe the first merging of the Grail story with apocryphal Christian sources—namely the Gospel of Nicodemus and the Acts of Pilate, which nests within it. Both these documents were omitted from the final canon of the New Testament (see chapter 7).

It seems to have been Robert who first suggested the idea of a family of Grail guardians. Joseph of Arimathea is the first guardian (not yet a king), followed by his son Josephus. De Boron then names Alain le Gros, twelfth son of Bron who was Joseph of Arimathea's brother-in-law, as the third keeper of the Grail. Alain's son is identified as Perceval in the *Didot Perceval*—though elsewhere Perceval's father is either Gamuret, in *Parzival;* Earl Efrawc in *Peredur;* or Bliocadran in the fragmentary story of the same name.[1]

Gerbert de Montreuil's Continuation tells us some of the backstory of how the Grail family came to be. In the section at the Castle of Maidens, the wounded Perceval with his sister are given a fuller account than that offered by Chrétien. After treating Perceval's wounds with some of the ointment used by the three Marys upon Jesus, Ysabel, the mistress of the castle, tells how her cousin and their mother, Philosofine, came with the Grail from across the sea and, because the land was waste and full of sinful people, angels bore a sacred vessel away to the house of the Fisher King. The implication here is that the Grail would have been lodged in the Castle of Maidens but had been taken for safekeeping to the Grail Castle.[2] This interestingly echoes the very background for

The Elucidation, where the two locations connecting the Graal are the Grail Castle and the Wells.

Later we learn from Chrétien that the Fisher King is over three hundred years old and that his name is Mordrain. While staying at an abbey, Perceval is told how forty years after Christ's death, the lands of a heathen king named Evalac of Sarras had been ravaged by a king of Syria. Joseph of Arimathea tells Evalac that he would be able to vanquish his adversary if he became a Christian, taking the name Mordrain. This fell out as Joseph had predicted, and Mordrain became a devout Christian. When Joseph later came to Britain, Philosofine, Perceval's mother, accompanied him. She brought with her "a trencher brighter than the moon and a lance that bled constantly," while Joseph brought "the most beautiful vessel ever seen." A wicked king named Crudel imprisoned Joseph and his followers; when Mordrain heard of it he sailed to ravage Crudel's lands. However, Mordrain was badly wounded and when Joseph showed him the Grail, in the hope of its healing him, Mordrain tried to peer into it, at which an angel with a fiery sword came and told him he had done wrong and that his wounds would never heal nor would he die until a true knight without sin relieved his burden, thus giving us the first Wounded King.[3]

The wonderful collapsing of time scale in this retelling, and the family relationships implied by it, gives us pause. According to this account, Joseph of Arimathea and Perceval's mother (significantly called by the Sophianic name, Philosofine) are contemporaries, and the connection between the apocryphal accounts of the aftermath of Christ's Passion and the time of Arthur is made even stronger.

De Boron's *Joseph of Arimathea* was created out of a blending of the canonical Passion narratives and the noncanonical fourth-century CE accounts found in the Acts of Pilate and the Gospel of Nicodemus. The vessel is presented as both the cup in which Christ celebrated the Last Supper *and* the vessel in which his blood is caught after the crucifixion. The cup passes into the hands of Pilate and is given by him to Joseph who, as a soldier in the Roman army, comes to ask for a gift in return for his long service. Pilate also permits him and Nicodemus to take the body of Jesus. Joseph catches the blood in the vessel as the body is prepared for burial.

However, while Christ descends first into Hell in order to free Adam and Eve and their faithful descendants before his resurrection, his tomb is broken open by the Jews who, fearful of the retribution that might fall on them for not guarding the now-vanished body, arrest Joseph and put him in prison, sealing it up. Joseph survives his long incarceration and is visited by Christ, who brings the light-filled vessel of the most precious blood to him. Joseph is bidden to keep the vessel, which he is told has three powers, upon which he may call for help when in need. De Boron dares not tell us about these, "I couldn't even if I wanted to, if I did not have the high book in which they are written and that is the creed of the great mystery of the Grail."[4]

Joseph remains imprisoned until the time of the emperor Vespasian, when he is found to be amazingly still alive and preserved as if he had only just been imprisoned. Released at last, he goes to the household of his sister Enigeus and her husband Bron. They are suffering from severe famine and so Joseph prays before the vessel and asks for guidance. He is instructed to set a table, like that of the Last Supper, with an empty place between Bron and himself to signify the seat of Judas. This place, he is told, cannot be filled until a son of Bron sits in it. Now Bron is told to go fishing and to bring the first of his catch. Meanwhile, Joseph is to lay the table, putting the vessel on it and covering it with the edge of the tablecloth. When everyone is sat, the company sense "a sweetness and fulfilment of their hearts."[5] Those who feel nothing are sent away, for it is their sins that have brought the famine upon all. Everyone asks about the vessel and what it should be called; they are told,

> Those who wish to name it rightly will call it the Grail, which gives such joy and delight to those who can stay in its presence that they feel as elated as a fish escaping from a man's hands into the wide water.[6]

All those who have eaten, including a man called Petrus, remain a long while in a state of grace. The years pass, during which Bron and Enigeus have twelve children and go to ask Joseph's advice about them. They are told that they should all be married but, if one does not wish to do so, he is to be sent to Joseph. The twelfth son, Alain le Gros, elects to remain celibate and is taught about the Grail's history. Another of Bron's company, the same Petrus who had been so deeply affected by the Grail, is sent ahead into the West to await Alain's coming. He will not be able to pass from life into death until that time but goes instead to the vales of Avalon. Joseph is instructed to induct Bron as the keeper and guardian of the vessel after him: "All who hear tell of him will call him the rich Fisher King because of the fish he caught."[7]

At this point, de Boron breaks off, leaving the reader wanting to know more about the Grail lineage. He takes up the story in *Merlin,* where we hear of the birth of the great enchanter, the coming of the Pendragons, and the establishment of a third table, the Round Table. (The first two are the table of the Last Supper and the table of Joseph.) Uther Pendragon wonders greatly about the empty place at the Round Table and is told that it will not be filled in his time, but that someone will come in his son's time.[8] When Arthur comes of age, Merlin tells him how Alain and Bron came to the isles of Ireland but that Bron (now called the Fisher King) is woefully ill. When a renowned knight comes and asks the question about the Grail's service, the Fisher King will be healed, and will impart the secret words of Christ to the new keeper of the vessel. With that the enchantments of the land of Britain will vanish and the prophecy will be fulfilled.[9]

De Boron then begins his *Perceval,* where we learn that Alain le Gros's son, Perceval, wishes to come to Arthur's court. The story of Perceval is then told, substantially as we know it, only now we are aware that he is of the lineage of the Grail family. We hear about his seven-year quest and are told that,

Chrétien de Troyes says nothing of this—nor do the other trouvères who have turned these stories into jolly rhymes . . . Merlin saw and knew exactly what befell Perceval each day and he bade [his master] Blaise record these adventures.[10]

Perceval comes to the Grail Castle on a path shown him by Merlin, entering into his grandfather's presence and finally asking the purpose of the Grail procession. As soon as he asks this question Bron, the Fisher King, is healed. Knowing that he will now die within three days, Bron tells Perceval about his ancestors and places the vessel into his hands. From it arises a melody and perfume so sweet that they feel as if they were in paradise. At the same time the enchantments upon the world were broken. Merlin takes his master, Blaise, to the house of the new Fisher King, Perceval. The Arthurian story speeds to its end with the breaking of the Round Table through the treachery of Mordred, and Merlin dictates the story to Blaise before retiring to his *esplumoir,* or moulting cage.

De Boron's superb skill in seamlessly attaching the apocryphal Gospel of Nicodemus to the Arthurian legends by means of the Grail is unsurpassed. It has a shapeliness and symmetry that only a good storyteller can bring to it. By making the story of Christ's Passion and its major relic into a vessel that "delights the heart of all worthy men," de Boron creates a healing of all ills. In two passages, he makes a play on the French words *Graal* and *agréer*—"grail" and "delight"—recalling the sense of hospitality that is part of the Faery Grail, yet also maintaining the sacramental and very Christian presence of the Holy Grail with its salvific healing.

By making Perceval the great-nephew of Joseph of Arimathea, de Boron ensured that we could never look at Perceval with the same eyes again: during the course of his adventures he changes from a hopeless young knight into a full-fledged Grail guardian.

From quite early on, the Grail lineage begins to be consciously woven into a pattern of secrecy. The early thirteenth-century text of *Parzival* by Wolfram von Eschenbach tells us that those born into the Grail lineage are subject to an extraordinary dynastic regulation. The children of noble families, who are called to the Grail when they are small, attain paradise when they live and die chastely, with only the Grail King marrying; but there are exceptions. To countries that need rulers, the girls are sent openly as spouses, while the boys are sent out secretly, being forbidden to tell whence they come, like mysterious secret agents.[11]

Apart from the covert secrecy and chastity, this is not much different from the usual arrangement of dynastic marriage in medieval times. In *Parzival* Wolfram also binds together the Grail legends and the Crusader ethic of his time by making the soldiers of the Grail into *templeisen,* or Templars, who defend the Grail and its places. These are men who do not marry but who are wholly in the service of the Grail.

The Grail family and its interconnections provide the legends with a means of agency and ancestral destiny. The lone Fisher King who starts out as an almost otherworldly figure in his undying, unaging court, elides easily into a biblical ancient whose ancestors remain unavenged, but whose descendants will bring healing.

THE LINE OF GRAIL KINGS

The lineage of the Grail Kings (and anti-Grail Kings) varies according to different storytellers, each of whom seeks to establish a different Grail family, giving the Rich Fisher a whole host of relatives, both forebears and descendants, thus imbuing the Grail legends with an ancestral guardianship. These patterns of Grail interrelationship become akin to those enjoyed by the royal houses of Europe who acted in concert in the defense of Christendom.

Within the *Lancelot-Grail* cycle, the *Estoire del Saint Graal* lists the following lineage for the Grail guardians: Josue (the first Grail King), Aminadap, Carcelois, Manaal, Lambor, Pellehan, and Pelles/Pellam, who rules over the Grail lands in Arthur's time and whose daughter, Elaine, is the mother of Galahad (fathered upon her by Lancelot). Thus, the Christian and Arthurian stories become forever linked, although the lineage does not pass further onward, as we shall see in chapter 8.

Another writer who took up the story of the Grail, adding a wide range of esoteric references, and claiming that Chrétien had got the story all wrong, was Wolfram von Eschenbach (1160–1220). Writing less than twelve years after de Boron, he named Titurel as the first of the Grail Kings, followed by Frimutel, Anfortas (his name for the Wounded King), Perceval, and last his son Lohengrin—a Swan Knight whose story resonates strongly with that of Brangemor, whom we read about in the previous chapter.

The German writer, Heinrich von dem Türlin, writing in his epic *Diu Cröne* (the Crown) around the time of Wolfram's death in 1220, makes the Grail family a cursed clan whom Gawain saves from a living death. Heinrich indeed gives us one of the most detailed versions of the Grail procession and its meaning. But it is to Gawain alone that the Grail King himself explains the truth. The passage is worth quoting in full:

> Sir Gawain, this marvel which is of God may not be known unto all, but shall be held secret, yet since ye have asked thereof, sweet kinsman and dear guest, I may not withhold the truth . . . of the Grail, may I say no more save that ye have seen it, and that great gladness hath come of this your question. For now, are many set free from the sorrow they long have borne, and small hope had they of deliverance. Great confidence and trust had we all in Perceval, that he would learn the secret things of the Grail, yet hence did he depart even as a coward who ventured naught, and asked naught. Thus, did his quest miscarry, and he learned not that which of surety he should have learned. [And thus] had he freed many a mother's son from sore travail, who live, and yet are dead. Through the strife of kinsmen did this woe befall, when one brother smote the other for his land: and for that treason was the wrath of God shown on him and on all his kin, that all were alike lost.
>
> That was a woeful chance, for the living they were driven out, but the dead must abide in the semblance of life, and suffer bitter woe withal. That must ye know—yet had they hope and comfort in God and His grace that they should come even to the goal of their grief, in such fashion as I shall tell ye.
>
> Should there be a man of their race who should end this their sorrow, in that he should demand the truth of these marvels, that were the goal of their desire; so would their penance be fulfilled, and they should again enter into joy: alike they who lay dead and they who live, and now give thanks to God and to ye, for by ye are they now

released. This spear and this food they nourish me and none other, for in that I was guiltless of the deed God condemned me not. Dead I am, though I bear not the semblance of death, and this my folk is dead with me. However, this may be, yet though all knowledge be not yours, yet have we riches in plenty, and know no lack.

. . . And know of a truth that the adventures ye have seen came of the Grail, and now is the penance perfected, and forever done away, and your quest hath found its ending.[12]

Again, we note that the Grail Castle's inhabitants are stuck in an unmoving state, and that they too await the coming of the joy, just like Bleheris and his companions in *The Elucidation*. As the day begins to dawn, the company slowly fade from sight, except for Gawain's two companions and the maidens who carried the Grail and the other wondrous objects.

And Sir Gawain was somewhat sorry, when he saw his host no more, yet was he glad when the maiden spake, saying that his labor was now at an end, and he had in sooth done all that pertained unto the Quest of the Grail, for never else in any land, save in that Burg alone, might the Grail have been beheld. Yet had that land been waste, but God had hearkened to their prayer, and by his coming had folk and land alike been delivered, and for that were they joyful.[13]

Here not only the Grail King, but also his entire family, along with their followers, appear to suffer. They have been dead for a very long while, and only Gawain's asking of the fateful question sets them free, making his question the trigger of a truly ancestral release, alike to the Harrowing of Hell! We cannot help remembering that the effects of Amangons's attack on one of the Maidens of the Wells provoked an attack upon them *all*, with everything that this entailed for future generations to come. In the *Diu Cröne*, Gawain is the one who relieves the great lamentation that afflicts all at the Grail Castle and beyond.

Heinrich's poem also includes a darker figure, who seems intent upon uncovering the secrets of the Grail for his own ends. He is called

Gansguoter of Micholde, the second husband of Igraine, Arthur's mother, with whom she elopes after the death of Uther Pendragon. Gansguoter creates magical castles and palaces for his new wife and her daughters, thus demonstrating his considerable powers. In this he resembles the building program of the Rich Company in *The Elucidation,* while elsewhere, in *Perceval,* the Castle of Maidens is protected by enchantments created by a clerk, "versed in astronomy."[14] Gansguoter may, in fact, be immortal since his sister is described as a goddess in the text, thus implying that he is a god. This is borne out when he challenges Gawain to one of the most famous adventures of his career: the Beheading Game is an ancient theme best known from the Middle English poem *Sir Gawain and the Green Knight,* in which the hero is offered the chance of striking a fatal blow at his adversary, only to see him rise and walk away unscathed, promising to return a year hence to take his own blow.

Gansguoter's character is variable throughout *Diu Cröne,* veering between light and dark in a way that may suggest faery ancestry. Here may lie an explanation for the negative figures that are ranged, again and again, against the extraordinary lineage of the Grail family in virtually every version of the story. These are anti-Grail Kings, devoted to the possession and subversion of the sacred relic in order to claim its power. They are akin to the Rich Company who, in *The Elucidation,* stand against Arthur and his knights.

THE DARK KINGS

Foremost among these negative characters are the black magician Klingsor (Clingchor) from Wolfram von Eschenbach's *Parzifal;* the invisible knight Garlon the Red, brother of King Pellehan, from the post-Vulgate *Merlin* and Malory's *Le Morte d'Arthur;* and of course, Amangons himself, who appears not just within *The Elucidation,* but in several other places, as we shall see.

Wolfram's Klingsor is himself a being of extraordinary lineage. He is the nephew of the Roman poet Virgil (author of the *Aeneid*) and a duke of Terre de Labur. He falls in love with Iblis, wife of King Ibert of Sicily, who has him castrated when he discovers the affair. Klingsor then flees to Persia to heal himself and begins a study of black magic. He becomes a figure of great power and uses his magic to create the *Schastel Marveile* (Castle of Marvels). There he captures and imprisons not only Arthur's mother, here called Arnive, but also Gawain's mother, Sangive, and his sisters, Itonje and Cundrie. He establishes the custom of the Perilous Bed or *Li Marveile,* which Gawain eventually destroys, and which is but one of the many testing objects sent against the quest knights, as the more ancient Celtic ordeals were for heroes of another age.[15]

In fact, it is Gawain himself who first encounters Klingsor during his long peregrinations in search of adventure. Wolfram claims to be uncertain of the exact location of the magician's dark enclave, sighting it either in Morocco or Sicily. Again and again, Gawain is drawn back to the Castle of Marvels, where he encounters a variety of tests and trials, all of them engineered by Klingsor, including the Perilous Bed.

Within the castle there is a mysterious pillar brought, it is said, from "Araby." It seems to serve almost as a kind of Grail and a camera oscura: just one of the many shadowy imitations created by Klingsor. Brought from the lands of Feirefiz and made of precious gems like diamond, amethyst, topaz, garnet, chrysolite, ruby, and emerald, the pillar entrances Gawain who cannot take his eyes from it:

> It seemed to him he could see in the great pillar all the lands around about, and it seemed the lands were circling the column and the mighty mountains collided with a clash. In the pillar he saw people riding and walking, others running standing still.[16]

Along the way Gawain encounters a Sabian queen who reads the mystery of the stars. She tells him how Klingsor built the castle to echo that of Arthur, whom he hated, and that within it he celebrated terrible parodies of the Grail feast. From this, Klingsor draws his dark power. For him, the Grail is a source of energy into which he can tap so that, although he never touches the stone, which, we remember, grants extended life, he is proficient enough in magic to re-create at least a part of the Grail's power for himself.

Klingsor's story is deeply woven into that of the Grail quest throughout Wolfram's epic poem; even the Fisher King's wound is ultimately caused by him. Once, he had desired Gawain's own amie, the Duchess Orgeluse, who at that time was loved by Anfortas, Wolfram's Grail King. Klingsor had stolen a great treasure (almost certainly a metaphor for sexual favors) from the duchess, then exhorted other men to win it back. Anfortas had done all in his power to do so, and in the course received the wound that would not heal from a red knight in Klingsor's service, who would later be slain by Parzifal.

But it was from Arthur's mother, Arnive, who had been herself imprisoned in the Castle of Marvels, just as she is sequestered in the Tower of Maidens in *Conte del Graal,* that Gawain learns the rest of the story. Years earlier, the magician had fallen in love with the wife of a neighboring king. When he and the lady are caught in flagrante delicto, the lady's husband exacted the direst revenge, having Klingsor castrated. Bearing a parody of the Fisher King's wound, Klingsor forever after hated all men. He traveled to Persia to learn black magic and created the Castle of Marvels to ensnare all good men and women. Only Gawain's bravery and determination overcame the evil wizard's wiles and, in the end, brought about the destruction of the castle. Dozens of brave people were set free because of this and the country around it became enabled again—once again echoing the healing of the Wasteland.

Wolfram's story is a strange one, mixing the Grail story with Oriental magic and myth, with Klingsor as a kind of magical Ottoman eunuch. The Castle of Marvels is clearly intended to be an imitation of the Grail Castle; while Klingsor himself is an anti-Grail King who not only parodies the realm of King Anfortas and suffers a wound to his virility, but enacts a kind of perverse Grail magic, drawing upon dark powers to re-create a sacred mystery that he cannot grasp. Like Amangons, he desires power and riches and beyond these the pearl beyond price, the glory of the Grail and its life-enhancing energies.

The second of these dark kings is named Garlon the Red, and we first encounter him in a continuation to the *Prose Merlin,* part of the *Lancelot-Grail* cycle. Here, as in Malory, he is the brother of King Pellam/ Pellehan/Pelles of Listenois, and thus a member of the Grail family. But he is a polar opposite of his brother, hating King Arthur's knights and enjoying killing as many of them as he can. Gifted with the power of invisibility, he rides down various knights and stabs them in the back. It is given to Balin le Sauvage, a poor knight from Northumberland who kills Arthur's cousin and is imprisoned as a result, to bring Garlon's evil ways to an end. Seeking to make good his reputation, Balin succeeds in drawing an enchanted sword from a scabbard and is released to go on a series of adventures that lead him to an encounter with Garlon who, while invisible, kills two men in front of Balin.

Sir Thomas Malory in his fifteenth-century *Morte D'Arthur,* which draws upon the *Lancelot-Grail* cycle, describes how Balin pursues Garlon to the castle of his brother King Pellam (elsewhere called Pelles) and kills him before the entire company. But the consequences are far more catastrophic than he could have supposed. Here is Malory's account of what happens next:

Anon all the knights arose from the table for to set on Balin, and King Pellam himself arose up fiercely, and said, "Knight, hast thou slain my brother? Thou shalt die therefore or thou depart." "Well," said Balin, "do it yourself." "Yes," said King Pellam, "there shall no man have ado with thee but myself, for the love of my brother." Then King Pellam caught in his hand a grim weapon and smote eagerly at Balin; but Balin put the sword betwixt his head and the stroke, and therewith, his sword burst in sunder. And when Balin was weaponless he ran into a chamber for to seek some weapon, and so from chamber to chamber, and no weapon he could find, and always King Pellam after him. And at the last he entered into a chamber that was marvelously well dight and richly, and a bed arrayed with cloth of gold, the richest that might be thought, and one lying therein, and thereby stood a table of clean gold with four pillars of silver that bare up the table, and upon the table stood a marvelous spear strangely wrought. And when Balin saw that spear, he gat it in his hand and turned him to King Pellam, and smote him passingly sore with that spear, that King Pellam fell down in a swoon, and therewith, the castle roof and walls brake and fell to the earth, and Balin fell down so that he might not stir foot or hand. And so the most party of castle was dead, through that dolorous stroke. Right so lay King Pellam and Balin three days.[17]

Merlin—at this point still on hand at the court of Arthur before his untimely withdrawal—comes to rescue Balin from the ruins and tells him that the spear he used to strike the blow was that which had been used to pierce the side of Christ, and that its inappropriate use has brought a curse upon the lands around the castle.

There are two things to note in this telling. First there is the way in which the Dolorous Blow comes to be struck—not only through Balin's impetuous actions, but also ultimately because of Garlon's actions, which demand that Arthur's knight deal with him. Second we see that the effect is local rather than general. It is the Grail King's lands that are laid waste rather than the whole kingdom of Logres, as we are given to understand elsewhere.

There is some confusion between the stories of Garlon and Klingsor here. The wound received by King Pelles is the equivalent of castration, and it is his inability to sire children that connects with the Wasteland. This probably harks back to older Celtic traditions in which the king must be whole in body in order to symbolically marry the land over which he rules (see chapter 7). The Grail King's wound is in the generative organs and brings desolation to his kingdom.

Chrétien himself seems to have been aware of this idea. The long and complex story of Gawain's quest for the broken sword, which takes up the second half of *Perceval*, grew in the telling and received its own history in the *Queste del Saint Graal*, where the sword is described as having once belonged to the Hebrew King David. From David, it passed to his son Solomon and is protected by a sheath made of wood from Eden's Tree of Life.[18] The same text relates the story of a king named Varlan—a name strikingly similar to that of Garlon—who acquired the sword in a time before King Arthur ruled over Britain and used it to kill the Grail King, Lambor of Listenesse. Varlan dies immediately when he returns the sword to its sheath, demonstrating once again that the misuse of any of the sacred hallows can cause death or wounding, as it did to Pellam, who is the Grail King in that text.

The way in which the wound is received seems important here. In *Perceval,* we learn that the Fisher King "*was wounded in a battle and completely crippled, so that he's helpless now, for he was struck by a javelin through both his thighs.*"[19] Garlon, Varlan, and Klingsor suffer either death or maiming, while in *Parzival,* Anfortas is wounded while defending the honor of his lady. Elsewhere, in the *Third Continuation,* we find, as a part of the story of the Broken Sword, the Fisher King explaining his wounding in a way utterly different to any of the usual accounts. Here, rather than the accidental wounding or the misuse of a sacred relic either to defend or empower, the king speaks of his brother Goondesert's death at the hands of Partinel, nephew of the evil King Pinogres, who kills him with the sword, which then breaks. When the body, along with the two pieces of the sword, is brought back to the Fisher King's castle, his niece, who is prescient, tells him that the blade will only be restored by the knight who is to come and who will avenge her father's death. Crazed with grief, the king takes the blade of the broken sword and "that very instant, made a cut through my thighs, severing every nerve. Truly I've been helpless ever since and will remain so till I'm avenged."[20]

Here the king causes his own wound and, like the Knight of the Swan Boat and others, must await the coming of his savior. Intriguingly, Partinel, who is Lord of the Red Tower, carries a shield emblazoned with his arms: argent, two maidens azure! (A silver field with two blue maidens.) Perhaps the author of the *Third Continuation* was thinking of Amangons's evil actions, or perhaps he had a wider issue in mind?

Though the anti-Grail Kings and their followers figure as the villains in the Grail legends, it is worth our while to appreciate how everyday chivalry was seen in a medieval context, because it was not just a feature of literature but of life also. While feudal chivalry places the king at the center of society, served by a series of lords who are his peers and companions, each of whom has a network of knights and resources who will support any action that the king commands, there were rules to the practice of chivalry.

The art and purpose of chivalry is succinctly summed up in *Gerbert de Montreuil's Continuation,* when Perceval and his sister visit a hermit. He tells them that a knight's sword has two cutting edges: one for the defense of Holy Church, and the other for protecting Christian people and upholding justice. But that if knights cut or capture innocent poor men, then it is the Holy Church's edge that is broken, that it is the earthly edge of the blade that has been raised.[21] This interdependence of holy and civil order is what the anti-Grail Kings violate at every turn.

In *Le Morte d'Arthur* the pledge sworn by the Knights of the Round Table is seen to be diametrically opposite to the actions of the anti-Grail Kings.

> The king established all his knights, and gave them that were of lands not rich, he gave them lands, and charged them never to do outrageousity nor murder, and always to flee treason; also, by no mean to be cruel, but to give mercy unto him that asketh mercy, upon pain of forfeiture of their worship and lordship of King Arthur for evermore; and always to do ladies, damosels, and gentlewomen succour upon pain of death. Also, that no man take no battles in a wrongful quarrel for no law, ne for no world's goods. Unto this were all the knights sworn of the Table Round, both old and young. And every year were they sworn at the high feast of Pentecost.[22]

As for Amangons, he carelessly violates every letter of this oath, which is why the Round Table knights wish to wipe all trace of him and his successors off the face of the Earth. The author of *The Elucidation* was almost certainly familiar with the work of Robert de Boron and perhaps also with *Parzifal* and *Diu Cröne.* He may well have been aware of one of the other stories then in circulation, including the *Lai du Cor,* in which a character named Amangons (or similar) played a negative role. Once again, we see the genius of the author in connecting disparate strands of story into a unified whole.

WHO IS AMANGONS?

So, what are the origins of Amangons, the great adversary in *The Elucidation?* There are several figures that bear the same or a similar name throughout the Arthurian canon, several dating from before the composition of *The Elucidation.* One of the earliest of these is the Irish hero and wonder-worker Mongan, son of the god of the Otherworld, Manannán mac Lír, who appears to be a likely candidate for the original horn-gifting King Mangon of Morrain, who as we saw in *Lai du Cor* sent a magical fidelity-testing horn to Arthur's court (see chapter 4).

Mongan's story appears in the eighth-century *Lebor na h-Uidre,* where we learn that he was begotten on an earthly woman, Kentigerna, by the Sea God Manannán mac Lír, who visited her by night to fulfill a prophecy that her husband, absent at the wars, might be spared from death if she slept with a stranger. When Mongan was only three nights old, he was removed by Manannán to the Land of Promise wherein he had his education.[23] Like the Mangon of the *Lai du Cor,* Mongan sends gifts from the faery hills to kings of this world though, beyond this, there seems no obvious connection between him and the rapine of Amangons.

Chrétien himself has a character whose name is strikingly like that of Amangons. This is Amaugin the Red, also known as Amanguins le Rois, who appears in the list of Arthurian knights taking part in a tournament in *Erec.*[24] This is not his only appearance however. He has a larger role in a story called *Le Bel Inconnu* (the Fair Unknown) by Renaut de Bage (1165–1230) composed around 1200. It is another of those tales dealing with knights drawn into Faery. We will recognize some of the themes from the Island of Women motif in this story.

In this version, the Fair Unknown of the title is none other than Gingalain, the son of Sir Gawain by Blanchemal, a faery woman whom Gawain meets in the forest. When a child is born, Blanchemal keeps both his own name and that of his father secret from him. In a somewhat similar variation on the Perceval story, Gingalain longs to be a knight after he finds a dead knight in the forest. He sets off at once for Arthur's court where he is knighted as "Sir Le Bel Inconnu." At this juncture, a messenger arrives requesting aid for the princess of Wales, Blonde Esmerée, who is besieged in her castle by the powerful enchanter Mabon. Le Bel Inconnu asks for the quest and accompanies the princess's lady-in-waiting, Hélie, to the castle. On the way, he encounters a knight named Malgier le Gris (Malgier the Gray) who seeks to marry la Pucelle aux Blanches Mains (the Maid of the White Hands), mistress of Ile d'Or (the Isle of Gold), who is discussed in terms that suggest she is either a faery woman or an enchantress.

Le Bel Inconnu easily defeats Malgier, and the Pucelle, who had fallen in love with him, offers him her hand in marriage. The Fair Unknown is not averse to the idea, but must leave to complete his task of rescuing Blonde Esmerée. She also offers to marry the Fair Unknown and seeks to keep him at her side, but he leaves to return to la Pucelle. At this point, as word of the mysterious young knight reaches Arthur's court, the king wants to lure him back, and it is here that Amaugin the Red suggests a tournament at the Castle of Maidens.[25]

When le Bel Inconnu hears of this he is desperate to go, but la Pucelle makes it clear she might not be waiting for him when he returns. Seeing his eagerness to prove himself, she relents and offers to help him with her magic. She transports him from her castle to the site of the tournament complete with horse, squire, and armor. He is, of course, victorious, but unlike many young men captured by faery women, he deserts la Pucelle and instead marries Blonde Esmerée—the author emphasizing that this was more to do with social than emotional reasons. Nevertheless, the story ends with Gingalain discovering his true name and parentage.

The part played by Amaugin may seem slight here, but it is his suggestion that the tournament should take place at the Castle of Maidens, implying that he had more than a passing relationship with the Faery realm. This might seem nothing were it not for the fact that the same character appears in *Diu Cröne* in connection with two chastity tests (one of which his lady, Aclamert, fails) and a white stag hunt. We cannot help noting that chastity tests, as we saw in chapter 4, may be signs of the broken Faery Accord, while the hunt for a white stag almost without exception leads to Faery. We have already seen that Mangon instigated the horn test in *Lai du Cor,* and we may also note that both Garlon and Amaugin bear the title "the Red"; Klingsor's own champion in *Parzival* is a red knight; while Partinel, who kills the Fisher King's brother in the *Third Continuation,* is known by the title "of the Red Tower." This may be no more than coincidence but, given the role each plays in the Grail story, may imply a deeper relationship.

Other mentions of Amangons's name can be listed, but seem to bear little relation to his character or actions in *The Elucidation.* There is a tournament in a late twelfth-century text called *Meraugis de la Portlesguez* that takes place at the castle of Li Rois Amagons,[26] and an Amaugins is mentioned briefly in *Vengeance of Raguidel.*[27] The anonymous French *Chanson du Chevalier au Cygne* of the twelfth century, which has links with both the story of Brangemor and Lohengrin, has an Amaugis or Amangon, one of several knights sent against the hero Elgya by the sorcerer Matabrune. An Amangon is also mentioned in the thirteenth-century romance *Le Bataille de Loquifer* and again in the thirteenth-century *Marvels of Rigomer,* which concerns a faery castle in which the best of Arthur's knights is imprisoned until Gawain sets them free. This part of the story is not unlike that of Chrétien's *Lancelot* but, again, the appearance of Amangons's name seems of little importance.

In the French Grail text, *Sone de Nansay,* dating from circa 1270, the hero Sone names his son "Margons" after the Irish Knight Templar Margon, who stands as godfather to the boy.[28] Margon acts as counselor to the queen of Ireland and has no sinister behavior, merely serving as a wise man who lives in service to a queen upon an island. Elsewhere, in the romance of *Meriadeuc,* there is an Amangon who is king of Greenland and father of Guenloie, Gawain's *amie.* The most significant aspect of this character is that he rules over a land from whom no one returns, which almost certainly makes him an otherworldly being.[29]

Turning for a moment to the *Continuations,* we find there two more characters whose names recall that of Amangons. In *Gerbert de Montreuil's Continuation,* Perceval fights the pagan Knight of the Dragon, who had a city built in the isles of the sea and filled it with people who do not believe in God. He besieges Montesclaire where lives the Lady of the Circle of Gold, daughter of King Esclador, in order to take her as wife. Perceval defeats the Dragon Knight, whose brother is King Maragon.[30]

Last, in the *Third Continuation*, Manessier mentions "li Rois Margons" as the enemy of a maiden who entertains Gawain and who is eventually overcome by him.[31] Margons is known as "the King of the Marshes" and "the King of One Hundred Knights," titles that recall the Margon of the *Lai de Cor* and the rapacious Amangons himself.[32] This seems to strengthen the sense of Gawain as one of the main actors in the routing of the Rich Company, since he overcomes King Margons and his evil reign. The King of the One Hundred Knights is an implacable foe of Arthur in Malory's *Le Morte d'Arthur*.

Each of these characters can be seen to act in a similarly negative fashion and several are in some sense responsible for the advent of the Wasteland, which, from a purely localized event, becomes more widespread and generally felt in the later Arthurian texts. By the time we come to the thirteenth-century story of *Perlesvaus*, or *The High History of the Holy Grail*, the failure at the heart of the Arthurian kingdom, which is illustrated by the Wasteland, has become more directly linked with the actions of Arthur himself, whose failure to take the initiative in the Quest—leaving it to his knights instead—is to be seen as a failure of will and the empowerment of his sovereignty. The clues to this failure will be explored more fully in chapter 7.

In considering these widely various figures, whose only connection seems to be their name, we may note that most live in a faery castle, or rule over a land of no return, or have otherworldly powers. In this way, they each have something in common with the most prominent of the anti-Grail Kings. There seems to be the shadowy outline of a single figure who stands behind most of those listed here. Taken as a whole, the lineage of the anti-Grail Kings looks back to a coherent image of an otherworldly king of great power who, when he encountered the Maidens of the Wells, took what he considered to be his by right.

DARNANT THE SORCERER

The mystery of Amangons's identity, beyond what we glean from *The Elucidation,* may never be resolved, but there is another possible view of him and his men, or perhaps of the Rich Company, in a text we have not looked at yet. Known as *Perceforest,* it is a vast, sprawling epic that tells the history of the kings and queens, knights and villains, who predate Arthur. It is an astonishing feat of imagination with more plot twists and adventures than an average detective novel. It has, like *The Elucidation,* been neglected by Arthurian scholars partly on account of its length (over a million words) and because it has only survived in a fifteenth-century manuscript, despite its original estimated date of composition in the 1300s.

Near the beginning of the story, the hero Perceforest, who is Perceval's grandfather—and therefore by extension part of the Grail lineage—encounters a band of dark and dangerous people who dwell in the forest. These are the family and followers of Darnant, described as,

one of the most accomplished men in the forests of England in sorcery, spells, and enchantments, and he did the most harm with them. Among his misdeeds he would take by force or love or magic any beautiful lady or maiden within his reach; in consequence, there are at least sixty bastards living in this forest, all of them knights, and every one of them engaged in magic.[33]

This is certainly a close parallel to the story of Amangons, for Darnant has been the lord of the forest for forty years, a position that he won in his youth by force of arms, overcoming the most valiant men. In every respect he has conquered, but he fears one name, for it is prophesied that a British king called Perceforest is going to kill him. In a combat with King Betis de Feson, we see the scope of Darnant's magical ability. As Betis is about to behead Darnant, he sees the dwarf of whom he previously dreamed telling him to cut off Darnant's head and to set free the forest and the land, but as he raises his arm for the blow, Betis perceives the head as looking like that of his own wife, who begs him for mercy. In that moment, Darnant reaches for his Welsh dagger and stabs the king, who realizes he's been enchanted, snapping out of his stupor in time to finally kill Darnant.

As Darnant's head is cut off, "evil spirits filled the forest with an appalling din," and Betis is acclaimed by the title "the King Perceforest," whom everyone has been awaiting. We also learn that Darnant has four brothers, each living in a great forest within England, and each having many children, but none as many as Darnant. This reads like a variant of the rape of the maidens with its consequent rise in the birthrate for the area. We remember also how in *The Elucidation,* we are told

> *And the king [Amangons] came to a bad end*
> *And all the others after him,*
> *And so were many punished.*[34]

A few pages later, Perceforest encounters a maiden named Lyriope, who tells him how "all of Darnant's men have used maidens, as soon as they're old enough, as beasts use one another."[35] There is little doubt that in *Perceforest* we are hearing a direct echo of the rape carried out by Amangons and his men, and what followed.

Darnant's wife has his body installed in a stone sarcophagus a league away from his castle, and arranges that no one should disturb his body by casting a spell "that made the body burn inside the tomb, and it produced such a foul smoke that it could be smelled from half a league away."[36] Like the damned in hell, Darnant burns, buried in the forest that also bears his name. This, together with the fact that each of his brothers also dwells in a forest, suggests a figure dating from a far older time than the mythical world of Arthur.

As if to further remind us of the parallels between Darnant and Amangons, as Perceforest is leaving the area he stops near a tent pitched beside a bridge, where he and his squires are entertained by two maidens dressed in white, who have already laid a table with dinner. These are not the Maidens of the Wells, but they are near enough to suggest that the anonymous author either knew *The Elucidation* or was drawing upon a lost source that had provided *The Elucidation*'s author with the basis for his portrait of the anti-Grail King. The actions and history of the People of the Forest, who are referred to throughout Perceforest as of *mauvais lignage,* or bad lineage, are so like that of Amangons and his men, this seems the only conclusion to be drawn. Like the Rich Company in *The Elucidation,* these folk stand for the direct opposite of the Grail family and the Knights of the Round Table.

Even the name, "Darnant" recalls the weed, darnel (*Lolium temulentum*): this weed, which grows in the same zones as wheat, is subject to a fungal infection that renders it poisonous. It is the darnel that is instanced in the saying of Christ in the parable of the tares, in the Gospel of Saint Matthew:

> Let both grow together until the harvest: and in the time of harvest
> I will say to the reapers, "Gather ye together first the tares and bind
> them in bundles to burn them: but gather the wheat into my barn."[37]

These stories with their rapes, otherworldly castles, islands, and marginal forests, suggest an ongoing generational battle between an Amangons-like figure and the forces of order. Perhaps this was a reason that Arthur, in the medieval Irish text *The Story of the Crop-Eared Dog* (see page 192) convened "the chase of the Dangerous Forest" every year? Could it be that Arthur's war against such evil customs as that of Darnant and Amangons is annually repeated between his realm and the denizens of the forest?[38]

We are now able to discern three clear zones of operation within *The Elucidation:* the zone of King Arthur and his knights representing the forces of order; the zone of Amangons and the Rich Company who perpetuate his *mauvais lignage* and make war against Arthur; and the zone of the Rich Fisher, keeper of the Grail Castle who stands in neither rank, but rather keeps his own enclosure. It is time to investigate the nature of the Wasteland and the Grail guardian of *The Elucidation* in more detail, and to understand just who are the Rich Company.

7

THE CAUSES AND CONSEQUENCES OF THE WASTELAND

Logres is a name of suffering, known for tears and weeping. It is known for suffering because they sowed neither peas nor wheat, no children were born there, no young girl married, no tree grew leaves, no field became green, no bird had fledglings, no beasts had young, and the king was mutilated until he had expiated his sins.

SONE DE NANSAY (TRANS. CM)

THE WASTELAND

Wasteland is the reverse of all that the Grail stands for: instead of nourishment, famine; instead of fertility, barrenness; instead of wisdom, disconnection. The Wasteland puts everyone in Logres into a state of bare survival. We have already discerned some of the mythic causes of the Wasteland in chapter 6, but its consequences have a much wider effect that is felt beyond the pages of these texts, in our own world.

The Elucidation uniquely gives us an alternative causation of the Wasteland that arises from the violation of the Maidens of the Wells, and the theft of their cups. As a consequence of Amangons's actions, the service of the wells ceases, the maidens appear no more, the country goes into decline, the land is laid waste, and the court of the Rich Fisher is lost. In this chapter, we will explore these consequences in more depth.

The concept of the Wasteland—a state of devastation whereby the land is rendered barren and depopulated—is largely absent from Chrétien. The consequences of Perceval's failure to ask the question fall mainly on the unhealing Fisher King, who would have regained his health and the rule of his land; the cause of this neglect is laid upon Perceval's sin against his mother, who has died on his account. His unnamed female cousin, whom he meets coming away from the Grail Castle, informs him that she grieves "no less for your misfortune in not learning what was done with the grail or where it's taken, than for your mother who has died."[1]

It is only later, when the Black Maiden comes to reproach Perceval at court, that he is told that by his neglect of the question, "Ladies will lose their husbands, lands will be laid waste, girls will be left in distress and orphaned, and many knights will die."[2]

But Chrétien gives us no further details of these things beyond a general social disorder whereby lands will be laid waste due to lack of governance. We do not hear about the land's general infertility.

The concept of Wasteland is developed much further in the *First Continuation* where the Wounded King relates how it was brought about by a knight who struck his opponent such a blow that the sword broke in half. "By that blow the whole land and realm of Logres, which had been held in such high regard, was laid waste."[3]

That a lack of fertility should result from the violation of the Faery Accord does not surprise us, but that the rape of the Maidens of the Wells is wholly missing from the rest of the Grail legends does. While this rape does not appear as the causation of the Wasteland, it is also not an isolated incident of violation. The Arthurian legends are full of blackhearted knights who imprison ladies for their pleasure, or pull maidens by their hair along the ground, fathers who slap their daughters bloody, partners who make their wives run around in a ragged frock, and many other enormities that replicate the historical evils of medieval times.

The abuse of women is what the Round Table knights are there to stop. In Chrétien's *Perceval,* we are told that the safeguarding of women was a point of honor; as Gawain explains to the rapist Greoreas, who once abducted a girl, "In King Arthur's land girls are protected; the king has given them a safeguard, and watches over them and ensures their safe conduct."[4]

Indeed, it was the measure of a civilization in medieval times that a woman could travel the whole country from end to end with treasure about her person and not be molested. The punishment meted out to the rapist Greoreas at Arthur's court was to tie his hands behind his back and make him eat with the dogs for a month, taking his food from the floor by his mouth alone.[5] We learn later that the maiden who was abducted by him is hardly satisfied by this minor punishment, and is downcast, depressed, and enraged that he is not more severely condemned.[6] In an incident that makes us seriously consider Gawain as the rescuer of the maidens, he liberates a household of maidens imprisoned by Greoreas, who have been made to weave and sew against their will: kept in ragged garments, half-starved and beaten, they appeal to Gawain and he frees them.

In *The Elucidation,* we are not specifically told about what happens to Amangons, only that

> *the king came to a bad end*
> *And all the others after him,*
> *And so were many punished.*[7]

While Amangons and his men meet a bad end, which might be considered punishment enough, the consequences of their actions remain with everyone in Logres. The Wasteland remains an ongoing condition, causing dearth, drought, and depopulation.

The causation of the Wasteland in the later Grail legends, as we have seen in chapter 6, is primarily as the result of the Grail King's wounding: sometimes this is the result of injury in combat but some-times it is self-inflicted, as the result of great sorrow or remorse. In the case of Klingsor in Wolfram's *Parzival*, it is even the means of gaining power, as he is castrated in a parody of the Wounded King. In the *Third Continuation*, the Fisher King wounds himself out of grief for the death of his brother. How are we to understand this self-harming in respect of the Grail legends? In terms of the Wasteland it can only make sense if we look back at the nature of kingship itself.

One of the many tributaries that has irrigated the Grail legends is that of the Celtic tradition, whose understanding of the rights and duties of a ruler can help us perceive the connections between Wasteland and Wounded King in a clearer way. Irish texts speak of the *banais rigi,* or wedding of the kingship, whereby the king was symbolically married to the land.[8] This marriage was the contract the ruler entered into with Flatheas (literally "lordship"), the Goddess Sovereignty, taking the land into his stewardship as a guardian and protector. According to bardic lore, the spiritual duties of a king were strictly entailed: if his rule was just, then his land and people were fertile and content. As the eighth-century Irish text *Audacht Moraind* (Testament of Morand) relates:

As long as he upholds justice, good will not be lacking to him, and his reign will not fail. . . .

By the prince's justice, every right prevails and every vessel is full during his reign. . . .

By the prince's justice, fair weather arrives fittingly in each sea-son, with fine and frosty winters, with dry and windy springs, warm showers of rain in summer, heavy dews and druitfulness in autumn.

For it is the prince's falsehood that brings contrary weather upon wicked peoples and dries up the fruits of the earth.[9]

Part of the king's contract with the Goddess of Sovereignty was outlined by the number of *geasa* laid upon him by men of wisdom at the beginning of his reign. A *geis* (plural, *geasa*) is a prohibition or obligation binding one on pain of the loss of honor, from the breaking of which a king might not only lose honor, but also harm the land. For a ruler, breaking one of the geasa imposed by Sovereignty implied fracturing the contract between king and land.

In an Irish story concerning Arthur, *Echtra an Mhadra Mhaoil,* or "The Story of the Crop-Eared Dog," Arthur says to his followers:

> Good people . . . there are many geasa upon me, and one of them is to convene the chase of the Dangerous Forest at the end of every seventh year. If the chase should prove favourable for me the first day, to leave the forest; if not, to stay the second day, and the third concerning the hunt. And I shall not break my *geasa . . . for he is a person without prosperity who breaks his geasa.*[10] (italics added)

As we saw earlier, such duties may well be incumbent upon Arthur in his long-standing war with the denizens of the forest (see page 187, chapter 6).

The prosperity of a ruler depended upon the keeping of his promises. All Indo-European sources are agreed that the one particular thing that broke the agreement between a king and the Goddess of the Land was if his body was subject to maiming or impairment. A king who was blinded or who lost a limb was immediately disqualified from ruling. We see this clearly in the *First Battle of Mag Tuiread* wherein the king of the Tuatha de Danann, Nuadu, loses his hand in battle. Although his physician fashions a prosthetic hand, his people will have none of him, and ask Lugh to step into his place.[11]

Keeping this in mind, we can understand the rationale behind the Wounded King and the Wasteland. Because the land and the king share one life, when the king is wounded, the land itself becomes infertile. If the king and the land are one, then we can see why *The*

Elucidation's unique cause of the Wasteland is so remarkable: it refers to *the wounding of the maidens,* not of a king. In this scenario, the maidens are agents of the Goddess of Sovereignty, the embodiment of the land. It follows that the wounding of the spirit of the land's representatives must automatically result in the withdrawal of fertility. The gravity of this violation goes even beyond the immediacy of the Faery Accord, since it offends Sovereignty, the Goddess of the Earth herself, giver of all life.

As we have seen, the many stories of the Land of Women that predate and interpenetrate the Arthurian legends reveal a region where a sovereign lady rules over an island of women: she is the one who gives judgment and rules wisely. But she only empowers one ruler at a time, bestowing her gifts on him. We see how Arthur's own legitimacy as king arises from the test of two swords: the Sword in the Stone, by which he is shown to his peers as the rightful heir to Logres; and also Excalibur, the sword that is given him by the Lady of the Lake. This dual acclamation by the peers of the land and by its spiritual guardians is essential for his kingship to be successful. It is unto the Lady of the Lake that Excalibur must be rendered when Arthur is wounded at the Battle of Camlann. It is unto her that he himself passes, going into Avalon where his mortal wound can be healed, just as Brangemor returns to his mother, Brangepart, in the *First Continuation* (chapter 5).

We can readily understand how, at the end of his earthly existence, Arthur himself ultimately becomes part of the myth of the Wounded King: ensconced in Avalon, outside time and accessible only to the needs of the temporal realms from whence he might, as Malory insists, be called back.[12] That Arthur may have already been seen as a wounded king is evidenced by references within the Spanish text of *La Faula* (see page 83, chapter 3).

We have already postulated a parallel location for Arthur at his court in the everyday world and for the Rich Fisher at his court in the timeless otherworld. Now we need to discover more about this mysterious guardian and his antecedents.

THE RICH FISHER

The figure of the Fisher King is known to us first from Chrétien's *Perceval*. Perceval first sees him fishing from a boat. The next time, it is at table where the king asks forgiveness for not standing to greet him, as he is unable. Since Perceval neglects to ask about this infirmity, he doesn't learn its cause until he is later berated by his cousin, the lamenting maiden, for not having asked about the Grail procession. She names the king as "the rich Fisher King" who has been wounded in battle and completely crippled because of being pierced through both thighs with a javelin. Because he can no longer hunt or go on horseback, he fishes as a form of recreation.[13]

The title "Fisher King" arises from a punning confusion within French language, whereby "to sin," or *pécher,* and "to fish," or *pêcher,* sit side by side and mingle meanings in this myth. At one level, the Fisher King is "the sinner king," and his wound is due to either his unworthy action or, according to the *Third Continuation,* his own self-wounding in an excess of grief over the killing of the best knight, his brother. He remains in a timeless condition for hundreds of years awaiting release from his suffering.

While we can understand how the Fisher King is also a sinner king, in the Christian sense of the legends, it is also worth exploring what his fisherman activities might be about. What does the Fisher King fish for? On one level, he casts his line for a fish, but at another, he is trying to reel in a seeker who will end his suffering; we can clearly see this manner of "fishing" in the *Lancelot-Grail,* where the Grail King, King Pelles, purposely sends his daughter Elaine into Lancelot's way so that the Grail winner, Galahad, might be engendered and thus end his grandfather's suffering.[14] In effect, the wounded Fisher King is attached to his own line, from which he himself cannot wriggle free.

The wounded Fisher King of Chrétien's *Perceval* has an even older correlative, as we hear when Perceval visits the cell of his hermit uncle:

> He who is served from the grail is my brother. Our sister was your
> mother. . . . I believe the rich Fisher King is the son of the king who

is served from the grail. Do not think that he is given pike, lamprey, or salmon; he is served with a single host which is brought to him in that grail. Such a holy thing is the grail that it sustains and comforts his life.[15]

This account lifts the curtain on the Grail family lineage that we explored in the account of Robert de Boron in the last chapter, one that is firmly showing us the Holy Grail at its most holy.

However, the Rich Fisher of *The Elucidation* is a figure utterly unlike the Wounded Kings of other Grail texts, since he does not seem to suffer from a wound. This fact is shared with no other text. It simply is not mentioned. The lamentation at the court of the Rich Fisher is wholly reserved for the procession of the mysterious body on the bier, about which we will speak further in chapter 8. The Rich Fisher belongs to an older mythic lineage, it would seem, one that is typified by its *richesse*.

The Old French term *riche* appears frequently in the Arthurian legends, usually to express the opulence of noble people, their clothes, and their surroundings. But in the case of the Rich Fisher there is a deeper sense in which the word is appropriate. We are told that "the rich country of Logres," (line 27) was a realm that once knew the custom of the Maidens of the Wells in times gone by, though it is not so now. The Rich Fisher, like the Celtic god of the underworld, is a purveyor of feasts and plenty. We also learn that the court of the Rich Fisher was responsible for the resourcing of the whole of Logres, for since the theft of the golden cups,

> *Nor could be found from now on*
> *The court of the Rich Fisher*
> *Which had been making the country resplendent*
> *With gold and silver, furs, gray fur,*
> *Rich brocaded silks,*
> *And meat and clothing,*
> *Of gerfalcons, merlins,*
> *Goshawks, sparrow hawks, falcons.*
> *Of old, when the court could be found*

There was throughout the country
Riches and great plenty,
Such as I have named,
That all be amazed,
Both poor and rich, by the wealth;
But now all was lost.
In the kingdom of Logres
Were all the riches of the world.[16]

We are not talking here about the mere economic loss of what is called by businesses today "the gross domestic product" of a land, for the Rich Fisher's domain is not a realm whose value is merely about stocks and commodities. The text is rather speaking about the loss of the flow of resources that normally fructify and irrigate the whole realm of Logres, thus making the Rich Fisher, like the Greek Plutos, the otherworldly source of all riches. The loss of this realm—which fructifies our world with all good things—results in dearth and need within Logres, as the land is laid waste and the waters retreat. Wasteland and loss of the Courts of Joy are the real result of the Dolorous Blow struck upon the Maidens of the Wells, showing us that the fracture of the Faery Accord displaces also the natural flow of resources from the court of the Rich Fisher to our world. In Celtic terms, this is a loss that has been wrought by lack of honor, as we saw above in the *Story of the Crop-Eared Dog,* where Arthur declared, "And I shall not break my *geasa . . . for he is a person without prosperity who breaks his geasa.*"[17]

The plenty that is provided by the Rich Fisher's court is in stark contrast to the Wasteland that is provoked by violation of the maidens. One of the major losses for the earthly realm of Arthur's world is loss of access to the court of the Rich Fisher: the inhabitants of Arthur's realm can no longer find the way to it, nor can the company of Bleheris discover its whereabouts—there is no joy without that connection. The quest to access the court of the Rich Fisher is, thus, the major quest in *The Elucidation,* whereby the knights go to the spiritual epicenter of the kingdom to restore plenty once again, but not to heal the Rich

Fisher, who does not appear to be wounded. We are told that Perceval

> *asked who the Graal*
> *Served, but did not ask*
> *About the lance, why it bled*
> *When he saw it, nor of the sword*
> *Of which half the blade was missing*
> *And the other lying on the bier*
> *On the dead body, nor the manner*
> *Of the great vanishing.*[18]

There is not a word about healing any wounds of the Rich Fisher in *The Elucidation:* rather the wounding seems to lie on the human side of things, but we do discover something that leads us to understand how the severance of the paths leading to his court is as a result of the breaking of the Faery Accord. The Rich Fisher uniquely appears in *The Elucidation* as a shape-changer, being a fisherman by day and a magnificent lord by night. Although commentators have generally discounted this factor as a mistaken understanding of the two appearances of the Wounded King in *Perceval* as fisherman and noble, we need to look at this much closer. The Round Table knights,

> *sought with great vigor*
> *The court of the rich Fisher*
> *Who knew much magic*
> *And could change his appearance—*
> *Some sought him in one shape,*
> *While others under another form.*[19]

Here, the knights seem to seek the Rich Fisher in a manner more familiar to us from the tales of the Scarlet Pimpernel, for his assorted guises are indeed bewildering. This shapeshifting tradition is found in one other Grail text, in *Diu Cröne*, where Gawain encounters a strange being called Gansguoter of Micholde who is a learned priest who has acquired magic.[20] He is the Grail bearer's uncle, one who terrifyingly changes shapes in quick succession, being able to take any shape he wishes. Not only does his body alter, but his dress also changes. We learn how he enabled Arthur's mother to escape from Brittany, becoming her second husband; he built for her the Castle of Maidens as well as the Grail Castle and made its revolving walls.

As we saw in the previous chapter, in an incident highly reminiscent of *Sir Gawain and the Green Knight,* in *Diu Cröne* Gawain is invited to play a beheading game whereby he will cut off Gansguoter's head that day, while Gansguoter will cut off his on the morrow. Gawain fortunately has the first strike with the halberd and beheads Gansguoter, whose body immediately searches about for his head and then walks away with it. On the next occasion, Gawain kneels for the return blow, but the halberd misses him twice, and he is only spared, we are told, because of his relationship to Gansguoter, who is the uncle of Amurfina, whom Gawain loves, and because Gawain's aunt, Igern, was Arthur's mother and Gansguoter's beloved, "whom he had won by fiddling and was taken to Madarp after Uterpandragon's death."[21]

Gansguoter's abduction of Igern reminds us of the Castle of Maidens in *Perceval,* where Igerna, Arthur's mother, rules over a household of maidens, widows, and unfledged young men in the Castle of Maidens, a place where Igerna takes her treasure. The sense of Gansguoter as a sorcerer who controls the castle by a series of enchantments clearly relates the Castle of Maidens and the Grail Castle in an incident that challenges Gawain as a Grail knight.

Gansguoter is both sorcerer and master engineer, the architect of several wondrous castles: one with an impenetrable moat where the walls of the castle are smooth as glass, and where the whole castle revolves: these features are standard architecture for otherworldly castles, as seen in the turning tower of Caer Sidi in the British Underworld.[22] Even the test of the beheading game is one to which we return, showing us the Celtic antecedents of the Rich Fisher, the only other Grail guardian who has this shapeshifting ability.

So how can a king also be a fisherman? We might take the idea of the Rich Fisher as a shapeshifter as a mere rationalization of the medieval mind, if it were not for a preexistent tradition in British myth.

We have already seen in chapter 6 how the anti-Kings of the Grail legends have a propensity to behave like mercenary, faery enchanters and to possess the power of invisibility. This tradition of the shape-changer who lives on the margins of the world goes back as far as *The Mabinogion* where Caswallawn (the British name for the Trinovantian war-leader Cassivelaunus, who withstood the Julian invasion of Britain in 55 BCE) appears as an enchanter. In *Branwen, Ferch Llyr,* Caswallawn is said to be responsible for overcoming the Island of the Mighty by dint of using "the Veil of Illusion, so that no one could see him slay the men, but the sword only they see."[23] This cloak of invisibility, like a magic mist or the *fé fiadha*—the faery cordon—makes another appearance in *Manawyddan ap Llyr* where a kind of Wasteland descends upon the realm of Dyfed. Manawyddan and his stepson, Pryderi, are feasting at the palace of Narberth when

> there came a fall of mist, so thick that not one of them could see the other. And when they looked toward the place where they were wont to see cattle and herds and dwellings, they saw nothing now, neither house, nor beast, nor smoke, nor fire, nor man, nor dwelling; but the houses of the Court empty, and desert and uninhabited, without man or beast within them.[24]

This sudden enchantment reminds us immediately of the sudden onset of the Wasteland. We have already seen how Manawyddan and Pryderi are significant to the Grail legends, both men possessing experience of the timeless realms of Caer Sidi, the fortress of inspiration in the watery underworld (chapter 4).

Caswallawn is not the only shapeshifter in British tradition. Uther Pendragon is described in Geoffrey of Monmouth's 1136 *Historia Regnum Britanniae* as the one who took on the form of Gorlois, Duke of Cornwall, in order to sleep with his wife, Igerna, and so engendered Arthur. Uther subsequently went into Welsh tradition as a shapeshifter.

This power of enchantment is heightened in the *Book of Taliesin*, where a poem is put in the mouth of the dying Uther Pendragon, who describes himself thus:

> *Am I not called Gorlassar (Blue Enamel)?*
> *My belt was a rainbow's circuit around the foe.*
> *Am I not a prince of shadows*
> *I, who appear with the two chief baskets? . . .*
> *Am I not the best enchanter*
> *of the Strong Door to ascend the mountain?*[25]

Here Uther's enchanting, shapeshifting power is in the form of a belt, or magic cordon, used to overcome his foes, just as Caswallawn uses his invisibility.

Caswallawn's mantle of invisibility is named as one of the Thirteen Treasures of Britain, now inherited by Arthur: "The mantle of Arthur in Cornwall. This made the wearer invisible, though he could see everyone."[26] In the *Dream of Rhonabwy*, the cloak becomes a carpet, which is called Gwen, or white: anything that is not white would immediately become so, effectively making the object invisible.[27]

This is all highly reminiscent of the invisible knight Garlon who, in the Continuation of the *Prose Merlin* from the *Lancelot-Grail* cycle and again in Malory's *Morte d'Arthur*, strikes at his enemies from under his own cloak of invisibility. Certainly, the older British legends have their Continental parallels but, in speaking of the Rich Fisher as a shapeshifter, *The Elucidation* brings us even closer parallels between Grail and anti-Grail Kings! The Rich Fisher of *The Elucidation* draws upon these older figures of Caswallawn and the lord of the underworld who feasts his host of heroes.

THE OTHERWORLDLY FEAST

At the court of the Rich Fisher, feasting continues unabated, unaffected by the Wasteland that so afflicts the temporal regions of Logres. Does the Rich Fisher himself sever contact between Logres and his court? Or is this an automatic effect of the violation of the Maidens of the Wells? To answer this, we must engage with the nature of the Rich Fisher's court and its location, since it is clearly separate from the ordinary world, for the Grail feast's provisions show no lack of supply.

After the Grail and other hallows are processed, the Rich Fisher sits down to dine:

> *Then the bread was given to them all,*
> *And the wine set before them*
> *In great gold and silver cups.*
> *Afterward, the Graal was seen,*
> *Without servant or seneschal,*
> *Coming through the door of a room*
> *And many were properly served*
> *In rich golden dishes*
> *Each worth a great treasure.*
> *The first course was set*
> *Before the king, and then served*
> *To all the others around in that place;*
> *And never were such marvelous*
> *Meals as were taken to them*
> *And the food that they were given.*[28]

This ability of the Grail to serve all by itself, without servitor, is also found in the *First Continuation,* where Gawain saw,

> *The rich Graal, which served*
> *And placed the bread speedily*
> *Before all the knights.*
> *Then it became as the butler,*
> *Serving the wine*
> *Into great cups of fine gold,*
> *Then was each table supplied*

> To the lords and their retainers,
> After which the others of the company.
> All this without a servant,
> Then was the second course served
> In great bowls of silver.[29]

In both *The Elucidation* and the *First Continuation,* the Grail seems to share this unique ability for self-service that is soon replicated in other places, including *Parzival*. In an almost futuristic way, food is dispensed automatically from the Graal, in much the same way as the maidens offered food to travelers, according to their preference.

The tradition of perpetual feasting seems to begin with Manannán mac Lír—the Irish counterpart of the British Manawyddan ap Llyr. As we saw in the *Fosterage in the House of the Two Pails* in chapter 4, the leader of the otherworldly regions, Manannán, provides the feast that sustains the life of the Tuatha de Danann faeries by creating a magical mist that obscures their realms from humans, and by giving the feast of Goibhniu, and Manannán's Swine. These latter are a pair of pigs who, no matter how many times they are killed, reconstitute themselves as long as none of their bones are broken. This ongoing and renewable feast sustains the land of Faery, without either aging or death, bestowing immortality upon them.

One aspect of the otherworldly feast gives us pause, since this is precisely what is said of Christ's body at the Passion. Instead of breaking his legs—the standard Roman method of quickly ending the suffering of crucifixion, in that the crucified person could no longer raise himself to relieve the strain upon his hands and lungs—Longinus's spear is thrust into Christ's side to cause a quick death. Water and blood issue forth, symbolically alluding to the water of baptism and purification, and the blood of atonement, remembered at the Eucharistic feast, by which Christians are sustained. The mythic requirement is that those whose bones are unbroken can be speedily resurrected.

The decision to leave Christ's bones unbroken is in fulfillment of the prophecy in Psalms 34:20: "He protects all his bones, not one of them will be broken." For these things took place that the scripture might be fulfilled: "Not one of his bones will be broken."[30] This instruction clearly refers back to the Passover meal, eaten hastily and in one house, whereat the leg of lamb is utterly consumed by those present. Also in Numbers 9:12 we hear how the Israelites "shall leave none of it to the morning, nor break any bone of it." Christ as the Paschal Lamb is considered to be a type of the Passover lamb.

Like Manannán, the Grail Castle's Rich Fisher in *The Elucidation* is a shapeshifter who hosts a feast that is endlessly repeated. However, unlike the joyous feasting of Faery, which is without guilt or pain, this Grail Castle feast is fraught with lamentation and the frustration of Grail seekers who fail to ask the right questions.

The Rich Fisher, as both the host of a perpetual feast and the witness of a lamenting Grail procession, is a strange mixture of otherworldly shapeshifter and Christian king, Even the Grail Castle itself, within the *First Continuation,* is reachable by a raised causeway and seems to be surrounded by water, just like one of the otherworldly islands of Celtic myth. We must look further back for the roots of the Rich Fisher, where we find an even older host.

BRAN: THE ORIGINAL FISHER KING

Within *The Mabinogion,* in *Branwen, Ferch Llyr* we encounter Bran, the titanic ruler of Britain, who is certainly one of the earliest mythic archetypes of the Fisher or Grail King. Bran is the owner of a cauldron of rebirth that he received from an otherworldly couple called Llassar Llaes Gyfnewid (whose name has the sense of "exchange of fire") and his wife Cymeidei Cymeinfol. Dead men can be reanimated by being placed in their cauldron. While Bran is in negotiations to give his sister, Branwen, as wife of the Irish king, Matholwch, the Irish ambassadors are so insulted by Branwen's brother, Efnissien, that Bran has to give the cauldron to the Irish, in recompense for their injured honor.

Later in the story, Bran hears how Branwen has been abused at the hands of her husband, Matholwch, and so he takes his army across to Ireland but, in the course of the ensuing debacle, the cauldron of rebirth is used to raise up dead Irish warriors who keep giving battle until only seven of the British party are left. Seeing that the cauldron is furnishing the Irish with yet more men, Efnissien has himself taken up and put in the cauldron as if he himself were dead and, stretching out within it as a living man, breaks it asunder. In the battle, Bran himself is mortally wounded, as Taliesin in his poem *Kadeir Taliesin* (Chair of Taliesin) tells us:

> *I was with the son of Iwerydd [Bran] in Ireland,*
> *I witnessed the immolation of Morddwyd Tyllon.*[31]

Now *Morddwyd Tyllon* means "the Pierced Thigh" and is a reference to the poisoned spear blow that Bran receives. When all seems lost, the mortally wounded Bran demands of his remaining followers that they behead him and take his head to the White Mount (possibly the site of the Tower of London or else Ludgate Hill) where they are to bury it with his face facing France. He prophesies to his loyal remnant:

> In Harlech you will be feasting seven years, the birds of Rhiannon singing unto you the while. And all that time the head will be to you as pleasant company as it ever was when on my body. And at Gwales in Penfro you will be fourscore years, and you may remain there, and the head with you uncorrupted, until you open the door that looks toward Aber Henfelen, and toward Cornwall. And after you have opened that door, there you may no longer tarry, but set forth then to London to bury the head.[32]

Everything falls out as Bran predicted, with the natural grief of the seven survivors put on indefinite hold as they listen to the birds of Rhiannon at the perpetual feasting, whereat the head speaks to them as if it had been still attached to Bran's body. This otherworldly suspension of time's flow unfortunately ceases as soon as a curious man of the company opens the forbidden door, whereupon time runs again and all the sorrows they had suffered come once more to mind.

This then is the earliest reference to the figure of the Wounded King that later reemerged in the Grail legends. Here we have a cauldron that revives the dead, a wounded king, and a perpetual feast. We can set beside it another tale, that of the ninth-century Welsh poem *Preiddeu Annwfyn*, the Raid on the Underworld, wherein Arthur himself aims to fetch back to his own realms the cauldron of Pen Annwfyn, Lord of the Underworld. Arthur sails in his ship Prydwen to seven locations to find the cauldron, in a voyage that is the very first Grail quest. The poem is narrated by Taliesin, who is also one of the survivors of Bran's foray upon Ireland. He tells us about the cauldron and the maidens who attend it:

> *My original song stems from the cauldron,*
> *By the breath of nine maidens was it kindled.*
> *The Chief of Annwfyn's cauldron, what is its power?*
> *Ridged with enamel, rimmed with pearl,*
> *It will not boil the coward's portion, it is not destined.*[33]

The fact that the Pen Annwfyn's cauldron is clearly designated for the use of heroes alone tells us that this is a vessel serving the greater dead, and that the feast that is enjoyed around it is the perpetual feast of the ancestors in the underworld. This is underscored by the fact that the cauldron's kindling is from the breath of nine maidens. These are maidens we have met before, of course: they are the otherworldly, faery women from whose hands hospitality is offered. They are the ones who automatically know whether someone is worthy or not.

The fact that *Preiddeu Annwfyn* has as its chorus, "Except seven, none rose up" from this dangerous voyage, reveals that Arthur's raid on the underworld for the cauldron and Bran's foray to Ireland are resonant with each other, with only seven returning from either adventure. This understanding was clearly made in the minds of the Welsh bards who recorded, in their triads, that one of the three fortunate conceal-ments of the Island of Britain was the burial of the head of Bran, whose purpose was to act as a palladium against invasion, but "Arthur disclosed the Head of Bran the Blessed from the White Hill, because it did not seem right to him that this Island should be defended by the strength of anyone, but by his own."[34]

In uncovering Bran's head, so that he might himself be the protector of the island, Arthur's hubris inadvertently leads him into the shoes of Bran: those who go on quest for objects of power and then remove their guardians must themselves become the guardian, is the rule here. Arthur's voyage to the underworld of Annwfyn is actually a quest for a cauldron, not a Grail, but we can see the remnant of an ancient *geis,* or sacred agreement, to uphold the protection of Britain throughout the Arthurian legends played out here. At the beginning of every feast, Arthur's *geis* is to not sit down to dine until he has witnessed a marvel: as expressed in Malory's *Morte D'Arthur,* "So ever the king had a custom that at the feast of Pentecost in especial, afore other feasts in the year, he would not go that day to meat until he heard or seen of a great marvel."[35]

A succession of Grail Kings unfolds throughout time, with Bran's own name becoming enshrined as the Grail guardian Brons, as we have seen in Robert de Boron's work. Bran's wounding in battle with the poisoned spear is itself an earlier version of the Dolorous Blow, but his subsequent demand to be beheaded and brought to the White Mount leads to a timeless feasting with the remnant of his followers.

Looking forward to the later Grail legends, we may then ask, what are the implications of the Grail King wounding *himself*? In all the ancient mythic narratives, there is no sign of this kind of self-harm, unless we are to look at the Phrygian myth of Attis who castrated himself after being exposed to the glory of the goddess Cybele.[36] For the Grail guardians, any wounds that arise are those taken in combat or battle. Self-wounding is something that arises from remorse, self-sacrifice, and as has been suggested by many scholars, a kind of inverse and perverted requirement to emulate the wounding of the Grail King. Klingsor's castration comes about as a punishment for sleeping with the wife of a rival king: it is only after this that Klingsor learns magic in Persia, thus replacing his manly powers with those of sorcery.

The suspended death of Bran, whereby his head lives on for seventy-eight years, is like that of the unburied knight in the skiff or the body on the bier: a body to be lamented but which seems not to be entirely lifeless. Bran's after-death task seems to be to oversee the perpetual feast of the ancestral dead and to protect the realm from invasion. This leads us to one further mystery that is associated with this protection.

In Welsh, the word *bran* means "raven." This gives Bran's command to bury his body at the White Mount an additional resonance, for this hill has been long associated with Tower Hill at the Tower of London. The legends concerning the ravens that are still kept at the Tower relate that Britain will not be invaded while they still live on the hill. Bran's head thus remains in memory as a palladium against invasion.[37]

The Grail Castle, which goes unnamed in the earlier legends, is called "Corbenic" in the *Lancelot-Grail*. In the original British language, *Corbenic* also signifies the "the raven's head." It is one of the many words associated with the Grail quest with which scholars and speculators have made hay: Corbenic, seen through French eyes, becomes *le corps bénit,* or blessed body; *cors bénit,* or blessed horn; or *cor bénit,* or blessed court. Bodies—sacred and other—drinking horns, and courts keep weaving the myth together, as we have seen. Truly, the legend of Bran underlies the Grail legends, providing a fertile seedbed for later development.

Bran's ongoing feast, like Manannán's, is akin to the Grail feast, but also the ancestral feast of worthy heroes. But when the resources that provide the feast are stolen, what other result can there be but Wasteland?

SACRED HOSPITALITY

Among most traditional cultures of the world, the respect for the stranger, whether traveler or pilgrim, is shown by the act of hospitality. The famous icon known as the Philoxeny (Hospitality) of Abraham, painted by the fifteenth-century Russian monk Andrei Rublev, depicts three winged angels sitting about a small table on which is placed a cup.

It depicts a famous act of hospitality made by Abraham at the oaks of Mamre to the messengers of God, whom he unknowingly receives as three strangers.[38] It is from such myths as this that many societies welcome the guest kindly, lest they entertain angels unawares.

Under the ancient laws of traditional and nomadic societies, hospitality once received put the stranger under the protection of his hosts, changing him from a stranger into a guest. The violation of sacred hospitality, when the guest offers violence or steals from the host, or the host from the guest, is considered everywhere as the grossest offense. It is in such a light that we must view the violation of the Maidens of the Wells who unconditionally offer the resources of the land to travelers.

The relationship of the Rich Fisher and the Maidens of the Wells is not made explicitly clear within *The Elucidation*. In a sense, the maidens and their roadside service of food and drink to travelers are but a window into the world of the Rich Fisher, a cynosure that is swiftly closed by the act of Amangons and his men. Travelers abroad in the land encounter the maidens when their hunger and thirst cause them to turn aside to one of the wells, where they ask for the food of their desire.

Let us consider the linkage between the maidens and the Rich Fisher, from the clues offered within the examples from the British tradition above. As we have seen, nine maidens warm the cauldron of Pen Annwfyn.[39] These nine maidens appear in different parts of the Arthurian legend and seem endemic to the northwest European tradition.[40] They appear as the Nine Witches of Gloucester, the women who school Peredur in arms, in *The Mabinogion*. They are seen in Geoffrey of Monmouth's *Vita Merlini* as Morgen and her otherworldly sisters who receive the wounded Arthur.[41]

That the nine maidens are warming the cauldron of the Lord of the Underworld with their breath shows us that we have the closest correlative between Rich Fisher and Maidens of the Wells: both the giver of the perpetual feast and the maidens who cook the food by their inspiration are involved with service of the cauldron. In this way, we can see that the theft of the maidens' golden cups and the severance of

Fig. 7.1. The Philoxeny of
Abraham, from an icon
by Andrei Rublev

the flow of prosperity from the court of the Rich Fisher that follows are utterly connected. Amangons's violation cuts away human connections to the hospitality of the earth and its otherworldly guardians, to sources of spiritual wholeness, and to the ancestral communion over which the Rich Fisher presides (see chapter 8).

The same mysterious service of the cauldron is also that of the Grail as we see in the *First Continuation* when Gawain witnesses the Grail procession a second time, "the rich Grail, without anybody carrying it, served them splendidly . . . it served at least seven full courses . . . richly and handsomely."[42] The food of one's desire is, of course, also served by the Grail in texts like Wolfram's *Parzival,* the *Lancelot-Grail,* and Malory's *Morte d'Arthur.*

The world of King Arthur, the everyday world that hears the story of the Maidens of the Wells' violation, is not the same world as that of the Rich Fisher, which is a world within (see chapter 4). The Rich Fisher is the keeper of the earth's resources, just as the Greek god Ploutus or Plutus before him is considered to be the God of the Harvest

Riches. The rape of the maidens causes the land in the everyday world to become

> dead and deserted,
> *So that it was not worth a pair of hazelnuts.*[43]

At a fundamental level, the richness of the land of Logres is portrayed as dependent upon the deep resources of the Rich Fisher's realm. In the earthly realm of Logres there is dearth and drought, but in the Grail Castle, the hospitality and renewed feasting continues unabated, albeit accompanied by a deep lamentation.

The theft of the resources of the land is a major theme in the British story of *Lludd and Llefelys,* from *The Mabinogion,* wherein the land suffers three oppressive enchantments that replicate the Wasteland of the Grail legends. The first is a cry that rings out every May Eve and causes women to become barren, and children and elders to drop dead; the second is the presence of a ubiquitous race who overhear everything that is done and who, thus, cannot be overcome; the third is the theft of food from the storerooms of Lludd, king of Britain.

Lludd goes to consult with his brother, Llefelys, king of France, meeting him in midchannel between their lands. At first, they have difficulty conferring from ship to ship due to the ever-present race of the Coranians who, by some mysterious spiritual means, muddle what one brother says to another; but by means of a speaking horn which is swiftly rinsed with the exorcism of wine, they are able to converse clearly once again.

Llefelys determines the causation of these three oppressions and wisely suggests solutions to overcome them. He concludes that the cry is caused every May Eve by two dragons that arise and fight each other: Lludd is to measure his kingdom and find its exact center, to dig a pit, and put a vessel of mead inside a box. The dragons will circle toward it, fall into it, drink the mead, and then can be closed up in the box and taken away and buried. The ever-present race of the Coranians can be neutralized only by placing crushed insects that he receives from his brother into the waters of Britain: while the native Britons will be unaffected, the ubiquitous race will be poisoned thereby. The third plague is caused

> by a mighty man of magic, who takes thy meat and thy drink and thy store. And he through illusions and charms causes everyone to sleep. It is needful for thee in thy own person to watch thy food and thy provisions. And lest he should overcome thee with sleep, be there a cauldron of cold water by thy side and when thou art oppressed with sleep, plunge into the cauldron.[44]

Lludd himself keeps watch until he finally sees a huge man in armor come into the storeroom, bearing a hamper into which he begins to put all the food. Lludd challenges him and they grapple, with the king overcoming the thief and swearing him to faithfulness in his service. Having successfully overcome all three oppressions, Lludd finally settles down to rule his realm in peace.

These three challenges seem to be tests that are sent against Lludd as a newly inaugurated king. The contending red and white dragons, which he manages to subdue, are taken away to Dinas Emrys and buried in Snowdonia, from whence they will break free again when the young Merlin is brought before Vortigern, the forerunner of the Pendragons: they are the forces of the land that Arthur himself later tames by his kingship. The unrestrained dragons depopulate the land by force of their terrible shrieking at the liminal time of May Eve, when the gates to Faery are open. Of the pervasive race of Coranians, who cannot be overcome because of their omniscience, we will have more to say below.

The sudden loss of provisions at the court of Lludd is a resonance of the Wasteland. The man who takes all Lludd's provisions reminds us of an early ninth-century Welsh poem known as *Uther's Death Poem*, suggesting another resonance between the Pendragons and the provision of plenty to the land:

> *Am I not a prince of shadows*
> *I, who appear with the two chief baskets?*[45]

These baskets may be a remembrance of the hamper that comes to remove Lludd's stores, a hamper that is well known from the list of the Thirteen Treasures of Britain, where it is named "the hamper of Gwyddno Garanhir. If food enough for one was placed in this, food for a hundred could be taken from it."[46] Gwyddno was the lord of Cantre'r Gwaelod, in what is now Cardigan Bay. His kingdom was protected from the sea by floodgates that had to be shut before high tide, but one day, Seithenyn, the keeper of the floodgates, became drunk, failing to close them, with the result that the sea rushed in and covered the land. Gwyddno is thus a king of the drowned lands beneath the sea, and his action in removing Lludd's provisions is resonant with the loss of his own lands to the sea.

The effect upon the land in *Lludd and Llefelys* is parallel to the state of Logres as we find it in *The Elucidation*: the cry of the dragons depopulates the land just as the Wasteland does; the ever-present race of the Coranians makes life impossible for the people, just as the Rich Company make peace a distant memory; while the riches of the land of Logres are stolen, just as the Rich Company seem to siphon off the resources of the land to create their own enclaves.

The devastations afflicting the land in *Lludd and Llefelys* are called *gormesiadd,* or oppressions, in Welsh, with the sense of being invaded and overwhelmed. In just such a way, the Rich Company invade and overwhelm the land of Logres.

THE RICH COMPANY

Whatever is sown in the earth is what comes up out of it at harvest time. In *The Elucidation* we have seen how the customary hospitality that binds humans and faeries into one accord has been ruptured. After this severance, Wasteland results and the Rich Fisher's court is lost. It is only found after the Round Table knights, inspired by the violation of the Maidens of the Wells to avenge them, find Bleheris and his company who themselves are unable to find the Court of Joy. After long quest, some of the knights succeed in finding the Rich Fisher's court, and Wasteland is once again replaced by fertility.

But, just when the story looks as if it is set fair again, at this high point of healing and rejoicing, there come out of the wells, not the Maidens of the Wells with their hospitable service, but the group of people known as the Rich Company:

> *Full of great ill will:*
> *Who came forth from the wells*
> *But they were not known.*[47]

Like a second and unwelcome harvest, the people who come out of the wells this time are very far from the maidens who hospitably issued forth previously. The behavior of the Rich Company is self-aggrandizing and ebullient. Their arising *after* the finding of the Rich Fisher's court obviously struck some listeners as a violation of a happy ending or an outrage that shouldn't have happened, for the narrator feels drawn to address their dismay:

> *To deny that these things happened*
> *Know this, through all the world*
> *That you won't find any such today.*[48]

Who precisely are these people of the Rich Company? They are not the folk from the Rich Fisher's court, but a race inimical to Arthur and the Round Table knights. In our list of what Wasteland brings to Logres, we included dearth, barrenness, and disconnection, but the Rich Company also sow dissention in the place where community once flourished, bringing greed, war, and oppression. The consequences for the realm of Logres are disastrous, causing a cessation of questing for four years, while Arthur and the Round Table knights deal with what arises.

The Welsh name for England, *Lloegr*—angelicized as Logres—had a particular linguistic echo for the French Arthurian writers who spoke of the Castle Orgueilleux, or Castle of Pride. For us too, this parallel is one we should not miss. From the word *Logres,* the Grail writers drew out its French echo, *orgellous,* or proud, which becomes the mission statement of the Rich Company. The land of Logres itself becomes a byword for suffering, as we hear from the *Sone de Nansay*:

> Logres is a name of suffering, known for tears and weeping. It is known for suffering because they sowed neither peas nor wheat, no children were born there, no young girl married, no tree grew leaves, no field became green, no bird had fledglings, no beasts had young, and the king was mutilated until he had expiated his sins.[49]

Logres' rich kingdom falls into Wasteland until it is restored by the quest for the Court of Joy, which is another name for the Rich Fisher's court. What comes out of the wells at the same time as this restoration is a group of people whom we would recognize as hedonists, content only with the riches that have been accessed.

The Rich Company set themselves up in opposition to the Round Table knights, and build for themselves strongholds and towns, including the great Castle of Pride that features so often in the quests of later Arthurian legends.[50] Inside it Round Table knights are held without parole.

> *The Rich Company,*
> *built castles and cities*
> *Towns, boroughs, and strongholds,*
> *And built for the damsels*
> *The rich Castle of Maidens;*
> *They made the Perilous Bridge too*
> *And the great Castle of Pride.*[51]

We have already explored the Castle of Maidens and the faery side of the Grail myth, but now we need to understand just what and who the Rich Company really are. If they really built the Castle of Maidens for the Maidens of the Wells, what do they do this for? The text tells us:

> *Therein each had his lady love;*
> *Many thus led a fine life.*[52]

Are we then to understand that the original Maidens of the Wells are held here as captives? Since they have faery origin, it would presuppose that the maidens in question survive, having longer life than those who are mortal. But surely the Rich Company, having come from the wells themselves, must also have some faery or semifaery blood? However, these oppressors are very different in character from the wandering company of Bleheris, who are likewise half-breeds.

Amangons's rape and theft of the cups serves to encourage his men to do likewise. Such acts are familiar to us from war zones the world over, where incoming forces use rape as an instrument of repression and contemptuous conquest. Any children born of such rape become those of the oppressor, thus overwriting the genetic legacy of the chosen partner of the woman who is raped. And this is how we imagine the Rich Company springing forth, as the shocking, secondary effect of Amangons's actions. The Rich Company is unlike Bleheris's company, for they inherit, not the hospitable virtues of the maidens, but rather those of Amangons and his men: values of violence and selfishness that help establish a totalitarian regime that is completely contrary to the Round Table knights and their king.

In British myth, there is a prior story about an oppressive and otherworldly race that bears repetition here. *The Welsh Triads* speak of three oppressions that came upon the Island of Britain, including,

> The people of the Coryaniaid . . . came here in the time of Caswallawn, son of Beli; and not one of them went back. And they came from Arabia.[53]

The Coryaniaid or Coranians, start to appear in the time of Caswallawn, he of the invisibility cloak, but they are finally dealt with by his son Lludd, as we saw above on page 210. What makes these invaders so oppressive is related in the story of *Lludd and Llefelys:*

> This race . . . was called the Coranians; and so great was their knowledge, that there was no discourse upon the face of the island,

however low it might be spoken, but what, if the wind met it, it was known to them. And through this they could not be injured.[54]

A further version of this text also adds of the Coranians that "their coin was faery money," literally, "dwarf's money": received as gold coin, it would quickly revert again to mushrooms, the substance from which it had been conjured.[55]

So, this gives us a portrait of a people who are ubiquitous, privy to any secret, and a threat to those who live in Britain. Examination of the name Coryaniaid gives us another clue, for it is related to the Breton word *korriganed* (modern, *korrigans*), or faeries.[56] The main component of this word is *korr* in Breton or *cor* in Welsh: both are words for "dwarf."

Already we have seen in chapters 4 and 5 how dwarfs play a leading part in the testing and irritation of Arthur's court, with their deceiving gift of the horn that spills itself all down the drinker. Their enjoyment of the results of their malice, while not of the same order as the disruption that the Rich Company create in the Arthurian realm of Logres, stems from an otherworldly source. Bleheris and his fellow wanderers do not engage with this disruption but seek earnestly for the Courts of Joy; but while the Rich Company stem from a similar mixture of races, they are more intent on maximizing their hold over the realm of Logres by means of commercial and martial domination.

Within our understanding of the Faery Grail, these two sets of relatives, Bleheris and his people, and the Rich Company, seem to virtually constitute semihuman, semifaery versions of the Seelie and Unseelie courts of the Faery realms (see chapter 5). While Bleheris and his wanderers can still hear the voices of the wells in their hearts, the Rich Company are immune to generosity or compassion. Their power bases lie in well-established castles to which they and their followers can retire, but the day is coming when they will be besieged and overcome.

We will be exploring what happens to the Rich Company in the end, when we examine their wars with Arthur in chapter 8. These people who share the same name as the Rich Fisher, but not his generous nature, arise in the wake of the Wasteland's healing, just as the story seems to be turning around. Why can they not hear their foremothers' voices? What does this mean?

LOSING THE VOICES OF THE WELLS

As any storyteller will inform you, without a dilemma a story can grow dull indeed, without any grit to act as its traction. Every major myth on which belief and hope have rested has a story about "how it all went wrong." In *The Elucidation,* that loss is the maidens' hospitality and the voices of the wells. What does this mean exactly? What are its implications? Just how do we hear the voices of the wells?

The voices of the wells do not seem to feature in any other part of *The Elucidation* save where we hear,

> *they lost the voices of the wells*
> *And the maidens that were within them.*[57]

This speaks of a general loss for the whole of the realm of Logres, a loss that applies just as much to Arthur's knights who, in their enthusiastic search to destroy Amangons's lineage, hopefully look out as they go to find any Well Maidens and their hospitality, but

> *No matter how they searched,*
> *They were unable to find them.*
> *Never voice could be heard*
> *Nor maiden seen to emerge.*[58]

What are the voices that we do hear in *The Elucidation?* The voices of the narrator and that of Blihis Bleheris, certainly. But it is not only these to which we need to attend. There is another voice here—the voice of the living earth itself, which speaks by way of the waters. Without water, we have Wasteland. When the waters flow again, the land grows lush with green and repopulation is possible. The voices of the wells are the faery voices that we hear no more or, to put it in more environmental terms, we no longer hear the call of the earth itself, nor can we hear with the understanding of the heart the eternal voices of the wider cosmos.

Primal connection to the harmony of nature, a paradisal state of total engagement with "all that is," is reckoned to be a condition that only children briefly experience. When we grow up, we lose this happy innocence, because we enter into a state of knowing. Once you have knowledge, you cannot put it back in the box again. You have to learn to live with it. The salve for the knowledge of experience is a wider compassion that is learnt through following a spiritual path. This loss has been exemplified for Western civilization in a mythic model that still has power to shape our world: the loss of Paradise.

For Christianity, Islam, and Judaism, the primal myth of how things go wrong is the story of the Fall from Grace, the disobedience of Adam and Eve, a myth that has had wide consequences for our world. Within Western Christianity, the Fall has underlain the doctrine of original sin, as defined by St. Augustine, whereby the primal parent's act of disobedience divides us from the grace of God: nothing can subsequently be in harmony, and everything, in the words of the poet Gerard Manley Hopkins,

> *is seared with trade; bleared, smeared with toil;*
> *And wears man's smudge and shares man's smell; the soil*
> *Is bare now, nor can foot feel, being shod.*[59]

The disrespect to the earth and its environment stems from that pernicious effect of the myth of the Fall's later developments in Christianity, for its implications are that no one and nothing could be pristine without divine grace and the atonement or sacrifice of Christ.

It is in such a context that the medieval Grail legends arise. If the legend of the Fall had sufficient seeds of hope within it, then perhaps it might have sufficed. But this was obviously not the case, and so the Grail legends arise in a totally independent and noncanonical way to stand beside the religious myth. We have to remember that at no time were the Grail legends officially or canonically recognized as any part of Christian doctrine; they do not even have the courtesy status of hagiography. Rather, the Grail legends remain separate romances, providing alternative, gnostic accounts about the way of return, and how we find the means to heal the original fracture.

Looked at another way, the myth of the stealing of the fruit from the Tree of the Knowledge of Good and Evil is very like the myths of the Greek Prometheus or the North American Haida, Raven, who both steal fire from heaven: they are the great thieves who bring knowledge into the world. Likewise, in the Gnostic scriptures, the great figure of wisdom, Sophia, departs from the pleroma or fullness of heaven, and from her is born the world that we inhabit.[60] It is only the Western churches' theological insistence upon the guilt and retributive judgment within the biblical account that essentially changes the focus. These thieves of sacred powers—Prometheus, Raven, Sophia—do the world a great favor, for they bring down knowledge that we learn to live with and use properly without burning our fingers.

People cannot live without hope. We need the saving stories and myths by which hope is kept alive and in which opportunities of healing are passed on to those who come afterward. It is an ancestral requirement and into this need seeds the Grail story. Although it wasn't until Robert de Boron that the Arthurian legends and the Passion narratives were tied firmly together. Even as early as the fourth-century Greek manuscript of the Gospel of Nicodemus, found with the apocryphal Acts of Pilate, we can discern another root of the early Grail beginnings: in the Oil of Mercy that Adam was promised as he was expelled from paradise, we can see echoes of the Grail.*

In the Gospel of Nicodemus we read how Adam, weary with work and heavy with years, calling his son Seth to him, begs him to return to the gates of paradise there to ask for the Oil of Mercy or Life that might soothe his pain. Seth is to speak to the angel with the flaming sword who bars the way back.

---

*An excerpt of *Apocalypsis of Mosis* can be found on Pseudepigrapha.com.

Tell him that I am sick of my life, and that I entreat him through thee in prayer, to send by thee assurance of the Oil of Mercy which the Lord promised me, when He sent me from Paradise.[61]

Seth is instructed in the way by his father:

And, that thou mayst have knowledge of thy way, thou shalt find on the road and that fair path the footprints of thy mother and father, withered, and dry, and scorched. When we came from Paradise, so manifold were our sins that no blade or herb grew on the road where we trod the earth with our feet.[62]

"By the dry, withered road" sounds remarkably like the Wasteland; Seth follows all the way back to Paradise and is enabled to peer through a wicket gate into paradise to ask for the Oil of Mercy with which to anoint his father.

Put thy head through the wicket of the gate, said the angel, and look in steadily to find what thou seest there. And when he put in his head he saw such loveliness that tongue could not declare the diverse kinds of fruits and flowers there, or such music to which he listened, and an organ such as no man ever heard. There he saw, too, a clear fountain, and from it four streams gliding.[63]

He is also given by the angel "three grains from the hollow of an apple from that tree" and is instructed, after his father's death, to "place these three grains under the roots of [Adam's] tongue, and from them will grow three rods." These will become a cedar for God the Father, a cypress for God the Son, and a Pine for God the Holy Ghost.[64]

These three rods are later taken by Moses as three rods of prophecy, which are later planted on his tomb. From here David later takes them and incubates them in a cave where they grow into a great tree in Jerusalem, until Solomon takes the wood to build the temple. The temple beam is cast down and his wife, Queen Sibylla, rescues it. In another later time, it becomes the wood of the cross. Eve also commands Seth to leave a memorial:

> Make tablets of stone, and other tablets of earth, and write on them my whole life, and that of your father, which you have heard from us and seen. If he judges our race by water, the tablets of earth will dissolve, but the tablets of stone will endure. If, however, he judges our race by fire, the tablets of stone will be destroyed, but the tablets of earth will be fired.[65]

These tablets with their *achiliacae,* "words written without lips," survive to us, for here in miniature is a story that will eventually be incorporated—in a slightly variant form—into the Grail legends in *Quest del San Graal,* wherein the timbers of the slips of wood taken from paradise (by Eve, in this instance) eventually become part of the Ship of Solomon that sails through time to bring aid to the Grail Seekers and to bring them to the fulfillment of their quest. In his *Morte d'Arthur,* Malory finally makes of these three slips of wood three spindles that adorn the mystical bed upon the Ship.[66]

By the skillful grafting of many hands, the story of the Fall from Grace and the nested ancestral stories of Adam's descendants bring the Crucifixion (the atonement that cancels the death-dealing effects of the primal disobedience of humanity) into a direct linkage with the Grail legends, which arise to "fix" the fracture that initially broke the harmony of paradise. In actual fact, the Grail legends are really a secondary or auxiliary fix, adding their own weight to the atonement of Christ.

Lying at the heart of this double mending is the ancestral requirement to ease the pain and suffering that call out from the times before times, in the suffering of the ancestors, and to send the possibility of healing forward to the descendants. Thus, the Grail story works on two levels: by adhering to the Christian atonement, it satisfies the conventional expectations of religion that were laid upon all people in the Middle Ages; but by including the folk themes of the food and drink that always satisfy, and the restoration of the waters that replenish the

Wasteland, the ancestral promise of the earthly paradise comes again. The people are fed both in spirit and in body.

We have explored the breaking of the Faery Accord that Amangons's act of rape and theft has fractured, and the possible healing of that breach in chapters 4 and 5: these are the mysteries of the Faery Grail. But the mysteries of the Holy Grail find their own roots in the Gnostic and apocryphal texts of the Passion and its antecedents.

The scene that was set up in *The Life of Adam and Eve,* where Seth planted the three seeds in his father's mouth to become the cedar, cypress, and pine from which the three rods will be taken, is wonderfully revisited in the *First Continuation,* where we are told how Gawain rides to the causeway leading to the Grail Castle: he rides through an overarching tunnel of trees made up of cypress, pine, and laurel, in fulfillment of the mercy that is sought by everyone.[67] Seth, as the quester for Paradise, is replaced by the Round Table knights, who each make their own attempt to find the merciful source of healing. Wasteland becomes a mere memory, as the trees and fields become lush with green once more.

And while we do not hear anymore the sound of the voices of the wells yet, in the *Didot Perceval,* the voice of the Grail itself is heard:

> And Bron the old placed the vessel in Perceval's keeping between his hands, and from the vessel there came *a melody* and a scent so precious that it seemed to them that they might be in Paradise with the angels.[68] (italics added)

The finding of the Courts of Joy in *The Elucidation* is not so well documented. To uncover their background and effect, we need to see how the painful tangle of Wasteland and devastation is finally undone.

8

IN THE PLACE OF THE ANCIENT HEART

Sit laus vobis	Praise be to you,
Qui loculum antiqui cordis	Who behold in the fountain
In fonte aspicitis.	The place of the ancient heart.
O vas nobile	O noble vessel
Quod non est pollutum	Which is never polluted
Nec devoratum	Nor never cursed
In saltatione antique spelunce.	In the ancient cave dance.
Et quod non est maceratum	And which is never ravished
In vulneribus antiqui perditoris	Nor wounded by the old enemy.

HILDEGARD OF BINGEN, *SIT LAUS VOBIS* (TRANS. CM)

FINDING THE COURT OF JOY

he words of the responsory for the angels above, written by Hildegard of Bingen in her *Symphonia Armoniae Celestrum* of 1140 to 1160, praise the spiritual powers that enable our world to keep its connection with the source.[1] No matter the evils befalling our world, whether they be Wasteland, rape, or devastation, there are always some beings who are attentive to the source: they may be the Grail guardians themselves, or those we encounter upon the way who illuminate the pathway of the quest. Each quester then becomes like a needle, sewing together the torn seam that joins our world with the otherworld: wherever they ply or wander awry, their individual attempts serving to bring that quest closer to its achievement.

Although the service of the maidens is no longer accessible to our world, the Grail itself remains inviolate in the regions of the Rich Fisher's castle. The direct communion with the land of Faery by means of the golden cup offered to travelers is broken, but the Grail, which offers the same bounty at each meal, is still working, albeit for a few. The problem is, how can it be rediscovered? *The Elucidation* explicitly and confidently tells us that

> *Each one of the guardians will tell*
> *The place where the court was found.*[2]

Sadly, they do not confess this location, yet this statement and the evidences of the nearest Grail legends to our text, suggest that the court of the Rich Fisher or Grail guardian is not found in one place, and that access to its location is subject to change. Again and again, the knights return via what they believe to be the same landmarks, only to find no such place as the Grail Castle. Even in *Conte du Graal,* after Perceval has failed to ask the Grail question, the castle in which he goes to sleep appears as unpeopled by morning.[3] It is his own personal experience of "the great vanishment."

Not only is the Grail Castle not a known location on a fixed map, but it is also so overwhelming, once you are within it that remembrance and normal common sense vanish. In the *First Continuation,* Gawain becomes engulfed by sleep even while the Fisher King is revealing to him the secrets of the Grail, and he leaves the next morning in guilty shame. When faced with holy things of great moment, the human ability to cope with multiple realities at the same time is somewhat circumscribed. Gawain's falling asleep echoes the sleep that happens to Gilgamesh in the Mesopotamian epic that bears his name: when confronted with the possibility of immortality, he dozes off and cannot stay wakeful.

When the sacred moment of realization is upon us, we lose focus.

When the sacred vanishes, you could say that it is our consciousness of it that is withdrawn, rather than the hallow itself that vanishes. Whenever we are in the right mode of consciousness, we can tune in and be present to it, but if we are out of tune then it isn't possible to view it.[4] Returning to the same doorway doesn't result in a fresh accessing of the Grail Castle's location, as many questers find.

This quest for the court of the Rich Fisher was set on by our storyteller Bleheris who, when he is first captured by the Round Table knights, tells them the story of the consequences of Amangons's actions, and how he himself and his fellows are descendants of this evil king and his followers, and how,

> *That they must wander so,*
> *Until God allows them to find*
> *The court from which joy will come,*
> *By which the country will be resplendent.*[5]

Unable to find it for themselves, the task has fallen on the Round Table knights. As we already heard in the last chapter, the Rich Fisher's realm has hitherto been the source of all good things that make Logres resplendent. Without the rich bounty that flows from this realm, no goodness can come into our world. Without Bleheris to inform them, the Round Table knights would perhaps have no knowledge of the Grail.

In chapter 3 we explored *The Elucidation*, lines 339–82, relating the seven branches of the story and their seven guardians. These lines are immediately followed by the assertion that these adventures, and especially the last of these, namely branch one, the Adventure of the Shield, bring about the Joy:

> *This adventure brought about*
> *The Joy whereby the people multiplied*
> *After the great destruction.*
> *Through these [adventures] were*
> *The court and the Graal truly found,*

How the kingdom was repopulated
So that the streams that had not flowed,
And the fountains that had sprang up—
But then had dried up—
Were now running through the meadows.
Then were the fields lush with green,
And the woods once more leafy
On the day that the court was found,
Where throughout all the land,
The forests became so great and so flowering,
And so fine and well grown,
That all marveled at it,
Who traveled through the land.[6]

This event is not told in its fullness in *The Elucidation* and we will explore it more fully at the end of the chapter, but what is this Joy that returns the land to fertility once again? How is it related to the Grail? In order to answer this with understanding, we need to examine the Irish myth of the three musical strains, which are recorded in the fourteenth-century text *Táin bó Fróech*.[7] These three strains—considered to be the three healing modes of music in Irish lore—grant three releases in Irish tradition: Suantrai brings sleep, Geantrai brings joy, Goiltrai grants tears.[8] The myth that brings these three musical strains into being concerns the labor of Boann, the eponymous goddess of the Boyne River in eastern Ireland, who brings forth three children at one birth.

> Boann of the sidhe was their mother. When that woman was in labor the first time, she was in weeping and sorrow because of the sharpness of her pains; the second birth was followed by smiles and joy because of the pleasure of her two sons; finally, she found sleep and quietness because of the heaviness of the last birth.[9]

Boann (whose name means "white cow") is the primordial being whose birth waters are magical. She is partnered by Nechtan, the keeper of a magical well, but she loves the Dagda, the creator of Brú na Boinne or Newgrange, the otherworldly hostel. It is Boann who uncovers the Well of Nechtan, the source of all inspiration, surrendering half of her own body to become the river as the medium through which inspiration can run. The river Boyne was anciently seen by Irish poets as the source of all poetic inspiration, and these three "children of Boann" are emblematic of the conditions arising from the playing of these three musical strains.[10]

Over and over in Irish lore, ambassadors from the realms of Faery come into our world and shake a musical branch with bells that possess these three modes, inducing the repose of sleep, the tears of sorrow, and the laughter of joy. A similar effect is shared in British myth where the three birds of Rhiannon come to impart their song to the surviving followers of the beheaded Bran, to put into the sleep of forgetfulness those in a state of traumatic remembrance.[11] These blackbirds also have the ability to bring tears and delight.

This musical gift from Faery comes into our world to relieve the human condition, bringing sleep after trauma, the catharsis of tears after pain, and the returning joy of laughter. Animals neither cry nor laugh, but humans do. These very abilities are often the flashpoint of friction between humans and faeries, according to many folk stories, for faeries see things through different eyes. We can perceive this best in the Welsh folk story of the *Lady of Llyn y Fan Fach*. A young man becomes the partner of a faery woman who emerges from a lake; the duration of their union is based on the understanding that if he strikes her three times, it will terminate. The three inevitable blows that he strikes involved two of the three strains: he slaps her thigh playfully the first time with a pair of gloves to encourage her to speed up as they ride; then he strikes her for crying at a wedding; finally, he strikes her when she laughs at a funeral.[12] She returns to the lake taking away her dowry of cattle, but leaving their offspring to whom descend her healing gifts. They become the Physicians of Myddfai, folk healers for generations. These children's descendants lived on till their last scion, John Jones, died in 1739.

These three musical strains of sorrow, sleep, and joy are wound through the Grail legends and are essentially part of *The Elucidation*. These are indicative of "the voices of the wells" that are lost to the realms of Logres: their loss causes sorrow, their searching often results in sleep—as we have seen with Gawain—and their finding brings the greatest joy possible. These three voices are heard over and over in the Grail legends.

Overlaying this ancient legend is a more medieval Arthurian source of joy that we must also consider. Chrétien's *Erec and Enide* is the first to frame the Joy of the Court within an adventure of lovers who misunderstand each other.

SOUNDING THE HORN OF JOY

Chrétien's story of *Erec and Enide* tells how one of Arthur's knights, Erec, married his love, Enide, and of the self-imposed challenges that he sets upon himself to prove how manly a knight he really is. The problem begins when Enide, looking upon her sleeping husband during their honeymoon, brings to mind the rumors that she alone is keeping him from the exercise of his knightly duties. She begins to weep at this thought and Erec, waking up, leaps to the mistaken conclusion that Enide has a secret lover for whom she is crying. Erec commands Enide to be silent and to follow him in her worst dress, as he sets out on a series of adventures, striding headlong into dangers that Enide, unable to comply with his command to keep silent, keeps warning him about. Several incidents bring him near death until Erec finally comes to the court of King Evrain, where he hears about an adventure so dangerous that he cannot cease his headlong pursuit until he has achieved it.

The adventure is innocuously called "the Joy of the Court," but King Evrain strongly discourages Erec from seeking it out, which of course only makes him yearn for it even more intensely. Evrain reluctantly conducts him to the place, as people from the court lament Erec's certain death in advance. All around the enclosed garden are evidences of the previous claimants of this challenge, their heads staring down from each stake:

The garden had around it no wall or fence except of air: yet, by a spell, the garden was on all sides so shut in by the air that nothing could enter there any more than if the garden were enclosed in iron, unless it flew in over the top. And all through the summer and the winter, too, there were flowers and ripe fruits there; *and the fruit was of such a nature that it could be eaten inside; the danger consisted in carrying it out; for whoever should wish to carry out a little would never be able to find the gate, and never could issue from the garden until he had restored the fruit to its place.* And there is no flying bird under heaven, pleasing to man, but it sings there to delight and to gladden him, and can be heard there in numbers of every kind. And the earth, however far it stretch, bears no spice or root of use in making medicine, but it had been planted there, and was to be found in abundance.

Through a narrow entrance the people entered—King Evrain and all the rest. Erec went riding, lance in rest, into the middle of the garden, greatly delighting in the song of the birds which were sing-ing there; they put him in mind of his Joy, the thing he most was longing for. But he saw a wondrous thing, which might arouse fear in the bravest warrior of all whom we know. . . . For before them, on sharpened stakes, there stood bright and shining helmets, and each one had beneath the rim a man's head. But at the end there stood a stake where as yet there was nothing but a horn.[13]

The last stake, King Evrain explains, is prepared for the next knight to attempt and fail the challenge. Before he departs, Evrain tells Erec about the horn:

Never has anyone been able to blow it. However, he who shall suc-ceed in blowing it his fame and honor will grow until it distance all those of his country, and he shall find such renown that all will come to do him honor, and will hold him to be the best of them all. Now there is no more of this matter. Have your men withdraw; for "the Joy" will soon arrive, and will make you sorry, I suspect.[14]

Left alone, Erec faces the red knight who comes forth to challenge him. Like a pair of action heroes, they exchange blows and lances until they are both terribly wounded. Finally, Erec's opponent is overcome and gives account of his life. He came to this garden because a childhood sweetheart asked of him a boon that he could not refuse her. After being dubbed a knight by King Evrain, the knight learned the consequences of his promise, that he was never to leave the garden and must hold it against any challenger who might conquer him. Though assenting to this, he was full of displeasure, and has realized that his sweetheart, "intended to keep me absolutely shut up with her all the days of my life." He acclaims Erec:

> You have given great joy to the court of my uncle and my friends; for now, I shall be released from here; and because all those who are at the court will have joy of it, therefore those who awaited the joy called it "Joy of the Court." They have awaited it so long that now it will be granted them by you who have won it by your fight. You have defeated and bewitched my prowess and my chivalry. Now it is right that I tell you my name, if you would know it. I am called Mabonagrain; but I am not remembered by that name in any land where I have been, save only in this region; for never, when I was a squire, did I tell or make known my name. Sire, you knew the truth concerning all that you asked me. But I must still tell you that there is in this garden a horn which I doubt not you have seen. I cannot issue forth from here until you have blown the horn; but then you will have released me, and then the Joy will begin. Whoever shall hear and give it heed no hindrance will detain him, when he shall hear the sound of the horn, from coming straight-way to the court. Rise up, sire! Go quickly now! Go take the horn right joyfully; for you have no further cause to wait; so do that which you must do.[15]

Erec immediately blows the horn and the joyful sound permeates the court and surrounding countryside bringing immense rejoicing, save for the damsel of Mabonagrain who weeps at the sound. All Enide's own sufferings are ended, and she is in accord with Erec once again, now he has been recognized as the supreme knight, but she still speaks kindly to the damsel and comforts her, learning that they are cousins. Erec and Enide return to their own domain where Erec, on the death of his father, becomes king.

This story in which Enide is cast as the patient wife—a genre beloved of the Middle Ages—reveals several themes that are already familiar to us from *The Elucidation:* the reluctant Mabonagrain, who is both a prisoner and defender of the damsel in the garden, and the horn as an instrument that brings joy. He is a direct correlative of the many consorts of the faery queen, and of Mabon, the youth from the beginning of time who similarly has been forgotten and lost sight of for generations, as we are told in *The Mabinogion* (and will see below). If we compare Mabonagrain's statement that he is "not remembered by that name in any land where I have been" with Mabon in the Welsh story, we can see the correlatives of the Great Prisoner:

Mabon the son of Modron . . . was taken from his mother when three nights old, and it is not known where he now is, nor whether he is living or dead.[16]

The Great Prisoner is almost forgotten because the memory has been lost.

We also note that what makes the court joyful in *Erec and Enide* induces tears in the maiden who is cast here as a human woman, but whom we recognize as a rationalization of the faery woman, retaining her mortal lover on the Island of Women. It is clear from the context of the mysterious garden, wherein the fruit can only be eaten within its boundaries, that this enclave is a part of the otherworld, an earthly paradise that is kept secure from all comers by Mabonagrain as its reluctantly indentured defender.

This earthly paradise, which is so sweet within, yet so strewn with the heads of those who've failed to bring the Joy without, recalls the Grail quest. The Joy that lies within the garden is so strong that it evokes the joy by which Bleheris and his companions shall be made free, at the finding of the court of the Rich Fisher. Did Chrétien foreshadow his *Conte du Graal* in *Erec and Enide*? Certainly, there are correlatives between the Castle of the Rich Fisher and the otherworldly garden wherein hangs the horn of joy, while the Joy that comes about as a result of the blowing of the horn is a coup du théâtre very close to the effect of the Grail's achievement: what has been stuck in time now flows into life again.

Chrétien intricately contrasts the freely given, dedicated love of Enide with the possessive love of the maiden in the garden, and the headlong wanderings of Erec with the stasis of Mabonagrain. But what we note here is that the breaking of the otherworldly enclave of the garden is signaled by the sounding of the horn that heralds the Joy. The events that have been unprogressive become susceptible to human time once again, signaling that we are seeing the interaction of faery and human time scales.

As we saw in chapter 4, the horn makes many appearances in the themes that irrigate the Grail story. The joy makes the court (*cort*) rejoice in *The Elucidation;* yet the joy is sometimes signaled by the horn (*cors*), as here in *Erec and Enide;* and sometimes the joy is about the returning of a body (*cors*), as we found in the return of Brangemor's body to Faery. The words for "court," "horn," and "body" in French, all pronounced alike, give us a thematically entangled and resonant set of characteristics.

Earlier in chapter 4, we saw how the vessel of faery hospitality in the *Lai du Cor* is a drinking horn, not a cup, and that it is brought to maliciously expose King Arthur and his unfaithful courtiers. Also in the *First Continuation,* we read how Gawain restores the stolen horn to the Maiden of the Ivory Horn whom he meets in the context of an al fresco picnic. The maiden sounds the horn, blowing the call that signals the end of a hunt, and they are dining together in a glade when the treacherous knight, Macarot of Pantelion, drags it from her neck. Gawain pursues and kills him, restoring the horn to the maiden who tells him that it was given her as a love token by a lover. Its powers confer the ability to be free of cold, thirst, and hunger, wherever its owner might be.[17] In this incident the horn can be sounded like a musical horn, yet it can also dispense food and drink, and so is much more like the cup of the Maidens of the Wells.

The testing horn that is brought to Arthur in the *First Continuation,* in an incident that echoes the *Lai du Cor* story, is called *Beneoiz,* or Blessing, but in variant editions of the text we also given *Boënet,* or Drink Well. There is both a stern testing of the unfaithful and a blessing that is conferred upon the constant of heart.[18] The horn of faithfulness rejects all of Arthur's court except for Carados alone, whose constancy to his wife Guinier is blessed by his ability to "drink cleanly, without spillage." If, as we have suggested in chapter 4, this horn is brought from out of Faery to test humanity, then surely it is Carados and Guinier who redeem human love in the eyes of Faery.

The joy that is had from the finding of the Court of Joy comes in deep contrast to the lamentation that exists at the heart of the Rich Fisher's castle itself: a sorrow that is witnessed by every Grail seeker who finds his way thither. About the body that is upon the bier, we read that

> *For three hours three times in the day*
> *There was therein such lamentation*
> *That no man would be so hardy*
> *Not to be frightened when he heard it.*[19]

Whence comes this lamentation? What is its relation to the Joy?

LAMENTING THE GREAT PRISONER

The Joy resultant from finding the Courts of Joy has its counterpart in an ancestral lamentation that is enduring. Scattered throughout the Grail myths is the theme of the Great Prisoner: one who is unjustly imprisoned, hidden, or secreted, one whose lamentations can be heard and who needs release. This theme is one that has become lodged within *The Elucidation* and the wider Grail texts. In order to see it in context, we need to return to an earlier story whose myth connects the undying but ever-wounded state of the Fisher King, and the mysterious body on the bier that remains unburied.

As we saw in *Erec and Enide* above, the name of Mabonagrain, the indentured knight whom Erec defeats, is a name reminiscent of a much older figure from Welsh myth. In the ancient British tale of *Culhwch and Olwen*, we hear about Mabon, son of Modron, who was stolen from his mother when he was three nights old, and whose rescue goes back to the roots of time.[20] Mabon is finally released from his captivity in Caer Loyw (the Fortress of Light, identified as the ancient British city of Gloucester) by the quest of Culhwch for helpers to enable his marriage to Olwen, the giant Yspadadden's daughter. Mabon is required for a critical part of the hunting of the monstrous ravening boar, Trwch Trwyth, whose comb and shears will barber the giant and overcome him, but there is a drawback, making this a seemingly impossible task. Since Mabon has been imprisoned all his life from the beginning of serial time, no human being knows of his whereabouts and his discovery can only come about by the aid of the Oldest Animals whose longer memories together lead to the Salmon, oldest of all, who recalls hearing a lamentation coming from the walls of Caer Loyw. Mabon is a key figure in a linked series of quests that enable Culhwch to be married to Olwen, as well as a pivotal force in overthrowing the oppressions of the giant whereby lamentation is changed into joy.

The story of Mabon does not stand alone, for in the Welsh stories of *The Mabinogion* and in the evidences of the *Welsh Triads*, we come across a succession of youths who are lost, snatched away by otherworldly forces, or just stuck somewhere in the otherworld.[21] Whether it is Pryderi, snatched into Faery and made to be the porter there, or else the legendary and forgotten Gweir, who in his captivity in Caer Sidi, within the depths of Annwfyn, cries out to all, there is a task to be undertaken. We have suggested elsewhere that, on some level, this captivity becomes the chief metaphor of bardic initiation, whereby the trainee bard is incarcerated in darkness to pursue his poetic theme, to be finally brought out into light, where his exploits may be recited to all.[22] But, on another level, the hidden or imprisoned youth is an exemplar of the powers of life put on hold, one whose innocence and prowess are unavailable to the world.

There are three kinds of incarceration in the Arthurian and Grail legends that support the *Elucidation*: first, the voluntary coming of a mortal man into the regions of Faery, there to become the king of the Island of Women, as we see in the legends of Guingamor and, potentially, of Gawain at the Castle of Maidens. Then there is the imprisoning of the Round Table knights by the Rich Company without parole, to rescue whom Arthur and his knights go to besiege Proud Castle. Finally, there is the unburied body on the bier.

We have already viewed in some detail the voluntary enclosure of men within the Land of Women in chapter 5, an act that is clearly echoed in the Grail legend's Castle of Maidens, and then further echoed in the imprisonment in *Erec and Enide* above. In the besieging of the Proud Castle, which we will look at in detail below, one of the main aims is to rescue the imprisoned Girflet, son of Do who has been captured by the Rich Company. After this is done, the power of the Proud Castle falls and the Rich Company departs, while Arthur is restored to the position of supreme king of Logres.

The fourth branch of *The Elucidation* gives us one instance of the unburied body, in the story of the dead knight in the skiff (see chapters 3 and 5): as we have seen from the evidences of the *First Continuation,* King Brangemor may not be dead, but rather in a state of suspended animation until his wounding is avenged. The return of Brangemor's body in the swan boat to the Faery realms overseas brings untold joy; it is a theme that the Arthurian legends will use again, when it comes to the mortally wounded body of Arthur being ferried in a boat overseas to the realms of Avalon.

The suspended animation of the Great Prisoner in Celtic tradition is like that of the Fisher King who, in the classic Grail legends, cannot move beyond or out of his suffering, which finds no relief. But in *The Elucidation* we have no wounded king, only the dead body on the bier that is lamented regularly three times a day until Perceval comes:

> *But I tell you in no uncertain terms,*
> *That he asked whose was*

The corpse in the hall,
And about the rich silver cross
That was processed before all.
For three hours three times in the day
There was therein such lamentation
That no man would be so hardy
Not to be frightened when he heard it.[23]

We are not told whose is this body, and the question we must ask is, can it be the body of Brangemor that is mentioned only as "the knight of the swan" in *The Elucidation*'s fourth branch? Since the Rich Fisher himself is not described as a wounded king in *The Elucidation*, in truth, the return of Brangemor's body to the land of Faery represents the only instance of a wounded man being healed by the finding of the Courts of Joy.

In *The Elucidation* and the *First Continuation*, the ancestral lamentation of the Great Prisoner is transposed to the lamentation over the body on the bier. But in Chrétien's *Perceval*, there is no mention of any such body: in the *First Continuation*—which is still our closest correlative with *The Elucidation*—this body has been removed from the incident when Perceval fails to ask the Grail question. When Perceval wakes, finding himself outside the Grail Castle, he meets his cousin, who is a maiden cradling the body of a dead knight in her lap, bewailing her lover's death. After catechizing Perceval about his actions and what he noticed in the Grail Castle, she berates him for not having asked the Grail question, and for the death of his mother, caused by his precipitate departure from the family home.

This transposition of the dead knight in the maiden's lap to the dead knight on a bier seems to have entered into the *First Continuation*, which ends with the incident of the dead knight in the swan boat. As we saw in chapters 3 and 5, in that crucial fourth branch story, the swan that has pulled the boat sets up a wailing and beating of wings in mourning for the dead knight.[24] The timing of this incident and its completion is on the Feast of All Saints, or November 1, which may well give us a clue.

The Celtic festival of Samhain (which we now call Hallowe'en), as the traditional time of remembering the dead, became the date of the dual feasts of All Saints and All Souls, on November 1 and 2 respectively, in the eighth century. In this way, both the Greater Dead and all common ancestors might be honored. Anciently, Samhain was a time when the doors between the apparent and invisible worlds were open, where the faery hills were open and communion between the worlds of the living and dead might be possible. Hiding under the Grail story is an ancestral loss that we only clearly see in *Peredur,* the Welsh parallel to Chrétien's *Perceval.* Here we are told that the Grail procession includes

> Two maidens, with a large salver between them, in which was a man's head, surrounded by a profusion of blood. And thereupon the company of the court made so great an outcry that it was irksome to be in the same hall with them.[25]

Peredur learns later from his uncle that the head in the dish is none other than that of his own cousin, and so the whole of his quest becomes more of a vengeance quest that overcomes the oppressions and enchantments that have fallen upon the land, rather than an actual Grail quest. The great outcry is clearly another instance of the lamentation. Despite the Grail texts being wound deeply with Christian themes of redemption—with lamentations over the blood pouring from the Holy Lance and with the vicarious sorrow over the sufferings of the Savior—the theme that persists beneath these is the sorrow for ancestral loss, and a requirement for ancestral vengeance or satisfaction, which is more in keeping with the Faery Grail.

The major emblem of this lack of restitution in the Grail legends is the mysterious sword that either keeps breaking or else is already broken in two pieces: the reuniting of these two halves is followed first by Perceval and then by Gawain. We are told in *The Elucidation* that Perceval,

> *asked who the Graal*
> *Served, but did not ask*

About the lance, why it bled
When he saw it, nor of the sword
Of which half the blade was missing
And the other lying on the bier
On the dead body, nor the manner
Of the great vanishing.[26]

In *The Elucidation*, the Grail procession is a sequence that replays over and over, like ancestral memories heard but unassuaged by any relief of healing:

When the service was done.
Then all crying ceased;
When everyone vanished.
The hall that was so great and wide
Remained empty and frightful.[27]

The vastation of this mysterious vanishing experienced by the Grail questers who fail to ask the question after the procession finishes, speaks to everyone in the place of the ancient heart, as Hildegard of Bingen calls it, because it partakes of the ancestral sorrow. The scene vanishes, only to begin again and again, in dreadful reproach. The vanishing signals the fact that the unquestioning seeker's chance to heal things is at its end for that occasion. The body on the bier is thus serially viewed, mourned but unburied, over and over. The one half of the blade remains on the bier, longing for the restoration of union with its fellow.

The two halves of the broken sword cannot be reunited by ordinary means because they represent the fundamental division that has come upon the world since Amangons violated the maidens and stole their cups, thus ending the harmonious relationship between humans and faeries. The person who exemplifies this division is the one upon the bier, the half-human, half-faery King Brangemor who gathers up all the symbolism of Bran the Blessed in his undyingness: as well as being the offspring of the mortal who steps into Faery to become one with it, Brangemor is the offspring of both worlds who lies lamented but unburied. Like the half-human, half-faery company of Bleheris who cannot find the Court of Joy, he lies in a coma like one dead, awaiting the fulfillment of the quest.

Burying the dead is also part of the Grail quest, as well as the clearing away of things that tried to flourish in the wrong places and were choked of life, or the overcoming of evil customs that seize life by the throat. Underneath the Christian Grail quest is an older sorrow. In the lamentation over the unburied body on the bier, we also hear the ancient sorrow at the failure of ancestral requital.

The Grail knights quest on behalf of those who are locked outside the story of hope, reconciliation, or healing, in order to move the stagnation of stasis into another, hopeful condition. In the many psychologically based commentaries upon the Grail legend, from Joseph Campbell onward, there has developed a very modern stress upon the individuality of the Grail hero's journey. However, this stress on the individual has served rather to point out the division of modern consciousness—often expressed as a vague loss of nature or of holism—from the collective. The living context of this division speaks of how we are split off from ancestral or faery roots: and those who seek for help today are often weakened or unable to heal because they do not think, work, or imagine from a collective basis.[28] How can we heal if we leave out the rest of the world from the equation?

The older and more traditional understanding of the Grail quest is of a collective, not an individual, task. The result of the Joy is not for one person, certainly not for the hero alone, but is intended for all beings. If the healing of the Grail is undertaken for vainglory or personal kudos, it is doomed to failure from the outset: only by unconditionally including all that is can the quest have validity.

Translating the early Celtic traditions about the Great Prisoner back into Grail quest terms, we can understand that the wondrous vessel cannot be accessed easily. The first entrant into the quest after the Faery Accord's fracture becomes stuck there in timelessness, just as the Fisher King does with the endlessly repeating Grail procession. The toil of the

Grail seekers is to serially endure the spiraling of their quest as they find the Grail Castle, neglecting to ask the rights questions, and losing the location time and again, until Perceval and Gawain find the way.

Within *The Elucidation* we do not uncover the backstory of the body on the bier, nor why he lies unburied. We are simply assured that the Joy will end the lamentation, though we can perceive the outcome with the help of many other texts.

In the *First Continuation,* we read about another prisoner whose imprisonment may well be related. During the feast of Pentecost when all the Round Table knights are assembled, Arthur looks upon the empty seat of a worthy knight. Perturbed and downcast, he absently cuts his own hand, wrapping it quickly to hide his wound from the company, but tears flow down his face until the perceptive Gawain asks what is wrong.

> *The king replied, 'You know well,*
> *That just a year ago, a folk*
> *Who made castles and cities,*
> *And strong towns and strongholds*
> *And the great Proud Castle,*
> *Strengthened themselves against us.*[29]

It turns out that Arthur is still grieving for the men lost in that battle and especially for his friend, Girflet son of Do, who has been imprisoned for three whole years in Proud Castle. He reproaches himself for feasting and wearing his crown in glory, while his friend lies suffering:

> *I swear before you all,*
> *That I will not sleep in a bed*
> *More than one night in any place,*
> *Until I save him, or find out if he is dead.*[30]

The extremity of Arthur's sorrow, expressed by his absent-minded self-wounding, reflects upon his kingship's honor: he cannot rest until he has attempted the rescue of the knight who lies in captivity in the Proud Castle—the headquarters of the Rich Company. The Round Table knights all agree to go forth and rescue Girflet. The siege of Castle Orgueilleux, the Proud Castle of the Rich Company, seems to have echoes of another, older siege in which Arthur and Kay figure. How they come there and what happens next, we will discover below.

THE WARS OF ARTHUR

In chapter 3 we promised to expose the evidences for our suggested restorations of some of the seven branches of *The Elucidation*'s cloaked stories. We have dealt extensively with branch four, the Avenging of Faeryland by Guerrehes in chapters 4 and 5. Now we need to focus upon these three stories that are interconnected:

Branch 6. The Unhealing Wound of Logres and the Battles of Arthur
Branch 3. The Wounding of Amangons's Son by Gawain
Branch 5. The Besieging of Castle Orgueilleux

We know it isn't possible to stretch the evidence and neatly tie down all the stories in a satisfactory way, with so little material to support *The Elucidation* save the *First Continuation,* its nearest cousin, but we must discover what we can.

We start with branch six, following the difficult time that follows the achievement of the Courts of Joy. When everyone should be rejoicing, Arthur finds himself in a difficult situation, for the Joy resultant from the finding of the Rich Fisher's kingdom is not unalloyed. No sooner has it been achieved than the Rich Company come forth from the wells, all 7,686 of them:

> *They built castles and cities*
> *Towns, boroughs, and strongholds,*
> *And built for the damsels*
> *The rich Castle of Maidens;*

They made the Perilous Bridge too
And the great Castle of Pride;

For nobility and lordship,
They created an order for themselves
Of the Peers of the Rich Company,
In their great pride set up
Against the Table Round;
It was well known by everyone.

Therein each had his lady love;
Many thus led a fine life.
There were three hundred and sixty-six
Who maintained the castle,
And each one of these had
Twenty knights whose leaders they were.
To the number no less than:
Seven thousand, and six hundred,
Plus four times twenty and six.[31]

The Rich Company, having so established themselves, proceed to put their power to work:

They rode through this country
And made war on King Arthur.
From the court, the good knight
Set off to put them to the test;
I know that, once they captured one
That they held him captive without parole.

King Arthur wanted to go there
To destroy and ravage the castle;
But all those who hated him
Attacked him at every point

And kept him engaged in the wars.
So none could go on quest
When the warfare was so great
That lasted more than four years,
As the stories tell us.[32]

These other descendants of Amangons and the Maidens of the Wells form themselves into a rival order of knighthood, becoming the implacable foes of Arthur's Round Table knights. The Rich Company also have their own power bases: they are responsible for building the Castle of Maidens and the Proud Castle. They take great pleasure in capturing and imprisoning any of Arthur's knights without parole. We are told that they attack Arthur and his knights at every point and keep him so engaged in the wars that no one can go on quest, ensuring that the wars last four years in total.

We may ask, why should there be wars at the very point of healing? Surely, things should be in a state of reconciliation? Looking wider into faery lore, we find the belief that wars within the human world are often preceded by wars within the faery realms.[33] We see echoes of this belief within the encounter that Arthur and Owain have in the Welsh story of *The Dream of Rhonabwy,* wherein every move in a chess match played between the two men (who appear in their otherworldly aspects in this dream, larger than life) has an immediate effect upon their own human troops of men, to the extent of killing them.[34] Because a state of attrition exists in the faery realms, it spills over into our world also. Just as Homer's *Illiad* asks of the Greeks and Trojans, "which of the gods set them on to quarrel?" so too the origin of Arthur's wars must be explored in the light of a faery causation.

The oldest written evidences for the existence of Arthur himself are based upon reports of his battles to defend Britain from invaders. Some of these reports are accounts of human conflict, but some of them are against otherworldly opponents also. Arthur is anciently associated with the besieging and attack of the Castle of Maidens, while in *The Elucidation* and the *First Continuation* we discover that he is similarly occupied against the Rich Company's Proud Castle, which we will examine further below. Let us look first at the ancient forerunners of this siege and Arthur's battles.

In the account of Arthur's twelve battles by the ninth-century British chronicler Nennius, Mount Agned is mentioned as one of the locations. According to Geoffrey of Monmouth, "Ebrauc [son of Mempricius] founded also the city of Alclud [Strathclyde] toward Albany, and the fortress of Mount Agned, which now is called the Castle of Maidens and the Dolorous Mountain"[35] (authors' brackets and amplification).

We note that both these latter locations—the Castle of Maidens and the Dolorous Mountain—appear also in *Perceval* as places of quest. When the Hideous Damsel comes to berate Perceval at Arthur's court, she specifically mentions these places, as well as echoing lines 417–18 of *The Elucidation* about the knights of Proud Castle and their lady loves,

> I don't know if you have heard of the Proud Castle, which is where
> I must go tonight. In that castle are five hundred and sixty-six great
> knights, each with his own lover, a fair, noble, and courtly lady. . . .
> Whoever aspires to be thought the finest in the world, that is where
> he would win his name.[36]

She also mentions Montesclaire, where a maiden is besieged, saying that whoever rescues her would win the greatest honor and be awarded with the Sword of the Strange Baldric. Gawain then decides to get to Montesclaire (a quest in which he succeeds), while Girflet son of Do decides to try the Proud Castle and becomes imprisoned; Kahendin goes off to climb Mount Dolorous, while Perceval, echoing Arthur's own pledge, penitentially promises to sleep nowhere two nights together until he has learned whom the Grail served and discovered more about the Bleeding Lance and why it bled.[37]

Mount Agned has been variously sited at Pennango, a hill in southern Scotland, near Teviot Water, or as an unlocated mountain called "Bregoin."[38] Medieval traditions also cite Agned as "Castellum Puellarum," the Castle of Maidens, near the Severn.[39]

The Castle of Maidens is also mentioned in the early Welsh poem *Pa Gur Yv y Portaur* (What Man Is the Porter?), which appears copied into the *Black Book of Carmarthen,* compiled in the early twelfth century. This tells of an assault upon the fortress of Dun Eidin, or Edinburgh, a city that is known in the record as Castellum Puellarum or Castle of Maidens.[40] Arthur attempts to gain entry while boasting to its porter about his men's exploits, notably those of Cei (Kay). Arthur promises to bring to the siege his best men, and the Porter retorts:

> Porter: *Into my house you will not come*
> *Unless you can deliver them [the best men in the*
> *world].*
> Arthur: *I can deliver them,*
> *And you will see them:*
> *The tough, the smooth*
> *And the fair, all three.*[41]

Cei boasts of Arthur's prowess against the force occupying the fortress:

> *At the mount of Eidin (Edinburgh)*
> *He fought against the dog-heads.*
> *By the hundred they fell,*
> *Every time a century of them fell.*[42]

"Dog-heads" may be mythically literal, merely insulting parlance, or else suggesting a clan that called themselves so or used emblems on their shields, we cannot tell: but the rest of *Pa Gur* discusses the attack by Cei upon a monstrous cat, Cath Paluc, so this may be a way of signaling that Arthur is fighting against otherworldly forces. There is an undertow of regret in Arthur's boast that so many of his men once,

> *Were defenders*
> *At Eidin (Edinburgh), on the disputed border.*

A lord would shelter them,
And where he could, avenge them.[43]

Overwhelming forces in *Pa Gur* have lost Arthur many men, just as they do in his wars against the Rich Company. Yet echoes of an even older conflict are heard in the ninth-century poem of *Preiddeu Annwfyn* (the Raid on the Underworld) in which we hear about Caer Goludd, one of the strongholds that Arthur attacks:

Six thousand men there stood upon the wall,
Hard it was to parley with their sentinel.
Three ship-burdens of Prydwen we went with Arthur:
Except seven none rose up from Caer Goludd.[44]

This ninth-century description of a siege is at some remove from the early thirteenth-century *Elucidation*, but Arthur faces a similar number of forces: the text says that the 366 leading knights of the Rich Company at the Proud Castle each have 20 knights serving under them, making 7,686 in total.

The Elucidation tells us that, although Arthur loses many knights, he also gains many from his encounters with the wandering company of Blihis and from his other quests:

King Arthur could not help
Losing many a good knight,
But he gained many good ones from it,
As the stories will tell you.[45]

It is time to return to the meaning of the sixth branch of *The Elucidation*, of which we are told,

the sixth [branch], without fail, is
About the great strife of the toil.[46]

We briefly examined this branch in chapter 3, but now we need to see it in the light of Arthur's battles. In the *Annales Cambriae* (Annals of Wales), one of the earliest British chronicles copied into a twelfth-century manuscript, we learn that

> Three names are generally given for the word "battle": *Gueith, Cat,* and *Bellum. Bellum* is the Latin, and *Cat* the British word for "battle." But *Gueith* is British for "strife," carrying the connotation of "struggle or toil." The earliest entry for Camlann calls it a *Gueith* or Strife, perhaps denoting a civil conflict or particularly bloody engagement.[47]

In *The Elucidation* the unhealing wound of Logres is caused by the earlier breaking of the Faery Accord by Amangons, and the Wasteland is healed by the rediscovery of the court of the Rich Fisher: but the battles of Arthur with the Rich Company cause a strife, an internecine *gueith* or conflict between the two kinds of being that will not cease until Arthur directly confronts it. His self-wounding at the thought of the imprisonment of Girflet son of Do, and his determination to liberate him that we read about in the last section of this chapter, connects the *First Continuation* with the earliest Welsh poem of *Preiddeu Annwfyn* where Arthur similarly hears the crying out of the Great Prisoner and goes on a perilous quest to liberate him:

> *Gweir's captivity in Caer Sidi was resonant*
> *With the tale of Pwyll and Pryderi.*
> *None before him was sent into it,*
> *Into the heavy blue chain that bound the faithful*
>   *youth.*
> *Because of the raid upon Annwfyn he sorely sang.*[48]

Arthur's toil in the wars against the Rich Company is an attempt to heal the wounds of the land, to bring out the prisoner; his besieging of their Proud Castle is a long remembrance of a much older myth that we can see in his earlier besieging of Castellam Puellarum in *Pa Gur* and his desperate adventures in the underworld realms in *Preiddeu Annwfyn.* These older legends speak clearly of sieges against other-worldly opponents. In their more medieval dress, the several besiegings within *Elucidation* and the *First Continuation* are rationalized into more human encounters, yet we must remember that Arthur's opponents are not human, but rather the half-faery, half-human descendants of the Maidens of the Wells and of Amangons. These are not the first wave of gentle, half-faery wanderers in the forest like Bleheris and his company, but a second wave of proud, exploitative, and unrelenting cousins of Bleheris, who give no quarter. Branch six of the story may well lie here.

The journey to Proud Castle is a part of the Grail story merely hinted at in *The Elucidation,* but it is the vital link between the healing of the Wasteland and the coming of the Rich Company. We must now look into the *First Continuation* to find out what is missing and how branches three and five are worked out.

THE FALL OF PROUD CASTLE

We left Arthur bewailing his imprisoned friend, Girflet son of Do, and making ready to ride out to liberate him, but we did not hear how Girflet came to be captured, only that he had the intention to set out to Proud Castle back in *Perceval.* Neither there, nor in the *First Continuation,* do we discover the circumstances of his capture, which happens offstage.

There follow adventures largely concerning Gawain and the life of Carados, creating a seemingly massive hiatus in the Grail seeking, but we need to understand the sequence in order to arrive at the end, so skillfully have these adventures been woven into the fabric of the story. The more we look into the *Continuations,* the more clearly we see that Perceval as the Grail winner is not alone. The *First Continuation* focuses entirely upon Gawain as the Grail seeker, with Perceval making one meager appearance at a tournament. It is also clear that this latter text is a major source for *The Elucidation,* though it works out in its own way. The phraseology of both texts bears strong similarities as do the themes that arise.

We must go back earlier in the *First Continuation,* ten years before the rescue of Girflet, where we are told that all the lords of the surrounding countries come to pay homage to Arthur, all except Brun de Branlant, whose castle is subsequently besieged by the Round Table knights. While scouting ahead, Gawain sleeps with the sister of Bran de Lis, one of Brun's lords, and conceives a son upon her—an incident that will come back to haunt him.

Just before Arthur and his knights set out to Proud Castle, the episode of the Drinking Horn is inserted in the *First Continuation;* this is the incident that we explored in greater length in chapter 4. In *Lai du Cor* Arthur was prevented by "a certain condition" from exacting any act of revenge upon the horn's sender, Mangons. But no such promise seems to be borne out in the *First Continuation,* where a scarlet-clad knight rides in, challenging Arthur to drink from a horn called Beneoiz (Drink Well) by filling it from a spring of water, saying that the horn will change water into wine. The story falls out exactly as it did in *Lai du Cor* with the honor of the now-drenched court being narrowly upheld by Carados and his wife, Guinier, as the only faithful couple at court. The positioning of this incident just before the besieging of Proud Castle seems to act as spur to Arthur's wars against the Rich Company, which are prosecuted upon Amangons's descendants.

Years later, when Arthur's company finally go to besiege Castle Orgueilleux and rescue Girflet, they ride through a wasteland, and Gawain tries to find a place where Arthur may shelter and be received honorably. He finally comes to a rich land with a deserted castle by a broad river. Beside a fountain near the bridge, there are two purple-clad maidens drawing water with golden pitchers.

> *Between four olive trees, there was a fountain which*
> *flowed,*
> *At which two demoiselles, in tunics of purple so very*
> *fine.*

Two vessels of sound gold they carried, that they filled
from the well.[49]

After greeting them both, Gawain asks for whom they fill these vessels, and is told, "to the good knight whom we follow, nor for any other do we pour." This response has echoes both of the ancient Goddess of Sovereignty who, in the early Irish story of *Baile na Scál* (the Phantom's Frenzy), may only pour for a rightful king, and also of the Maidens of the Wells who serve travelers. It gives us a very different picture of what happened to these maidens after their carrying off by Amangons: in medieval parlance, once a maiden slept with a man, he became her lord, as these royally dressed women seem to acknowledge.[50]

Gawain finds the castle beautifully and richly appointed with sumptuous foods, including a hundred boar's heads on *silver graals,* or platters, but with no one present to ask about hosting the king, he returns over the bridge to ask of the maidens at the fountain, "who seemed like faeries," but they are no longer there.[51] We have found the erstwhile Maidens of the Wells, now serving the lord of the Proud Castle, as described by *The Elucidation:*

Therein each had his lady love;
Many thus led a fine life.[52]

Gawain now leads Arthur and the knights into the deserted but richly appointed castle from whose environs all people seem to have vanished—just like the vanishment experienced at the Grail Castle—and then he sets eyes upon a shield hanging on a peg; still transfixing the shield is the stump of a lance with its colors. Immediately he recognizes this as a remembrance of his encounter with the family member of Bran de Lis that he killed in combat, and with whose sister he has slept. He admits his bad behavior to Arthur, saying that he would have married the lady but, since he has killed Bran de Lis's kin, there can be no recourse but to fight him the next time that they meet.

Just at that moment, a dog bounds up and Kay begs the honor of possessing it as a companion for Huden, his own hound. Following the dog, he comes into a large garden where Bran de Lis is sitting in a large company; it is he who is the lord of the rich castle to which Arthur and his men have come.

According to custom, Bran de Lis and Gawain begin to do deathly battle in the hall, to work out the wrong that lies between them, but at that very moment, Bran's sister accompanied by her child fathered by Gawain enters. Seeing the conflict, she sends the boy into the mêlée to prevent her brother and her lover coming to blows. To the horror of the company, the boy darts between the flashing swords and, in order to prevent his injury, Arthur calls off the assault, promising recompenses to Bran de Lis, who now finally pays Arthur his liege homage.

The castle of Bran de Lis is described in terms that make it a rich castle indeed, with money tables piled high with currency from across the known world, from Normandy to Arabia, Byzantium, and Africa. The inference seems to be that Bran de Lis was once one of the Rich Company, still holding out against Arthur until this point. This reading is confirmed when Bran is told of Arthur's mission to rescue Girflet, and that the Round Table knights don't know whether he is alive or dead: Bran tells them that their lost knight is indeed a prisoner and promises, now that he has given his homage to Arthur, to ride to Proud Castle as soon as possible. Throughout this passage, Bran de Lis continues to be the interpreter to Arthur of all that happens at Proud Castle, betraying from his great knowledge of their ménage, that he was once of their number.

Arthur's party set off and arrive before Proud Castle at midsummer. At sight of the Round Table knights, the bells of the castle start summoning help to signify they are besieged. Three thousand pennons immediately crowd the battlements while other armed men in huge companies ride swiftly to the castle to defend it.

This three thousand is less than the 7,686 members of the Rich Company so numbered in *The Elucidation,* but it is still a formidable array. At the edge of the grove where they are encamped, Arthur and his knights visit the cemetery where the slain knights from previous conflicts are buried. The knights also note the four olive trees that demark the boundary of the tournament: any knight who passes beyond their arena will be held to be vanquished.

Since we have only vestigial detail from *The Elucidation,* we must assume that the defenders of Proud Castle are none other than the Rich Company.

The outcome of the siege is to be decided by a series of jousts, knight against knight. Lucan the butler is the first to ride out on behalf of the Round Table against a lone knight who defeats him, taking him prisoner. Although Arthur is upset, he rejoices that now Girflet will have immediate news that a rescue attempt is being mounted on his behalf. Girflet is indeed heartened, but tells Lucan of the many knights who've died at the hands of the Rich Company.

The next morning, Bran de Lis rides out and successfully overcomes one of the Rich Company, one his erstwhile companions. That night is the midsummer festival of Saint John, the traditional time of faery revels, and the Round Table knights hear the watchmen on the battlements of Proud Castle sounding their horns and pipes. Kay is awarded the next joust and finds himself forced back beyond the arena of the four olive trees, a vanquished man, and is mocked by his own side for being a loser.

The next day, a great ringing of bells peals out and Bran de Lis confirms that it is a Saturday, a time when the Mother of God is worshipped and that there will be no jousts that day. Gawain accordingly disports himself in the countryside, riding into a glade with a palisaded tower and moat where he finds a well-built knight musing so deeply that he refuses to return his greeting. Gawain then meets a lady dressed in white and gold who bemoans the fact that she has killed the finest knight, without equal, by not keeping her word to him. Returning to camp, Gawain describes his encounter and Bran de Lis explains that the distracted knight he saw was none other than the Rich Souldoyer, or Rich Soldier or Mercenary. (*Souldoyer* gives us the English word "soldier," literally, "one who takes the *solidus* or coin.") Bran de Lis also adds that the lady whom Gawain met is loved so much by the Rich

Soldier that his strength and courage have been considerably reduced—information that proves useful to Gawain, whose own strength doubles at midday and even more so at midsummer. No sooner has Bran spoken than a host of over twenty thousand come out of the castle to meet the Rich Soldier who is conveying his lady within.

Yvain has the honor of the next joust, capturing one of the newly dubbed knights of the Proud Castle, a man who had till the night previous served the Rich Soldier's lady as a page, but who had not yet earned the riches of his mistress's lover. Gawain asks him who is to joust next day and is told that the Rich Soldier will certainly be next.

Finally, Gawain himself jousts with the Rich Soldier, or Rich Mercenary, who is revealed to be the head of the Proud Castle. Because Gawain's strength (drawing upon his mythic status as the ancient Welsh hero Gwalchmai, the Hawk of May) waxes toward midday, and this is midsummer when his strength is invincible, he easily overcomes the Rich Soldier who yields to him. Fearful of losing his lady's love, the Rich Soldier then begs Gawain to go along with him to the castle and there pretend to submit himself as prisoner to the Rich Soldier's lady. If Gawain so assents then no man of the Proud Castle will ever oppose Arthur again, he swears. Taking a risk, Gawain complies, to the fearful surmise of Arthur and his men who, seeing Gawain being led away, really believe him to be captured.

In an adroit pantomime, Gawain kneels before the Proud Castle's lady, submitting his sword to her, like a captive, while the Rich Soldier asks his lady to make ready another castle for them in which to be private and, as soon as she has gone, gives orders for both Girflet and Lucan, who has also been imprisoned, to be released. When Arthur and his men see their long-lost comrades returning, they rejoice. The Rich Soldier, having saved his honor before his lady, finally submits to Arthur and gives him the Proud Castle.

From this siege in the *First Continuation* we may conclude that the Rich Souldoyer is the leader of the Rich Company—a mercenary who is the inverse ratio of the Rich Fisher. The sudden powerlessness of the Rich Soldier reminds us of how the Grail King of *Parzival* is maimed in his attempt to keep the favors of Orgeleuse, the Lady of Logres. It also recalls the aggressively defensive Mabonagrain from *Erec and Enide*, who weakly agrees to remain within the garden to ensure that the Joy of the Court never arrives, until Erec overcomes him.

In the *First Continuation,* there is little of faery and a lot more of chivalry. The breaking of the Rich Company seems too easy, hinging as it does upon the subservient love and fear of the Rich Soldier's being dishonored before his mistress by being vanquished. So, what then happens to the Rich Company? At the end of *The Elucidation* we are told,

> *through all the world,*
> *That you won't find any such today.*[53]

Does this mean that the Rich Company are no more, or that they have retired from the world, or that the Round Table knights wiped them out—as they once swore to do to Amangons—or just that they revert to individual citizens again? Or does Arthur become their liege lord, after their submission, entering into a form of chivalric transformation from bad to good knights? Let us see what happens.

THE BREAKING OF THE RICH COMPANY

After these four long years of war with Arthur, we are told,

> *Then was in that day abandoned*
> *The court, and the Rich Company*
> *Went hunting in the forest,*
> *Those who wanted to hawk*
> *Following the good rivers.*
> *Just so are the people of good upbringing:*
> *Some paying court to the ladies,*
> *Others preparing to do so.*
> *And they took their ease there*
> *Throughout winter until summer.*[54]

Now this passage is almost entirely replicated in the *First Continuation*, where we are told that, after the siege of Branlant when the city was starved out, the Round Table knights, the thirty peers, and the knights of the watch "all resorted to their favoured pastimes, some going hunting in the woods and rivers, others courting girls and ladies in the women's quarters."[55] But here it is the Round Table knights who so disport themselves, we notice, not the Rich Company as above in *The Elucidation*.

The extraordinary climb down from being the Rich Company who inhabit the Proud Castle and the Castle of Maidens, and who maintain the Perilous Bridge, to simply folk who go hunting in the forest is almost bathetic. The carefree descent into hunting is reminiscent of retired people going on a winter holiday, rather than the humiliation of a people under submission. The fact that they are said to spend the winter hunting is wholly correct in medieval terms, since winter was the season for such activity, with the hunters putting up in rustic style at hunting lodges. What, finally, are we to make of this?

The Elucidation speaks of "the court being abandoned"—we may well ask, does this mean the Rich Fisher's court? Or is it speaking of something else? Since there is no evident connection between the Rich Company and the court of the Rich Fisher, it doesn't seem likely. Certainly, the Rich Company have rich possessions and holdings, but they are of a different order to the Rich Fisher. By relinquishing the Proud Castle to Arthur's possession, the Rich Company make off to the countryside.

Thinking back to the premedieval Welsh story of the dog-headed opponents in Arthur's siege of Dun Eidin, in *Pa Gur* we see a huge disparity between those otherworldly denizens and the Rich Company's more human-seeming inhabitants and castles. But we are reminded that *The Elucidation* speaks of the fifth branch as being about "the anger and loss of Huden." We discussed in chapter 3 how Huden is the name of Tristan's dog and how we had no extant story to account for this branch. It is our contention that the fifth branch is about the siege of Proud Castle and the breaking of the Rich Company, based upon the preliminary adventures preceding this siege.

The Rich Soldier, who goes unnamed in the *First Continuation*, loses his lands largely as a result of the betrayal of the Rich Company by Bran de Lis, who switches sides to Arthur's camp. Kay is awarded Bran de Lis's dog by Arthur and then follows the hound through the enchanted castle empty of people, yet prepared for a huge feast, to discover Bran. It is through Bran's combat with Gawain and the necessity to bring peace between them on behalf of Gawain's child, that Bran de Lis is reconciled with Arthur, leaving only the Rich Soldier as the leader of the Rich Company.

This besieging of the Proud Castle has become a simple human story in the *First Continuation*, resulting in the supremacy of Arthur's kingship of Logres:

> *Just as you have heard from me*
> *About King Arthur, as I told you,*
> *That he had four years of war*
> *Against the people of his country;*
> *But all that drew to an end,*
> *There was not man or neighbour*
> *Who did not do his will.*
> *This known, by force or by agreement,*
> *Thus were truths proved;*
> *But know that it was named*
> *To the shame of them and the honor*
> *Of the king, as most people know.*[56]

The Elucidation's sense of Arthur's wars as being "against the people of his country" implies a kind of civil strife, in which he comes out triumphantly over unruly forces. The ancient texts flag up this supremacy, notably in the Old Welsh poem *The Battle of Llongborth* in the *Red Book of Hergest*, which features the Dumnonian leader Gereint ap Erbin (the original of Chrétien's Erec from *Erec and Enide*), where Arthur is described as *ameraudr*, or emperor:

> *In Llongborth I saw Arthur*
> *And brave men who hewed down with steel,*
> *Emperor and conductor of the toil.*[57]

Llywiaudir llafwr, or conductor of the toil, is the earliest salient function of Arthur as a battle leader. His supremacy in battle overcomes all opponents, including these rebellious half-mortal, half-faery members of the Rich Company who have refused to acknowledge him. As those who live in Logres, they are as much his subjects as any others, forcing him to fight a civil war to bring them into subjection. In *The Elucidation,* the Rich Company issue from the wells, making us suspect that they are, like Bleheris and his people, blent of the race of the maidens and also of the knights of Amangons but, unlike Bleheris's folk, they have all the petty and acquisitive traits of humans and little of those of faery.

When we look back at the history of faery we can see that, on the breaking of the Faery Accord, two kinds of faeries come out of the record: what are called the Seelie, or blessed court, and the Unseelie, or unholy court (see page 154, chapter 5). The Seelie court maintains good relations with humans and largely do no harm, but the Unseelie court tend to acts of malice or sorcery.

Arthur's wars against the Rich Company can be seen in this context: ultimately, the battles have been against the Unseelie court—these are the ones who have sent the test of the drinking horn, and an array of other tests to maliciously show up Arthur's court for unfaithfulness and lack of constancy in their love. The defeat of Proud Castle and the overthrow of the Rich Company finally revolve around this same point of faithful love: if the Rich Soldier is seen to be overcome in the eyes of his lady, then he is virtually a dead man in terms of his honor. He persuades Gawain into pretending to submit to the lady of Proud Castle by this ploy:

> *I have a sweetheart*
> *Truly, who I love more than my life,*
> *If she were dead, if I were to hear such a thing,*

> *Then I would kill myself.*
> *If I might beseech you of your nobility,*
> *By courtesy and by prowess,*
> *To give to me, without killing her, my sweetheart,*
> *Then I avow that, rightly or wrongly,*
> *No one will ever oppose you again,*
> *Not one man of the Proud Castle.*[58]

War born out of Amangons's desire for the maidens and their gold cups set this affair on, and it is love for the maidens that brings the war to a close, at least within the *First Continuation*. As *The Elucidation* relates,

> *Because of the maidens, I would say*
> *Were many battles fought throughout the land.*[59]

These many battles finally end with a coming to terms that allows the Rich Company to step down without loss of face, using the old game of keeping the lady sweet, of remaining on her terms, that we have seen worked out from the Celtic faery lore into the Arthurian legends. In these games, Gawain has come out ahead of all the other questers. It is Gawain who becomes "king of the castle" at the Castle of Maidens, where he is invited to remain its lord; it is he who overcomes the Rich Soldier, leader of the Rich Company; it is he who is the liberator of the prisoners, Girflet and Lucan, and now it is he who must press on to the Grail Castle via a series of interlinked adventures.

GAWAIN AND THE GRAIL MYSTERY

The time has come to see how another of *The Elucidation*'s seven branches plays out: the seventh branch, which is about the Quest of Gawain for the Bleeding Lance. This can only be done by examining the *First Continuation*, as we have only the scaffolding of the story in *The Elucidation*.

Riding back to Bran de Lis's castle, after the siege of Proud Castle, Gawain learns that his young son has been kidnapped by an unknown band of men. The company make plans over dinner to hunt for the boy. But at twilight, as Arthur and Guinevere play at backgammon out of doors, there rides by, without any acknowledgment of them, an unknown and unarmored knight bearing a baton, signifying that he is on peaceful mission. The queen demands to know who he is. First Kay and then Gawain attempt to accost him. The knight begs to be excused, saying that he cannot turn aside from his urgent mission, as he is the only man "this side of the sea" who can accomplish his task, which he doesn't reveal.

Gawain swears that he himself, were he the last man alive, would carry out the knight's mission, and eloquently persuades him to turn aside and greet the queen. Since Gawain's prowess speaks for him, the knight complies. But as they approach the queen's pavilion, Kay launches a javelin that strikes the unknown knight through the body. We assume that Kay attacks him because his own previous and rude attempts to persuade the knight were unsuccessful. Crying out in his death agonies, the unknown knight says:

> *Ah, Sir Gawain, I am slain!*
> *Truly it is a sinful wrong*
> *That I've been killed under your protection.*
> *If God pleases, you will, I think,*
> *Do all that you have promised.*
> *If I die, take then*
> *My arms as your accoutrements,*
> *Take my destrier as your mount,*
> *Go wherever he leads you,*
> *Taking care to not turn aside.*[60]

He then expires and Gawain gives orders for the knight to be unclothed: at the sight of his body, someone exclaims, "God, where can he have been born, to have been so fair?"[61] As everyone mourns the unknown knight—and the culpable Kay quickly makes himself scarce—Gawain dresses himself in the dead man's armor and sets out to fulfill the deceased's unknown errand, to the astonished sorrow of the crowd.

We never hear who this knight is, nor upon what errand he was so urgently riding; we only note that he was unarmored, bearing the baton of a herald on a mission of peace. Could this be a possible link to the unassigned story of branch three that, in *The Elucidation* is given as,

> *The next [branch] is the third, of the hawk*
> *Of which Castrars had great fear;*
> *Pecorins the son of Amangons*
> *Carried all his days the wound on his forehead?*[62]

We earlier assigned this branch as "the Wounding of Amangons's Son by Gawain." Can this be supported? Since the positioning of the unknown knight's death lies between the fall of the Proud Castle and Gawain's journey to the Grail Castle, it seems important to consider it a possibility. The unknown knight comes as a peacemaker who cannot turn aside from his mission; he is assaulted by Kay while under Gawain's protection. The nature of the knight's death is reminiscent both of the ancient Welsh story of Lleu from *Math ap Mathonwy*, stricken through with a lance, and also the blow struck by the invisible knight, Garlon.[63]

The mysterious dead knight's mission is taken up by Gawain. As we've seen from page 85, it is Kay himself who receives a wound from the hot peacock juices whose scar becomes a reproach for the rest of his life in the episode leading to the siege of Proud Castle, but there is no mention of Pecorins. The muddled themes of which *The Elucidation* speaks are not wholly borne out here, but somewhere in the mud lies the broken and misplaced fragments of this lost story. The fact that the knight's body is so beautiful that people wonder if he is of another race gives us a hint that we might be looking at an ambassador—but whether he is from Faery or from the Rich Company, we cannot tell. Let us see where Gawain is led, to see if we are justified.

Through the dark night, Gawain rides on until the horse stops him

at the Perilous Chapel at the crossroads. A single candlestick illuminates this foreboding place when a monstrous hand comes through the
window and snuffs out the light. His horse gallops off with him into
the stormy night, but of

> *The great marvels which he found*
> *All night, wherever he rode,*
> *Should no man tell;*
> *For those who have great desire,*
> *Know that these are the work of the Graal,*
> *So great a sin and terrible wrong*
> *Would come to those who attempt to tell of them,*
> *Save as they should be told.*[64]

Gawain's borrowed horse rides on all night and all day, traversing the
entire length of the whole country, until at twilight he is brought to
the sea where a causeway covered in trees awaits, at the end of it shines
a light, like the burning candle of the Perilous Chapel. He has come
finally to the Grail Castle. This is where the unknown knight was riding. Although Gawain has ridden till night, giving the horse its head,
the causeway is long and the light no nearer.

Finally, the way brings him into a great hall wherein a crowd of
people greet him as the long expected one. But as they dress him in
a hall robe, they surround him, muttering that he is not the one. He
experiences the great vanishment: as the crowd is suddenly withdrawn
from view, he notices the bier with the sword broken in half upon the
body. Then come the mourners in procession, bearing a silver cross,
who begin the office of the dead. The mourners vanish and then scores
of servants come to prepare the table, ahead of the Wounded King and
his supporters.

Gawain witnesses the coming of the Grail, watching it as it serves
bread and wine and other courses at each place; we are told that if the
diners do not care for one course, then another is brought, just as in *The
Elucidation* where the Maidens of the Wells provide a similar service:

And if the meal did not please him,
Many others were brought him.[65]

Then the diners also vanish, leaving Gawain alone with the bier, and
now he sees the object of his quest: the lance, whose streaming blood
runs down into a golden pipe at its base and from thence, via a pipe of
emerald, borne out of the hall. Two boys appear carrying candelabra,
followed by the Wounded King who bears the half sword that Gawain
took from the dead knight. The Wounded King laments the body,

Ah, noble body lying here,
For whom this realm is laid waste,
God grant that you be avenged,
So that the people's joy is restored![66]

The Wounded King invites Gawain to join the two halves of the
sword together, but the knight is unable. The king kindly tells that
Gawain is unable to do so, and that another knight for whom they
have been long waiting, will achieve this. This knight is, of course,
now unable to come because Kay has already killed him: Gawain has
taken up his task, but is not the appointed one who can mend the
sword. Now Gawain, who has had no sleep for two nights, asks about
the lance—the mission that he first undertook in *Perceval,* as well as
about the bier and the sword.

The Wounded King confirms that the lance is that by which
Christ was struck in the side, which will bleed without cease till
Doomsday. The second blow—the one struck by the sword that no
one has yet repaired, and which has done such harm—he is told, has
been the destruction of many a king, prince, noble, lady, and maiden.
The whole land was destroyed by the blow that the sword dealt. He
goes on to tell how the Grail was the cup that Joseph of Arimathea
had brought to the Crucifixion, in which he caught Christ's blood,
storing it away until he fled from persecution to the land where he
might live in safety:

> *The White Island was that country,*
> *So it was well called,*
> *A part of England*
> *Which the sea closely held and enfolded.*[67]

Joseph's lineage has kept the Grail since, with the Fisher King and Perceval being of his line. But the Grail King is unable to tell Gawain more, since he has not mended the sword, although he acknowledges that the dead knight must have recognized Gawain's eminence in entrusting him with bearing the half sword hither. He is telling Gawain about the knight who struck the Dolorous Blow with the sword by which the Wasteland has been caused in Logres, when Gawain falls deeply asleep and hears no more.

He wakes in great shame in a marsh beside the sea, for the second time, determined to ask more directly about the Grail and the bier in more detail, vowing to mend the broken sword. He sets off and, as he rides, something marvelous begins to happen. But because he has asked some of the questions, the results are immediately seen in the land:

> *Never have eyes beheld*
> *A land so richly flourishing*
> *In wood, water, and meadowland.*
> *In this way was the wasted land*
> *Which had been completely empty of all good things*
> *The night before, as God so willed,*
> *During that night—as was fitting—*
> *Had restored the rivers to their courses,*
> *And all the woods, to my best knowledge,*
> *Restored to greenness once again,*
> *And all because Gawain had asked*
> *About why the lance bled.*[68]

People acclaim Gawain as he rides back to the court of Arthur:

Sir, you have killed us and healed us.
You should be happy and joyful . . .
For the benisons you've brought us,
But, on the other hand, you should hate yourself
For failing to hear about
The Graal, of whom it served.
Of the great joy which should have been
In the future, no one can speak,
You should mourn it distressfully.[69]

Their joy at the return of the green and fertile land is blent with sorrow at Gawain's failure to ask about the Grail and its purposes. So it is that his Grail quest results in an incomplete healing, with the land restored, but something fundamental not quite resolved, for Gawain has failed to hear what the Grail was for. Once again, a quest knight has brought a measure of joy to the court, though not all the healing that was sought.

This depiction of the Wasteland's healing is nearest to that shown in *The Elucidation:* a complete overnight transformation. Here in the sequence of the *First Continuation* that we've been following, only a partial joy comes about after the besieging of Proud Castle. This was Gawain's second visit to the Grail Castle, where his earlier witnessing the procession and attempt to mend the broken sword came to nothing at all. He is now in a better state of understanding than he was when, back in *Perceval,* he swore to fetch the Bleeding Lance and bring it back to Guigambresil: this is a holy object that cannot be diverted to mere human use, nor a relic to be brought back as a souvenir (see chapter 3, page 79).

All we can do is wonder at the identity of the dead knight whose arms Gawain took. It is by these arms that the folk of the Grail Castle recognize him as the destined Grail winner so that, after an initial recognition, once his armor is stripped off, they understand immediately that he is "not the one." The Wounded King says that this person has been long expected but has not shown up. Who he is remains a mystery, as the author of the *First Continuation* states that he will tell us nothing about the dead knight whose arms and horse went with Gawain to the Grail Castle. So here we have the thread of an unknown Grail seeker, who might be one of the half-faery denizens of the Rich Company—as his fair body seems to dictate—or some other person unknown.

It is not till the *Third Continuation* that we hear more about this mysterious dead knight. A maiden on a mule comes to remind Gawain of his forgotten quest, announcing herself as the sister of the knight whom Kay killed and whose mission Gawain took up. Gawain journeys with her until they come to her castle where the immense wailing from its occupants tells them King Margons has overtaken the castle. The maiden on the mule then relates how she was going to marry her own knight when Margons determined to marry her to his own son, Quagrilo, to her great disgust. When Margons hanged her beloved, she had Quagrilo captured and stuffed into a mangonel, to be catapaulted back into Margons's own tent. Margons accordingly threatens her with amputation of her breasts and the leveling of her castle, but Gawain saves the day and overcomes him, sending him to submit himself to Arthur, to the maiden's great disgust.[70]

The name of the evil king, Margons, once again echoes that of Amangons. Here it seems we have yet another thread of the continuing story, wherein the maiden on the mule takes revenge on behalf of her erstwhile sisters, the Well Maidens. The discrepancy between the *First Continuation*'s statement that her partner was the knight killed by Kay, and the *Third Continuation*'s that Margons hung him, we must put down to a lack of scrutiny on the part of the continuator!

To conclude, Gawain spends many years on adventures and quests. Years pass and he finally encounters a young knight with whom he jousts, only to discover that it is his own lost son, who receives from his father the name "Lionel." (This is a curious choice, since this is the name of the well-known brother of Lancelot.) They both return to Arthur's court at Carlion, to great rejoicing but, while they are being greeted, an unknown man comes into the hall and carries off the arms of the dead knight and his horse, to Gawain's great sorrow. What belongs to Faery or to the otherworldly Grail realms, has to be returned there. Here the narrator tells us,

> *The story must here divert*
> *And another branch begin,*
> *Which I will relate without delay*
> *Word for word, I'll tell and say. . . .*
> *All in order, with utmost care . . .*
> *I'll not have it heard without telling*
> *In its proper order, at the right time,*
> *Exactly as the story reveals.*[71]

This replicates the continual assertions by the narrator of *The Elucidation* that the story will be revealed in order. The *First Continuation* then ends with the branch four story of Guerrehes, and Brangemor in the Swan Boat, or what we have indentified as the Avenging of Faeryland by Guerrehes, dealt with in chapters 4 and 5.

As we have seen above, we have in the *First Continuation* the clearest working out of branch seven, Gawain's Quest for the Bleeding Lance and his partial success in healing the land. But we cannot support, without further evidence the ascription of branch three to him; the story of the hawk and the scarring of Pecorins remains a lost story to us. In its working out of the Grail procession and the Grail King's explanations, we see the clear influence of Robert de Boron in the ascription of the lineage of Joseph of Arimathea to the Grail family—as we saw in chapter 6.

Here, both Grail and Bleeding Lance are firmly revealed as relics of the Crucifixion, although the Grail still purveys food and drink with all the generosity of the Well Maidens' hospitality. Of the body on the bier we remain ignorant. It is not until a third continuator brings his deductive powers to conclude all the unanswered mysteries of the previous stories with tidy answers in the *Third Continuation* that we hear that the stricken body on the bier is none other than the Fisher King's brother, who is killed by a blow from the sword; the Fisher King then severs the sinews in his own legs in sorrow and the Wasteland is brought about. This is all in keeping with the later medieval Grail legends.

However, these latter rationalizations run counter to *The Elucidation,* with its alternative "dolorous blow" caused by the rape of the Well Maidens by Amangons. Here, the skillful fusing of faery lore and Christian mystery has grafted the two traditions together, with *The Elucidation* remembering an older tradition and enabling it to continue via the newer.

The fact that the *First Continuation* ends with a double healing is significant. The partial healing of the Wasteland affected by Gawain's questions is immediately followed by the story of Brangemor, the dead knight in the swan boat, who is finally returned to Faery by the persistence of Guerrehes; these two deeds seem to satisfy both the Christian and the faery demands of the story.

For the Grail to operate and the Courts of Joy to spread their fertile delight once more, it requires questers who can access the place of the ancient heart and bring the healing. It is time to go deeper.

9

THE GRAIL REVEALED

The One filled a mighty krater with Creative Intelligence and sent it down, appointing a Herald to make this proclamation to the hearts of men: "Immerse yourself in this krater, whoever is drawn to it, having faith that you may ascend to the One who sent down this krater, realizing why you came into being." Those who heard this proclamation, merged with Creative Intelligence and became perfect and complete because they had received gnosis.

CORPUS HERMETICUM BOOK 4, 4 (TRANS. CM)

THE HALLOWS

Throughout world myth, special objects of power have been the object of quest, war, and healing. Jessie Weston was one of the first to note that the main objects of the Grail quest are similar to those found in other cultures, from the four emblems of the Dhyani Buddhas, right through the four treasures of the Irish faeries, the Tuatha de Danann, and to the emblems that characterize the tarot suits: the sword, staff, cup, and stone.[1] These hallows represent aspects of the universal understanding, as adamantine objects that make their appearance both within the apparent world at certain moments, as well as within the human imagination.[2]

Within *The Elucidation* we view certain of these hallows, or holy things, during the Grail procession: the Bleeding Lance, the Sword upon the Corpse on the Bier, the Silver Cross that is processed, and the Grail itself. We are assured that,

> *When the good knights will come,*
> *Who found the court three times,*
> *Then may be heard,*
> *Point by point, without making anything up,*
> *The truth of whom the wells served,*
> *And who the knights were,*
> *And why the Graal served,*
> *And of the lance that was bleeding.*[3]

These mysteries cannot be discovered so easily, as we have seen, and each requires that the quester pose his questions, since it is by questioning that healing may be wrought: but, as we have also seen, finding the right place to ask those questions doesn't always work out so well. We are told that "it was Perceval the Welshman" who,

> *asked who the Graal*
> *Served, but did not ask*
> *About the lance, why it bled*
> *When he saw it, nor of the sword,*
> *Of which half the blade was missing,*
> *And the other lying on the bier*
> *On the dead body, nor the manner*
> *Of the great vanishing.*
> *But I tell you in no uncertain terms,*
> *That he asked whose was*
> *The corpse in the hall,*
> *And about the rich silver cross*
> *That was processed before all.*[4]

We have seen that in the *First Continuation* it is Gawain who actually asks about the Bleeding Lance, and who arrives with the counterpart half of the broken sword upon the bier. Of the corpse upon the bier, we do not hear very much, but we notice that both it and the body of Brangemor in the swan boat are the unburied bodies who are the lamented witnesses of the unhealing Wasteland, earlier combatants in the Grail wars.

The Elucidation tells us that Perceval asked about the Grail itself and about the body and the silver cross, but we do not have these stories unfolded, not even in the *Third Continuation,* which is where most of the mysteries are deductively unraveled.

We have already seen how everyone experiences the great vanishment, but it remains one of the mysteries about which the Grail seekers fail to ask. We are told that after the procession of the hallows, the great lamentation that is being made ceases and then everyone vanishes, leaving a vast, empty hall. Neglecting to ask the question is like looking a gift horse in the mouth. As the Hideous Damsel says in her berating of Perceval, "Fortune has hair in front but is bald behind."[5] This refers to the ancient instruction that on being offered some great fortune, one must seize it with both hands, or lose the opportunity. Within *Perlesvaus* the knights encounter a bald maiden, who acts as a kind of walking representation of the Wasteland: a reproach to the questers who don't comprehend the consequences of their actions in not asking the question.

The great vanishment is also tied to the Siege Perilous of *Gerbert de Montreuil's Continuation* where Perceval comes to Arthur's table and finds an empty and magnificent chair upon which no one is sitting. It was sent to Arthur by the faery of Roche Menor who made Arthur swear that the chair will be placed ready on every high feast day and that the one who sat in it without fear would win the praise and esteem of the whole world, as well as learn about the secrets of the Grail and the Lance. In this text, the Perilous Seat thus has a faery precedent, quite unlike Robert de Boron's depiction of the Siege Perilous as the seat of Judas, the betrayer at the Last Supper.[6]

In *Gerbert* we learn that six knights who have sat therein to date have been swallowed up. Perceval determines to sit in the seat, whereupon the chair groans and the earth beneath cracks open, while the chair remains suspended with Perceval in it. Before it closes up, from a cavernous pit deep below arise the six previous and unworthy sitters in the chair who are pulled out to safety. In this way, Perceval accomplishes a kind of harrowing of hell of his own.[7] The rescued knights thank Perceval saying, "The faery knew very well that the one who was to complete the Grail quest and know its outcome has such a true and fine heart that he would free us from the abyss."[8]

Perceval's harrowing of hell is of a different order from Christ's action of descending into hell to redeem the ancestors but, in the context of the Grail quest, it is as significant. Gerbert seems to be telling us that the Faery Grail that was stolen by Amangons, and the mysterious Holy Grail of the Last Supper and the Crucifixion, have a finder who brings joy back into the world again, and that a faery woman prophesied his coming by the test of the Siege Perilous.

The Seat Perilous acts as a faery ordeal, a test of fitness for Grail seekers. In eighth-century Ireland we find many such ordeals or hallows that test truth in cases of judgment.[9] As we saw in chapter 4, these are paralleled in Faery by tests of fitness: tests of faithfulness to one's lover, which are followed in later medieval tradition by the chastity tests. Such tests of fitness litter faerytale: trees that must be shaken when they are ripe in the German tale, *Mother Hölle;* or golden cauldrons that cause the grasper to become stuck to them in *Manawyddan ap Llyr;* even the Tree of the Knowledge of Good and Evil in the garden of Eden. These are all tests that assess the quality of those who encounter them.

Among the many challenges posed by various maidens and others en route, the questing knights are often tested by the very hallows they have come to seek, whose mystery overwhelms them to such a degree that they are rendered dumb in the face of their wonder. Unable to ask even the most basic question about these holy things, they lose the opportunity and so prolong the agony of the Wasteland and the lamentation over the unburied body.

From among the many tasks that are set upon the questing knights, we draw forth this quatrain, which might have gone otherwise unnoticed. They are required to find out,

The truth of whom the wells served,
And who the knights were,
And why the Graal served,
And of the lance that was bleeding.[10]

Gawain's questioning may well have brought forth a partial healing of the land, so that it is regreened and fertile once again, but there is still something lacking: no one has asked about the "truth of whom the wells served." Among the begged questions, we have to ask, do we have one Grail or two within *The Elucidation?*

THE SERVICE OF THE GRAIL

It is clear from our text that there are two appearances of the Grail at work: the cups of the Maidens of the Wells represent a primal hospitality that nourish the wayfarer, while the Grail of the Grail Procession in the court of the Rich Fisher feeds only those who dwell or visit there. So, are these cups the same vessel or a different vessel? To answer that question, we have to discover exactly what the Grail does. We are told that the Grail was seen,

Without servant or seneschal,
Coming through the door of a room
And many were properly served
In rich golden dishes
Each worth a great treasure.
The first course was set
Before the king, and then served
To all the others around in that place;
And never were such marvelous
Meals as were taken to them
And the food that they were given.[11]

In *The Elucidation* the service of the maidens is extended to all travelers but, after the breaking of the Faery Accord, that service is suspended indefinitely. It is only within the court of the Rich Fisher that the Grail comes to serve those who sit at table. As in the *First Continuation* "the Grail serves all by itself," without any servitor to bring it round, but we are not told by what agency it does so.[12] It remains, in both instances, a vessel that purveys food: the ultimate vessel of wondrous hospitality.

The *Lai du Cor* incident in the *First Continuation* and the Maidens of the Wells' cups in *The Elucidation* reveal one end of the story of the cup or horn of faery hospitality, while the Holy Grail appears throughout most of the rest of the texts as the default vessel of the legends—blent of the vessel that caught the blood of Christ at the Crucifixion and the Cup of the Last Supper—presenting the other end of the story.

It is only in Chrétien's *Perceval* that we first hear about a more obviously sacramental use of the vessel when Perceval visits the cell of his hermit uncle, who tells him,

> He who is served from the grail is my brother. Our sister was your mother. . . . I believe the rich Fisher King is the son of the king who is served from the grail. Do not think that he is given pike, lamprey, or salmon; he is served with a single host which is brought to him in that grail. Such a holy thing is the grail that it sustains and comforts his life.[13]

This withdrawn king is kept alive by being fed a single host every time the Grail circulates; like a mystic or saint, he needs no other nourishment, just as King Arthur is described as being in the thirteenth-century Spanish text *La Faula*.[14]

However, when we look back at the earlier correlatives of the Grail in Celtic tradition, we find that they are ultimately cauldrons that purvey food—as in the cauldron of Pen Annwyfn that only purveys food to heroes—or else brews up alchemical potions that purvey wisdom, as in the story of Ceridwen's cauldron; or, like the cauldron of Bran, bring the dead back to life.[15] These functions are also part of the Grail's abilities.

The Faery Grail in *The Elucidation* is ultimately about the giving of food as a ritual of hospitality that creates communion between faeries and humans: the wisdom that it purveys is the neighborly consideration of all life that arises in human awareness as a consequence. Those who offer and drink from the cup in peace are the children of one universe, in communion with the natural world even as their ancestors were, who enjoy the ancestral feast. When the rules of faery courtesy are broken by violence, rapine, and theft, the Faery Accord is broken. This is ultimately what causes the blight upon the human world that we call the Wasteland: the riches of the Rich Fisher no longer flow. Humanity enters in a warfare with Faery, displaced people wander the land without protection, and even the court of Arthur is visited by mocking and embarrassing tests. Fertility fails when the waters of the Faery Grail are withdrawn: but when they flow again, the land becomes fertile and is repopulated. People are brought once more into communion with their ancestral belonging.

The Holy Grail is ultimately about the provision of food that feeds the body but also the spirit, bringing humanity into communion with the divine: this is a wisdom that makes kinship between God and humanity through the redemptive mediation of Christ's sacrifice on the Cross. When this communion is ruptured, Wasteland, violence, and terror rule the Earth, bringing war, famine, and depopulation. When this communion is reestablished, then Christendom is restored under a single ruler, King Arthur; under his suzerainty, the weak are once more protected from brigandage, commercial exploitation, and merciless depredation.

Faery Grail and Holy Grail are thus kindred vessels: one operating under the older dispensations of nature and Faery, the other under the newer dispensation of Christianity. The effect of them both is the same in the everyday world of court and castle: the world is regreened and made fertile, the wars stop, and peace returns. The spiritual communion within people's hearts is framed differently, but it is ultimately consistent in respecting one's neighbor.

It is a reminder of the time when Christ was asked which of the commandments was the most important; he replied,

Love the Lord your God with all your heart, and with all your soul, and with all your mind. This is the first and greatest commandment. And the second is like: Love your neighbor as yourself. All the law and the prophets hang upon those two commandments.[16]

Is this what the Maidens of the Wells were promoting at the beginning of this story? Let us find out what happened to them and answer that question.

WHAT HAPPENED TO THE MAIDENS OF THE WELLS?

The question of what happened to the Maidens of the Wells subsequent to their rape has never before been posed. In the collapsing and multi-woven time scales of the Grail legends, we are tempted to forget them by placing them at the beginning of *The Elucidation* as merely the victims of Amangons. That they might appear again in the story may have passed us by.

Throughout the Grail legends, there are two sorts of people who exhort, explain, and direct the Grail questers to their goal: these are largely hermits and maidens. The hermits act "as constants throughout the deserted places of the quest, and as social companions who put the knights back on the path."[17] They also unravel dreams and mysteries, give backstories and exhort to godliness those knights who fall exhausted into their hermitages. As for the maidens that the knights encounter, they more often give reasons for distraction from the main quest, having to be rescued, aided, or brought to places of protection—but not all of them.

The first clue to this is found in *Perceval* where the Hideous Damsel comes on muleback to Arthur's court at Carlion to berate Perceval for his failure to ask the question; she is described as having black hair and skin, a beard, discolored teeth, and with a hump both front and back. We may remember how she berates him for losing the opportunity to ask the question and heal the Wounded King. She then declares,

I don't know if you've heard of the Proud Castle, but that's where I have to go tonight. In the castle there are five hundred and sixty-six knights of worth . . . each of them has his love with him, a noble, fair, and courtly lady.[18]

She thus entices the Round Table knights to go thither, to joust, and to seek out the peak of Montesclaire where a maiden is besieged: whoever raises it and frees her will win the greatest honor and be allowed to gird on the Sword of the Strange Hangings. This sets the rest of the knights to go off on quest.

The Hideous Damsel is harsh-tongued and ugly, provoking the knights to deeds of arms, just like the dwarf messengers we have seen before in *Diu Cröne* and other texts. Like them, she appears to have an otherworldly origin. But we ask the question, why is she traveling to Proud Castle? Does she live there?

In Celtic tradition, the appearance of the Loathly Lady or Hideous Damsel signals the manifestation of Sovereignty herself, the Goddess of the Land. Time and again, heroes encounter her under her most hideous guise and are put in positions of exacting test, whereby she challenges their fitness for the quest.[19] The final test in most of these stories is the ultimate one: the hero must either kiss, sleep with, or—in the case of Gawain in the Middle English story *Sir Gawain and Dame Ragnell*—marry with the Loathly Lady.[20] In all cases, the effect of any hero taking her up on this challenge is that she then changes into the most beautiful woman alive and acknowledges him as the victor.

Is the Hideous Damsel merely the instrument of the Proud Castle, sent to lure out knights to seek the adventures there, or is she a messenger of the Grail itself? Subsequent Grail writers, notably Wolfram von Eschenbach in his depiction of Kundry, employed the Hideous Damsel as a Grail messenger who finally delivers the hope and relief of the Grail's achievement.[21] In most medieval writings, her ugliness—all thought of the testing Goddess of Sovereignty forgotten—is seen as resonant of the Wasteland, as we see in the Bald Damsel of *Perlesvaus* or the sorrowful Queen of the Wasteland in Malory.[22]

The maidens that Gawain discovers along his quest each presents her own challenge; the many instances where he aids or is led by a maiden are too numerous to mention, but we note two of these, which both bring about the same result. In the *First Continuation,* his encounter with the woman who was raped by Greoreas—an incident that brings the rape by Amangons to mind—ends with her leading him to a castle wherein are twenty maidens held captive. They have been forced by Greoreas to weave and sew in his sweatshop, under terrible conditions, punished, starved, and tormented. At their rescue, they demand that Gawain become the lord of the now liberated castle. Kindly refusing, he passes onward.[23]

In *Perceval* the contrary Maiden with the Mirror, otherwise known as the Proud Maiden of Nogres, whom Gawain encounters on the way to the Castle of Maidens, would exhaust the patience of a saint, but Gawain somehow forebears to strike or curse her, as we have seen in chapter 5. It is she who leads him to the Castle of Maidens where, again, he is invited to become the lord of the place.

The Castle of Maidens, as we saw, is a place of multigenerational mistresses, where the mothers of Gawain and Arthur still live in a semi-otherworldly manner, yet under an enchantment. This place is said, in *The Elucidation,* to be one of the many castles built by the Rich Company: it is the environment of maidens, widows, and squires who can never attain knighthood, caught in a time warp from which only the test of the Perilous Bed will deliver them.

Ultimately, Gawain's ability to overcome the Rich Soldier, leader of the Rich Company at the Proud Castle, and to bring healing to the Wasteland at the Grail Castle is surely in some measure due to his previous success at the Castle of Maidens, where he is acclaimed by the women there as the one who causes time to run on once again, so that squires might become knights, widows have their provisions, and maidens become wives. This part of the Amangons legacy is successfully overcome by Gawain.

Strongest of all evidence that the Maidens of the Wells are still at their work is the moment when Gawain meets two maidens at the castle of Bran de Lis,

Between four olive trees, there was a fountain which
flowed,
At which two demoiselles, in tunics of purple so very fine.
Two vessels of sound gold they carried, that they filled
from the well.[24]

Surely these are the very Maidens of the Wells we met at the beginning of *The Elucidation?* But here, they say that they will only pour water for the lord of the castle, Bran de Lis, the knight who, at this moment, is still a member of the Rich Company. Here they are, still serving from the wells, yet not as formerly. The communion that faery hospitality once brought is here suborned to the use of one man: the cup of common service has become privatized. We have to assume that this is the state of affairs in the other castles held by the Rich Company, who emerge as the secondary wave of semimortal descendants of Amangons and the maidens. After all, Amangons stole away the maiden and used her cup for his service thereafter.

Do the maidens have any part in the Holy Grail itself, we might ask? In *Gerbert de Montreuil's Continuation,* we hear how Philosophine, the name given to Perceval's mother, first brought the Grail to the Castle of Maidens in the company of Joseph of Arimathea:

We brought the grail—a sacred thing indeed—to this land when we first crossed the sea . . . but it was taken to the house of the good Fisher King.[25]

We are told that its transfer is due to the land being full of sinful people, and so for safe keeping it is taken to the keeping of the Fisher King. This is the only place where we hear about the Grail coming to the Castle of Maidens first, but Gerbert's Castle of Maidens with its holy and chaste damsels is a very different kind of place to the castle that Gawain enters, with its multigenerational mistresses, with its long-departed mothers, and unknown sisters. But it is interesting to see the Faery and Holy Grail traditions briefly entwining in this way.

As we have seen, the maidens who appear in the Grail story can be both helpful and unhelpful, but with all the yearning of those who once served the wells, they actively cause the Round Table knights to seek out solutions by going on quest. Like the nine maidens who warm the cauldron of the Celtic underworld, their inspiratory breath blows, exhorting the knights to virtuous deeds that will deliver the world from Wasteland, and into a condition that allows the communion that was once the result of the service of the wells to be resumed.

It is not the same service as in times of yore, but it enables those who have been unfaithful to their purpose to return to a renewed condition of faithfulness and communion with all that is holy. Through the tangled and multiple time scales of our story, let us see how its inhabitants emerge.

THE INHABITANTS OF THE STORY

At the beginning of chapter 4, we explored some of the locations and times at work within *The Elucidation*. With a greater sense of the sequence of events and how they unfold, we can now see that there are several different time lines in operation here:

- The times before when the maidens dispensed hospitality
- The time of the Wasteland, and the wanderings of the children of Amangons and the maidens
- The time of Arthur and his Round Table knights and their quest
- The time of the Joy, when the Rich Fisher's court is discovered
- The time when the Rich Company come forth and the wars begin

In the land of mythic imagination, these time scales cannot be categorized by anything more than sequence. The hospitality of the Wells is happening within the—we know not how distant—past, removed from the time of King Arthur. Within the period of the Round Table knights, only the *story* of the shutdown of the wells is known. Two waves of people issue from the disruption of Amangons's theft and rapine: the first to emerge are the company of Bleheris, who may have been wandering many generations, we cannot tell. The second company, the Rich Company, arise only *after* the court of the Rich Fisher is found, making an unsettling coda to the story. It is Bleheris's folk, and their testimony, who bring distant myth nearer to eyewitness account, serving to act as the spur to quest for the court of the Rich Fisher. It is the Rich Company's prosecution of war that causes Arthur and his knights to engage with them until Arthur finally wins.

The different groups of people who inhabit *The Elucidation* are woven together, creating a set of interlocking patterns. Based upon the time lines above, here is a brief working out of the story:

1. *Time of Hospitality:* The court of the Rich Fisher is findable

   Recipients: **Dispensers:**
   Wayfarers   Maidens

2. *Time of Wasteland:* The court of the Rich Fisher becomes unfindable

   Violators: **Wanderers:**
   King Amangons & his Men   Bleheris's Company, born of the
                               Maidens & Amangons

3. *Time of Quest:* The court of the Rich Fisher laments

   Storytellers: **Questers:**
   Bleheris's Company   Knights of Round Table

4. *Time of Joy:* The bounty from the court of the Rich Fisher flows freely

   Wanderers become Settlers?
   Maidens and Knights born of Well Maidens & Amangons

5. *Time of the Wars:* The bounty of the court of the Rich Fisher is misused

   Origin of Riches: **Exploiters of the Riches:**
   The Rich Fisher & his Court Rich Company
   Combatants:
   Knights of the Round Table v. Knights of the Rich Company

6. *After the Fall of Proud Castle:* Peace

At Peace:	Returned to Forest:
Knights of Round Table	Rich Company

The connecting factor in these six time zones is the court of the Rich Fisher, which we are told purveys all good things to Logres. The communion enjoyed between human realms and those of the Grail Castle within the first of these time zones is gained by the open hospitality of the Maidens of the Wells, through their golden cups. The court is lost in the second zone, typified by the wandering of Bleheris's company. It is regained by dint of Bleheris's testimony, setting the Round Table knights to quest for it in the third zone. In the fourth of the time zones, that bounty begins to flow again, possibly causing Bleheris's company to become settlers, only now the vessel that feeds people is the Grail, not the wells. In the fifth troublesome time zone, war begins between the Rich Company who emerge from the wells as the secondary wave caused by the incident from the second time zone; this company sets itself up in rivalry to the Round Table knights. They have no lack of provisions and resources with which to make a power base, but are finally overcome by Arthur.

What happens to the wandering maidens and knights of Bleheris's company, the offspring of victim and perpetrator? We are not told whether they can finally become settled in the lands of Logres where King Arthur rules, or become part of the court of the Rich Fisher, or return to Faery, although we are told in line 159 that Arthur "gained many good knights" from that encounter, suggesting an alliance of forces. Their wanderings seem to be occasioned by the breaking of the Faery Accord: as the descendents not just of their faery mothers but also of the human fathers, they cannot settle in any one place, being unwelcome in Faery and without land or possession in the human realms. For them, the court of the Rich Fisher becomes an unfindable location.

We have likened the semimortal, semifaery peoples of Bleheris's company to representatives of the Seelie court, those faeries who are more kindly disposed to humans; while we have liked the Rich Company to members of the Unseelie court, half faeries like their cousins, but with more of our human acquisitiveness about them. As a secondary wave of "people of the wells," the Rich Company are troubling. With the acuity of their faery omniscience they can outmaneuver Arthur's knights; with their human entrepreneurialism, they create a series of castles and retire into them in astounding luxury, but without a shred of compassion or humanity. In the *First Continuation* also, we are shown that the Rich Soldier, the leader of the Proud Company, becomes a follower of Arthur's, and that his men are sworn to be obedient to Arthur's rule, solely as the result of not being shamed before his lady.

Faery and Holy Grail both feature in this story, fusing an older myth with a newer one. The double healing—both of the Wasteland and of King Brangemor—at the end of the *First Continuation* seems to tie together both sides of the story, serving both the Christian and the faery legends. Since Brangemor's name includes that of Bran—who, as we have seen, is the oldest of the Wounded Kings—this seems doubly appropriate.

As Gawain has been on the Quest for the Bleeding Lance, relic of the Crucifixion and emblematic of the redemptive blood of Christ, so Guerrehes has simultaneously been on an unknowing quest that results in his retrieval of a lance that had killed—and will revive again—the semimortal Brangemor, and will kill his assailant. The body on the bier in the Grail Castle and the body of Brangemor upon the bier at Arthur's court have a mythic parallelism that bring both Holy Grail and Faery Grail together in the most extraordinary way.

It is of this lance that we must now speak, for its role, long foretold in *Perceval*, brings us intelligence that is difficult to hear, but that we must heed if we are to understand the real mystery of the Grail.

THE PROPHECY OF THE LANCE AND THE GRAIL QUEST

Back in *Perceval*, the vassal of the king of Escavalon laid upon Gawain the quest for the Bleeding Lance, with this warning: "It is written that the time will come when the whole kingdom of Logres, which was once the land of the ogres, will be destroyed by that lance."[26]

The hallows each have both healing and destructive powers, depending upon the way in which they are accessed or used, but this foreboding prophecy, with its punning hinge of Logres/ogres, is never fully achieved in *Perceval* or its *Continuations*. However, when we consider the full arc of the Grail legends within the Arthurian story as a whole, the effect is still the same.

It is ultimately the Grail legends that presage the fall of the Round Table: Malory writes of the way in which the chivalric rage for going on quest for the Grail effectively depopulates the court, leaving it weak and ripe for exploitation by Mordred in his *Morte d'Arthur*. Few knights return from their quest; with their attention turned to things of spiritual fulfillment, they neglect the task of chivalric guardianship that keeps the land safe. But there is an even more serious flaw that enters into our considerations of the Grail.

In the light of Christian eschatology, we can see that the quest for the Holy Grail and the Bleeding Lance lead inexorably to the end, not only of the realm of Logres, but of *all* things. The worldview of Western Christianity, that creation is spoiled and cannot be redeemed until doomsday, when everything will be rolled up, is presaged by the words of Isaiah: when everyone is judged, "All the stars in the sky will be dissolved and the heavens rolled up like a scroll; all the starry host will fall like withered leaves from the vine, like shrivelled figs from the fig tree."[27]

This rolling up of the scroll of creation is the ending of the story, but no such necessity is seen in the light of faery viewpoint. Because the Faery Grail is a hallow of hospitality and fellowship, the union it brings doesn't require that things end, only that the exchange and communion are repeated in a seasonal and renewable way. The ancient Faery Accord doesn't require us to stop telling the story, or to tidy it away. The early Grail writers, in the words of Manessier, author of the *Third Continuation,* "sealed all in parchment," so that the words of this story might still come to us: they did not perceive how barren an ending would later come to overshadow the earlier traditions of hope that *The Elucidation* extends to us.

These two viewpoints result in different ends. The Grail legends, which became much more Christianized as time ran on, show us how Perceval is overtaken and replaced by Galahad as the chief Grail winner, with Perceval himself succeeding to the role of Grail guardian, passing into a celibate and heirless conclusion, while Galahad dies a virgin and enters into a nirvanic union with God. Meanwhile back at Camelot, the Round Table knights are overthrown by the machinations of Mordred and the Orkney clan, and Arthur is mortally wounded at the Battle of Camlann. It is only within Wolfram's *Parzival* that the Grail family proliferate, becoming involved with the India of the mysterious Prester John, while the majority of our Grail finders remain childless.[28]

The mysteries of the Grail become boundaried in a very limiting way in the *Second Continuation*, where we are told that the secrets of the Grail are,

> a most sacred thing, and should not be spoken of by any lady, young or old, or any girl; nor even by any man born, unless he's an ordained priest or a man who leads a holy life . . . of the wonders which no man could hear without shaking and trembling and turning pale with fear.[29]

This is wholly at odds with *The Elucidation*'s promise that the service of the Grail

> *has been known but hidden,*
> *The good that it served will openly*
> *Be taught to all people.*[30]

From the evidences of the Grail texts, it seems that the questing of Perceval and of Gawain present two very different traditions. Perceval is sometimes depicted as having a sweetheart, Blanchfleur, whom he both meets and misses in Chrétien's *Perceval*. While subsequent continuators of the story attempted to get the couple married, their marriage seems to remain unconsummated, in true ascetic fashion, and Perceval has no offspring.

The many narrators of the Grail legends had already knowingly tagged their hero with not only the achievement of the Grail quest, but also with the future role of Grail guardianship. As subsequent Grail legends attest, the Holy Grail cannot be found by a married man, but only by a virgin—an understanding that is even more underscored by the time Perceval becomes subordinate to Galahad who, as the chief Grail winner of the *Queste del San Graal,* is the ultimate virgin. This disruption of the ancient rules of quest can be wholly put down to the Cistercian reworking of the *Lancelot-Grail,* which begins, at the very onset of the Grail quest, with a total prohibition on any knight setting forth on quest with his sweetheart or wife in tow. It is clearly designed to be a quest for single or celibate men only: a quester becomes necessarily like a priest, under this dispensation.

However, we must not forget Dindrane, Perceval's sister who, in the *Lancelot-Grail,* is actually the first to find the Grail. She is, however, a hermit who receives the Grail vision after she has declared vows of chastity.

At the other extreme, we have seen how Gawain makes his way to the Castle of Maidens and is invited to be its lord and protector, a pattern that seems to follow the more ancient tradition of the bravest hero who makes it into the regions of Faery (chapter 5). When we turn to his career, we find Gawain is continually rescuing, if not sleeping with, young women, even forming relationships with faery women, according the lays of Marie de France. Sexuality is never far from the surface in Gawain's courteous championship of women.[31] Gawain's line continues, following the fertile path of Faery, which renews all things through the changing cycles of nature in every season.

The episode of the testing horn of the *Lai du Cor* is actually repeated, in brief, within the *First Continuation.* Its placement, just before the besieging of Proud Castle and the rescue of Girflet and his fellows, is significant. Both in the *Lai du Cor* and in the *Lai du Mantel,* as well as in the *First Continuation,* it is the beloved of Carados who, alone of all women, proves to be the most constant of partners. Carados is about to drain the horn without spillage, and his unnamed wife is able to wear the testing mantle of constancy without its shrinking up and exposing her nakedness, because they both faithfully love each other. It would seem that Carados and Guinier, as she is called in *First Continuation,* are the perfect lovers.[32]

In the light of the Faery Accord that we explored in chapter 4, Carados and Guinier restore the trust of faery in humanity through their faithfulness to each other. Their singular success acts to redeem the whole of the Arthurian court, for they win out in both the faery testings. They stand out as exemplars who can restore the Faery Accord.

Underneath the Holy Grail myths lies the theme of the disobedience of Adam and Eve who eat of the fruit of the Tree of the Knowledge of Good and Evil, but beneath the Faery Grail of the Horn of Joy are Carados and Guinier who redeem human love from the taint of betrayal. In mystical Christian theology, the "happy fault of Adam" was redeemed by the coming of Christ; and the "Ave" of Mary, who assented fully to his birth through her body, redeems and reverses the "Eva" of disobedient Eve.

ARTHURIAN AND BIBLICAL CORRELATIVES OF SALVATION

	Faithless Pair	Testing Object	Faithful Pair
Arthurian:	Arthur & Guinevere	Drinking Horn	Carados & Guinier
Biblical:	Adam & Eve	Fruit of the Tree	Jesus & Mary

The Holy Grail myth, because of its fusion with the Christian tradition, leads the Arthurian legends to their ultimate conclusion: to the loss of the Round Table and the passing of Arthur. In their place is set an alternative quest leading to spiritual wisdom that prepares the way to heaven with the blessed, into communion with God through the Church.

The Faery Grail myth, based in a primordial understanding of the living Earth and using the Arthurian legend as its vehicle, leads to a very different outcome. The intermingling of human with faery creates an integrated world, reminding us of the renewing season's promise, wherein love and faithfulness bring trust. It offers a communion with all creatures within the earthly paradise of Faery.

RESTORING THE VOICES OF THE WELLS

But no matter how they searched
They were unable to find them;
Never voice could be heard
Nor maiden seen to emerge.[33]

Can the voices of the wells be finally and successfully restored? If we could hear them again, what would they say? What does the loss of the voices actually mean for our world? We have followed the quest of others who have sought to restore those voices, but can we ourselves do any better? Can we be enabled to envision things within a common, ancestral understanding, to hear the voice of the earth itself and behave as if the commonwealth of all mattered above all things?

On one level the loss of the voices of the wells signals the severing of the Faery Accord between humans and faeries, whereby those of different kinds and natures can meet together in the most basic common exchange of hospitality—what feeds, nourishes, and quenches our thirst, both of body and of spirit. On a deeper level, the yearning for Faery is not a narcissistic craving for nirvanic accomplishment after which we become perfect and pass out of life. It is an urgent requirement to be included within a perspective of the earthly paradise that exists outside of time, to enter a simple and tranquil unity in which every living being is equally respected as a child of the Earth. The goal of all spiritual enlightenment is to enter into a communion where the small individual is part of the greater and blessed whole.

It is when people fall out of the communion with the Faery Accord or with these revelations of spiritual wholeness, that acts of violence re-create the Dolorous Blow. Every time the Grail procession and the awful lamentation is witnessed by any visitor in *The Elucidation*—and we are told that this happens three times a day for three whole hours—an opportunity is provided for something to be resolved over and over. So, when Perceval and other knights neglect to ask the Grail question, "whom does the Grail serve?" or about the details of the procession and what they signify, they let slip a chance to heal what is amiss.

This same opportunity to halt the world's sorrow is happening every moment, in any region of the time-bound world. The opportunity to stop or question a harrowing event that is repeating and repeating may not occur to anyone who remains caught in a time-bound existence: but it is an opportunity offered to those whose quest takes them out of time into the precious present moment.

Perceval does eventually ask the right question and the finding of the court of the Rich Fisher and its wonders do their work, but this solution is not permanent. The unvarnished truth of the Grail myth is that the evil wrought of bad decisions recurs and recrudesces: it is not obliterated. Small errors become larger ones as time wears on, and the fabric of the worlds falls apart as the communion of the Faery Accord is forgotten or violated. Like many mythic narratives that polarize the creative and destructive powers against each other, *The Elucidation* relates the consequences of self-serving actions that forget to listen to the "voices of the wells," which continually are singing the vision of a world where our gifts of innate intelligence and common sense are bound by a love and compassion of all who are alive.

In whichever part of the many variant Grail stories we chose to look, we find the same signature of the seven branches of the story:

1. Once there was a wonderful and fertile time of peace.
2. Then a violent deed broke that original image so that this plenty was withdrawn.

3. The land was laid waste and evil things were abroad.

4. Echoes of the original fertility show themselves in the shape of the Grail hallows to different people.

5. The task of questers is to seek for the Grail and its accompanying hallows and to ask the all-important question that will interrupt the suffering caused by the violent deed that originated the Wasteland.

6. When the hallows are discovered and the question asked, this brings to a halt the suffering, restoring the Wasteland and life returns to peace and plenty.

7. Those who go on quest for the hallows rarely return to ordinary life but live in a withdrawn location . . . until the time of peace and plenty is again interrupted by a violent deed and the whole cycle begins again.[34]

The pattern of the Grail quest is thus an ongoing and recurring action happening at any moment: as Sallustius said, "myth is something that never happened and is happening all the time."[35] The cause of unheeded or violent actions upon the world cannot be healed, we are told, "as long as the world lasts."[36] The solution then is to step *outside of time* in order that the restoration can be made: precisely what the myth of *The Elucidation* does, empowering us to be active in situations that have become stalemated within time, by turning back time and returning to the quest for the original nourishment.

Restoring the voices of the wells is accomplished when we make attempts to return to the primal communion between the world of time and the world of eternity by listening and attending. Each quest for what is holy and healing may be as many branched for each individual as the guardianship of this story with its seven cloaks. We may go in one of many guises along the spiritual path, each following his or her path of the spectrum that illuminates and heals. We each have different paths to follow, but they are in service of the Grail that is served by us.

Wherever we live in the world, at whatever time and place, this myth is somewhere being worked out in one of its seven branches and you are part of it. If you chose to go on quest, then you will doubtless find those who previously went on quest, who are now occupying the place of the many Grail hermits, knights, ladies, and others who are ready to be the mentors, guides, and supporters of those who come next. When your quest is done, who knows what ancestral role you too will fulfill?

THE REAL FUNCTION OF *THE ELUCIDATION*

This leaves us to consider what is the true function of *The Elucidation*. This brief text—the shortest of all Grail stories—is one that many scholars have marked as unsatisfactory because it doesn't replicate the party line of the bigger, more impressive Grail texts. It fails to explain or elucidate easily. As a result, *The Elucidation* has been spoken of with slighting contempt or discarded impatiently as irrelevant to the main trajectory of the more important Grail corpus. Like the all-important cornerstone that was rejected, *The Elucidation* proves to be a text that we should never discard, since it is a compendium of them all.

In her own appreciation of the work of Grail scholar Jessie Weston, the Arthurian scholar Janet Grayson has suggested that *The Elucidation* is exactly what it proposes itself to be, a complete introduction to the Grail myths:

> If it be the record of an insult offered by a local chieftain to a priestess or these rites, in consequence of which they were no longer openly celebrated in that land . . . would that not be the logical introduction to the tale of one who found or knew not what he had found?[37]

Like the nesting boxes of Tolkien's own world of Middle Earth, in which the *Hobbit* and the *Lord of the Rings* are contained within the even bigger framework of the *Silmarillion* so, too, the many Grail variants and continuations in their proliferation are somehow contained within the seemingly tiny text of *The Elucidation*.

This very sense of "little bigness"—wherein something apparently small contains something absolutely universal—is the uncanny but unmistakable mark of a true myth, and is a sign that we are involved with faery lore since, in the otherworld, time and space become of little account when we enter into the heart of the myth. As in the Hindu myths, where Yasoda, seeing her baby Krishna eating clay, looks into her son's mouth to remove it and suddenly views the whole universe within his mouth, we too can look into *The Elucidation* with the same awe and acknowledge that there are "millions of skies" within it.[38]

Collapsed into a mere 484 lines, the whole Grail myth is encompassed within its fragile but adamantine frame in truly mind-shattering ways. Containing the whole myth, *The Elucidation* requires us to hold in the same story, two forms or appearances of the Grail, in an embrace of total and accepting gnosis, wherein dichotomies collapse under an appreciation of the whole picture. As Christ says in the Gospel of Thomas,

> When you make the two one, and when you make the inside like the outside and the outside like the inside, and the above like the below. And when you make the male and the female one and the same, then will you enter the Kingdom.[39]

The kingdom as presented in the Grail legends is full of visions of strange and wondrous matters. How were these understood and received by the questers? For them, the world was already set into Christian mode whereby wonders could only be "approved and Christian" or "forbidden and non-Christian." Despite this, *The Elucidation* persists in giving us two different visions of the Grail—from both earlier and later perspectives—and still talking about them both in the same way.

What arises within mythic imagination is experienced as being "entirely true": it is only when that same understanding is commandeered by some group or other as being "the only true vision" that we have division. In truth, there is no division in what we experience and how it really is.

Like the krater or mixing bowl of creation that is eulogized in the

Corpus Hermeticum in the quotation at the head of this chapter, whoever is drawn to the Grail finally becomes immersed in it. Such is the power of the Grail itself that, wherever or however we experience it, the Grail is sent for all. It does not belong to any one authorized body or specialized person. Like the Grail story itself that still remains outside the compass of canonical theology, the Grail is an unconditional visitant to anyone who seeks to enter into a state of unity.

Within *The Elucidation,* the parallel traditions of the Faery and Holy Grails sit side by side. Dismissed as a mere afterthought to the Grail myth, this short poem contains the synthesis of the whole Grail myth, honoring both sides of the earlier and later traditions that here meet together, as the storyteller relates:

> *The good that it served will openly*
> *Be taught to all people.*[40]

The task of reconciling the human and faery worlds, and the task of healing the breach between the time-bound world and the timelessness of the Grail realm are not contradictory, but complementary. They each lead us to consider the duties of the human state and our relationship with our original wholeness and holiness—these words have the same meaning, although our dualistic world applies them differently. *The Elucidation* brings us face to face with the consequences of our actions, the outcome of human greed upon the universe, but it also gives us methods of reconciliation and healing. If we follow the way of our quest, the world will no longer be Wasteland.

This book has been but a brief peering through the wicket gate into the deeper mysteries of the Grail, in which we have lifted the curtain a little for you to look inside. Throughout *The Elucidation* we are given the promise that "all people" will know or be told about its mysteries. Well, we have played our part and the story is with you, now. Be aware that the secrets of the Grail that have been hidden and are now revealed only open in the deep places of the ancient heart and in the mythic imagination. From its depths, its teachings come forth and can nourish the spirit, just as the Maidens of the Wells originally served the wayfarers in the times before King Arthur. In the words of this allusive text,

> *adventures will come,*
> *To those . . . who will seek,*
> *What has never been found*
> *In this country, nor told before.*[41]

May your own quest lead you home to the holy earth!

Envoi

> *Take these, O holy Earth,*
> *take those, all honored one,*
> *who are to be the mother of all things,*
> *and hereafter may you lack nothing!*[42]

APPENDIX

THE ELUCIDATION
IN VERSE

his version of *The Elucidation* is offered so that the reader might have a sense of the French original: put into verse by Caitlín Matthews, please note that it is merely a reading version that follows the general scansion and rhyme scheme of the original. For an exact line by line translation see pages 33–59.

> Now to begin our noble tale,
> A high romance without fail:
> Most pleasing story that ever was told—
> It is the Graal, for none of old,
>
> 5   Should tell the secret nor yet sing;
> Because revealed would be such thing,
> The story shown before all was said,
> That none should boast that he had read,
>
> At fault he'd be, and far astray,
> 10   Just as the sages to us say,
> So, simply now we'll pass it by.
> For if Master Blihis did not lie,
>
> Of its secret, none should tell,
> So listen, hear how it befell,

15 And you will learn by every word
    The most pleasing story ever heard.

    Seven guardians will be unfurled,
    Whose rule governs throughout the world
    Every good story heard or told,
20 As these writings will unfold.

    Who these seven guardians will be,
    How their deeds will turn the key,
    For never before to you was told
    This story which to you unfolds.

25 Great noise and rumor, I you tell,
    How and why destruction fell
    Upon Logres, that rich land,
    Many once knew on every hand.

    The kingdom turned to mighty doubt,
30 The land lay dead and emptied out,
    Not worth two nuts, to value come;
    The voices of the wells fell dumb.

    As for the maidens who dwelt inside,
    By them was served on every side,
35 All those who strayed upon the road
    By night or day, from their abode.

    If thirst or hunger upon him smote,
    The traveler need only change his route,
    Towards the wells, where he might ask
40 Whatever he, in plate or flask,

    Of finest vittles that pleased him best
    That might be given at his bequest,
    Provided he ask in gentle wise.
    Then from hence there would arise,

45   A maiden serving from the well,
He could not ask a sweeter belle—
A cup of gold within her hand,
Meats, pies, and bread, I understand.

Another maiden to serve his wish,
50   Bringing a napkin and a dish
Of gold and silver in which was brought,
The meal and drink that he had sought.

Whoever arrived to take a meal
At well-side, all were greeted well.
55   And if the food did not quite suit,
Then other meals were brought, to boot.

All as desired, each had his wish,
With joy and plenty in cup and dish.
And so, together, the maidens served,
60   With joy and gladness all who turned

Out of their way, to seek and greet,
Who came there to the wells to eat.
King Amangons broke that custom's deed,
Violating them, that cowardly thief;

65   Others, with violent hands rending,
Took their example from their king,
Whose duty should have been to guard,
Than break their peace, with heart so hard.

With violation he did take
70   A maiden's flower with his rape,
He took away her golden cup,
Carrying it and the maiden off.

Ever after he made it him to serve.
From this, much ill did issue forth;

75   No maiden from the wells served more
      Nor from the well came as before,

      Not for any traveler who came by,
      Who might upon the maidens cry.
      Amangons's men copied his deed.
80   God! Why was there not then seen

      Some honorable man upon that scene?
      When Amangons, of frightful mien,
      Raped the maidens of the well,
      Whichever one he found *plus belle.*

85   His followers raped them, in his way
      Taking their golden cups away.
      Hence, from those wells came not again
      Maidens to serve the traveling men;

      Most wisely, this you should know,
90   Sir, whyfor it happened so:
      The land sunk down into a decline,
      Its king to a bad end came, in time,

      And all the others after him,
      Who followed him down pathways dim.
95   Waste was the kingdom, empty, thrawn,
      No wells, no tree in leaf was born,

      The meadowlands their flowers did lack,
      And every waterway died back;
      Nor could be found for ever after,
100   The eminent court of the Rich Fisher,

      Which had enriched the country wide
      With gold and silver, furs so fine,
      With rich brocades and watered silk,
      With meat and all habiliment;

105 With falcons swift and merlins small,
Goshawks, and birds of prey, besides.
Of old, when that court could be found
There was throughout that country round

Riches and plenty, so great store,
110 As I have hereto named before,
Wondrous it was, who saw that wealth,
Both rich and poor, when once was health.

But lost were all these riches fine.
In Logres realm, as men opine,
115 Were all the riches of renown.
The knights that served the Table Round

Lived in the time of Arthur, king;
Since when, no greater have been seen.
These goodly knights who fought all wrong,
120 So worthily, so proud, so strong,

So vigorously in adventure,
That, soon as they had heard it, sure,
The story of how this tale befell,
They vowed they would restore the wells.

125 Together swearing, they would find,
And in their keeping, justly kind,
The maidens who had served the ways,
And the cups they carried, in those days;

They swore they'd smite the lineage
130 Of all those men who'd wrought damage,
All who had stopped them coming forth
Of the wells, whence they came no more.

If they could take one man of them,
They'd string him up or cut him down.

135 They prayed, gave alms, and even more,
Prayed God, that he would yet restore

The wells, before the custom burst,
Exactly as they'd been at first.
And for the honor they would make,
140 Requesting service for their sake.

Alas, no matter where they went,
They could not find where they'd been sent;
And never after was voice heard,
Nor ever maiden did emerge.

145 But such adventures did they find,
That many marveled in their mind.
For in the forest, wandering free
Maidens of such great beauty—

And knights within their company,
150 Well-armed upon their destriers,
Together where the maidens rode;
Ready to fight upon the road,

Any who sought to steal them away;
Many a knight was killed upon the way.
155 Because of the maidens, I understand,
Were battles waged across the land.

King Arthur, in truth, for all his might,
Could not help losing many a knight,
But many he gained, and good ones, too,
160 As these stories here will show.

The first knight to drop his sword—
Blihis Bleheris was he called;
Conquered he was by Sir Gawain,
By his prowess, he showed full plain.

165   To Arthur, king, was this knight sent,
And to his court he swiftly went.
He mounted up without delay,
But no one knew him on the way,

Nor was his face known to the king.
170   But such good stories did he sing,
That no one listening fell asleep,
Such stories live in memory's keep!

The court demanded then to know
About the maidens who with them rode,
175   Through the forest; they'd not been there,
So rightly demanded who they were,

Asking about them, night and day,
Listening close what he might say,
And willingly to learn what more,
180   They stayed awake to know the lore

Of maidens fair, and worthy knights,
Questioning what were their rights.
Bleheris said, "Your mighty wonder
Concerning the maidens that with us wander,

185   Ranging throughout the forest wide,
You ask of me, why do they ride,
And what the country of their birth.
And truly now I'll tell you first:

We all were of the maidens born,
190   Those beauteous ones of ancient dawn,
That King Amangons did enforce.
Which harm will never, ever be

Made good until the world's last day."
Knights of the Table Round did pray,

195   That by courtesy and high honor,
        By their prowess and their vigor,

        They vowed by force that they would free
        The wells, restoring them completely,
        These knights and worthy men.
200   "The truth I'd like to tell you then:

        All we who travel all together,
        Knights, maidens too, in every weather,
        Who wander far about this land,
        Through forests far, within one band,

205   Know we must wander ever so,
        Until, God help, we find and know
        The court from which all joy will rise,
        By which the land will be made bright.

        Your own adventures will arrive,
210   To all of you who'll quest and strive,
        To find what has been never found,
        Within this land, nor told around."

        Great gladness made they everyone,
        To hear the tale that he had spun.
215   Then right away, and in agreement,
        They held a mighty parliament,

        Those goodly knights of Arthur's court,
        Each of them his place had fought;
        They quested far with mighty strength
220   The Rich Fisher's court to find at length,

        For he knew magic, necromancy,
        And he could shapeshift, at his own fancy,
        Some sought him far under one guise,
        Others in yet another wise.

225 Sir Gawain to the court he came
     In that time of Arthur's reign.
     He found that court, beyond the waste,
     As we will tell in the right place.

     The joy he found, we will record,
230 By which all realms were then restored.
     But first before him in that place,
     A gentle knight of youthful face,

     Most young and of a tender age;
     Yet none more strong within his gage
235 Throughout the world could ever be found.
     He came then to the Table Round,

     The youthful knight of whom I speak,
     Whose prowess overpassed the peak
     Of all knighthood's most noble fountain,
240 By the eminence of a mountain.

     Thought at first of low degree,
     Then most noble, finally,
     He sought throughout that mighty land
     —As one of many, you understand.

245 It was he who found it, verily,
     As many of you now agree:
     The Welshman, Perceval, the same,
     Who questioned, asking the Graal by name,

     Whom it did serve, but failed to ask,
250 Why bled the lance—neglectful task—
     Nor when he saw it, why the sword
     Had one-half blade within that court,

     While on a bier the other half lay,
     On the dead body, cold as clay,

255 Nor of the vanishing in that hall.
     But to you now, I tell you all,

     That knight asked, whose the body was,
     Upon the bier, that sorry corpse,
     And also about the silver cross,
260 That went before, to mark the loss.

     Three times, three hours, every day,
     Those lamentations scratched the sky,
     No man so hardy who could bear
     Nor be not frightened by such care.

265 Four censers round it there did hang,
     Four candelabra in their rank,
     About the corners of the bier,
     When that service did appear.

     Then all the crying abruptly ceased,
270 And vanished all before the feast.
     And that great hall so vast and wide,
     Fearfully emptied on every side.

     Down fell the blood in steady stream,
     From a vase upon the lance, it seemed,
275 Issuing through a silver spout.
     The people returned, who'd been without,

     Into the palace, with the knights.
     These were the finest meals, by right,
     Of any in the world's renown.
280 Then out there came, wearing his crown,

     The king whom none had known before;
     From a chamber, clothed as never you saw,
     In noble vesture, all adorned,
     Of workmanship not seen before,

285 His robe and his rich adornments,
   So great his gorgeous habiliments;
   A ring upon his hand he'd placed,
   His sleeves so long were tightly laced,

   A golden circlet round his brows,
290 Whose stones were worth a thousand pounds,
   A buckled belt about his waist,
   No finer man within that place,

   I challenge you far to find.
   Many might puzzle in their minds
295 If in the day they'd seen him led:
   —A fisherman they would have said.

   Soon as the king was sitting down,
   Was seen at every table around,
   The seated knights within that hall,
300 Then bread was given to them all.

   Before them each their wine was set,
   In gold and silver goblets let.
   Then came the vessel of the Graal,
   No servant bore it, nor seneschal;

305 Alone it came from out a room,
   And many were properly served full soon,
   In golden dishes set before,
   Each worth a treasury's mighty store.

   The first dish set before the king,
310 Then afterwards was everything
   Served to the others who sat there;
   Never were seen such marvels rare,

   As meals were set before each one,
   That food whose quality cannot be sung.

315   At length a mighty marvel came,
         For which none could prepare the same.

         Of it now, I cannot speak,
         For Perceval soon must tell of it
         Within the middle of this tale.
320   Great villainy and shame, I rail,

         To break so good a story up
         Before it ends: it's too abrupt.
         But when those good knights will arrive,
         Who found the Fisher's court three times,

325   Then may be heard, and point by point,
         Without dissembling, nor out of joint,
         The truth of whom these wells do serve,
         The names of the knights and which they were,

         And why and how it served, the Graal,
330   The bleeding of the lance as well.
         I'll tell you truly, without fear,
         What there was upon the bier,

         That sword. I'll tell you everything,
         I will not flinch, omit nothing—
335   The vanishing and lamentation,
         All will be told in every nation,

         People all will hear it told,
         How this story will unfold.
         Listeners all, I'll truly sound,
340   How seven times that court was found,

         In the seven cloaks of the tale;
         The meaning, I'll show without fail.
         In these seven branches, know,
         Each one a guardian who will show;

345   Each of these guardians will you tell,
The places where the court befell;
Before, these things could not be told;
Now in these writings, I unfold.

I'll name these guardians, every one;
350   Omitting nothing from my song,
Their names, descriptions I will tell,
Beginning to end, as it befell.

The seventh branch, that pleases most,
About the lance of ancient boast,
355   With which Longinus struck the heart
Of the Holy King, with piercing dart.

The sixth branch, now I will reveal,
About the great strife of the toil.
The fifth branch now, I tell in turn,
360   Of Huden's loss, whose anger burns.

The fourth, the stories of the Swan;
Who came at first to Glamorgan;
No coward he who came ashore,
The dead knight that the swan boat bore.

365   The next, the third, tells of the hawk
Which caused Castrars to greatly balk;
Pecorins, son of King Amangons,
Upon his forehead bore the wound.

Unto you all, I've named the third.
370   The second is not ever heard
In good storytellers' relation:
That's the tale of the Great Lamentation,

How Lancelot du Lac came at last
To the point, his great strength lost.

375   And the last story, after all:
      Since I have summoned to recall.

      To you all, I must relate
      You'll not hear me extenuate—
      It is the Adventure of the Shield:
380   No better story will you yield.

      These seven are the natural
      Stories, proceeding from the Graal.
      This adventure bought, I will relate,
      The Joy, whence lands repopulate,

385   After the mighty destruction.
      Through these stories' conduction,
      Both court and Graal were truly found,
      And all the realm with life abound.

      So those streams that ceased to flow,
390   The fountains that once appeared so
      But which had come to sudden cease—
      Now through the meadows ran with ease.

      Then the fields came lush with green,
      The woods yet leafier were seen
395   On the day the court was found,
      Where, everywhere throughout the land,

      The forests flourished wide and great,
      So beautifully, as to create
      Much marvel in every band
400   Who traveled far throughout the land.

      Then came there back a people strange,
      Of great ill-will against us ranged,
      Forth from the wells they did emerge,
      Unknown to all, they were a scourge.

405 Castles they built and cities tall,
Towns and strongholds for their hall,
And for the damsels they had built
The Castle of Maidens, with them filled;

The Perilous Bridge they also made,
410 The Castle of Pride they then upraised.
For power and to uphold their border,
For themselves they created an order

Of the Rich Company, they were the peers,
So in their pride they did appear,
415 In contempt of the Table Round;
And all awaited a great showdown.

Each had his lady love inside;
And over a fine life did preside.
Three hundred and sixty-six were they
420 Who kept each castle in that way;

Each castle had its own command,
With twenty knights to be its band,
No less a company than this:
In thousands seven, in hundreds six,

425 Plus twenty and six by four more times.
And if you would gainsay these crimes,
Know well, if you look through the world,
No such company will you find unfurled.

Throughout the country then they rode,
430 On King Arthur's realm, a war they sowed.
The good knight rode out from the court,
To test them all, to put at nought;

If they should capture Arthur's men,
Without parole, they did them pen.

435 King Arthur longed himself to go,
To ravage the castle and beat his foe;

Those who hated him did assail,
At every point, they did not fail;
They kept him at war, without any rest,
440 So none could go or seek on quest.

And then the warfare grew so great,
Four years it lasted, without abate,
Or so the stories do us tell;
Like he who wrote this book as well.

445 And so, I tell you, one by one.
I'd like to show, now I've begun,
In what way the Graal did serve—
Because this service was preserved

By a good master, and to me shown.
450 Till now it has been hidden, but known.
Now will that benefit, openly
Be taught to all people, sociably.

Believe, from me you have heard true,
455 About King Arthur, I tell to you:
It was four years he fought that war
Against these peers he did abhor.

But finally there came an end:
No man nor neighbor, not yet friend,
Who did not finally submit,
460 And come, by force or agreement,

Within one bond of peace;
But know you well, as all agree,
Some named and shamed;
Not the king's honor, not his, the blame.

465   Abandoned they within that day,
        Their court: the Rich Peers went to play,
        Hidden within the forest dark,
        All those who would put up their hawk,

        Following the river's course along;
470   Such goodly folk, like in a song,
        Seducing ladies by their charm,
        The others preparing to them harm.

        In forest's depths they took their ease,
        Through winter's blast and summer's breeze.
475   Now Chrétien will begin to tell
        This parable that you know well,

        These efforts won't have been in vain,
        For Chrétien labored long in pain,
        To put into verse this tale's account,
480   By order of his grace, the count,

        For every royal court and hall,
        To know the story of the Graal,
        The book of which the count was giver.
        Pray now that Chrétien does deliver!

NOTES

Texts translated by Caitlín Matthews are marked "trans. CM."

INTRODUCTION.
REVEALING AN UNKNOWN GRAIL STORY

1. Meyer and Robinson, *Nag Hammadi Scriptures.*
2. Thompson, *The Elucidation.*
3. *The Elucidation,* 192–93. References are to lines.
4. Jones, *In Parenthesis.*
5. Chrétien de Troyes, *Perceval, ou le Conte du Graal,* 6204–9, trans. CM. References are to lines.
6. Brown, *The Origin of the Grail Legend.*
7. Baigent, Leigh, and Lincoln, *Holy Blood, Holy Grail.*
8. Steadman-Jones, Pegler, and Matthews, *The Nanteos Grail.*
9. Sallustius, *Concerning the Gods and the Universe,* xliii.
10. Chrétien de Troyes, *Perceval, ou le Conte du Graal,* 1–7, trans. CM.
11. *The Elucidation,* 445–52.

CHAPTER 1. THE STORY OF THE GRAIL

1. Bryant, *Perlesvaus.*
2. Matarasso, *The Quest of the Holy Grail.*
3. Bogdanow, "Robert de Boron's Vision of Arthurian History," 19–52.
4. Izquerdo, "The Gospel of Nicodemus."
5. James, trans., *The Apocryphal New Testament,* 96–145.
6. Izquerdo, "The Gospel of Nicodemus."
7. Cabaniss, "Joseph of Arimathea."
8. Matthews, J., "The Grail before the Grail."

9. Saint Augustine, *Confessions* 6.3.

10. Bryant, *Complete Story of the Grail,* 214.

11. La Tour Landry, *The Book of the Knight.*

12. Matthews, J., *The Grail: A Secret History.*

13. Bryant, *The Complete Story of the Grail,* 273.

14. De Boron, *Merlin and the Grail.*

15. Von Eschenbach, *Parzival, a Knightly Epic.*

16. Malory, *Le Morte d'Arthur.*

17. Weinraub, *Chrétien's Jewish Grail.*

CHAPTER 2. *THE ELUCIDATION OF THE GRAIL*

1. Bryant, *The Complete Story of the Grail,* 344–45.

2. *The Elucidation,* 70.

3. Matthews, J., and Knight, *Temples of the Grail.*

4. Chrétien de Troyes, *Arthurian Romances,* lines 61–68.

CHAPTER 3. THE STORYTELLER AND SEVEN CLOAKS OF THE STORY

1. *The Elucidation,* 17–19.

2. Hindman, *Sealed in Parchment.*

3. *The Elucidation,* 95–98.

4. *The Elucidation,* 387–97.

5. *The Elucidation,* 17820–32; Roach and Ivy, *First Continuation,* trans. CM.

6. *The Elucidation,* 129–30.

7. *The Elucidation,* 195–98.

8. *The Elucidation,* 207–8.

9. *The Elucidation,* 170–72, 186, 180–82.

10. Matthews, C., *Healing the Ancestral Communion.*

11. Weston, *The Legend of Sir Perceval.*

12. Bryant, *The Complete Story of the Grail.*

13. Gerald of Wales, *Description of Wales,* 252.

14. Brugger, "Bliocadrin," in *Medieval Studies,* 153.

15. Weston, *The Legend of Sir Perceval,* 289.

16. Hahn, *Sir Gawain: Eleven Romances and Tales.*

17. Matthews and Matthews, *Encyclopedia of Celtic Wisdom.*

18. Matthews, C., "The Voices of the Wells."

19. Chrétien de Troyes, *Erec and Enid,* trans. CM.

20. Matthews, C., *Mabon and the Guardians of Celtic Britain.*

21. Bullock-Davies, *Professional Interpreters;* Kinsoshita, *Medieval Boundaries.*

22. Matthews, C., "The Voices of the Wells."

23. Corley, *The Second Continuation.*

24. Duggan, *The Romances of Chrétien de Troyes,* 187.

25. *The Elucidation,* 4–9.

26. Jacobs, *Celtic Fairy Tales.*

27. *The Elucidation,* 445–52.

28. Weston, *From Ritual to Romance,* 138.

29. Weston, *From Ritual to Romance,* 138.

30. *The Elucidation,* 315–22.

31. Hindman, *Sealed in Parchment.*

32. *The Elucidation,* 353–57.

33. *The Elucidation,* 353–56.

34. Morris, *Cursor mundi: A Northumbrian Poem of the XIVth Century,* lines 16834ff, trans. CM.

35. Lacy, *The Lancelot-Grail,* vol. 1, 51.

36. Corley, *The Second Continuation.*

37. Corley, *The Second Continuation.*

38. Von Eschenbach, *Parzival, a Knightly Epic,* chapter 9.

39. Matthews, C., Afterword to *The Holy Grail and the Eucharist.*

40. Matthews, C., *The Holy Grail and the Eucharist,* Afterword.

41. *The Elucidation,* 273–75.

42. Roach, *The Didot Perceval,* 17402–10.

43. Chrétien de Troyes, *Perceval: The Story of the Grail,* 196.

44. Chrétien de Troyes, *Perceval, The Story of the Grail,* 66.

45. Weston, *The Legend of Sir Perceval;* J. Matthews, *Sir Gawain: Knight of the Goddess.*

46. Pollmann, *Chrétien de Troyes und der Conte del Graal.*

47. *The Elucidation,* 358–59.

48. Bryant, *Complete Story of the Grail,* 218.

49. Matthews and Matthews, *King Arthur: One Hero, Many Faces.*

50. Willams, *Annales Cambriae.*

51. Matthews, C., *King Arthur's Raid on the Underworld.*

52. Torroella, *La Faula.*

53. Chrétien de Troyes, *Perceval: The Story of the Grail,* 17.

54. Chrétien de Troyes, *Perceval, The Story of the Grail,* 270.

55. *The Elucidation,* 359–60.

56. Malory, *Le Morte d'Arthur.*

57. Chrétien de Troyes, *Perceval: The Story of the Grail,* 140, 176.

58. Weston, *Sir Gawain at the Grail Castle.*

59. Weston, *Sir Gawain at the Grail Castle.*

60. Bryant, *Complete Story of the Grail,* 180–83.

61. *The Elucidation,* 361–64.

62. *The Elucidation,* 70.

63. Chrétien de Troyes, *Arthurian Romances,* verse 32130.

64. *The Elucidation,* 365–69.

65. *The Elucidation,* 225–30.

66. Weston, *Sir Gawain and the Lady of Lys,* 286.

67. Matthews, J., *Sir Gawain: Knight of the Goddess.*

68. Von dem Türlin, *The Crown.*

69. Genesis 4:9–17.

70. Gaffney, *Gnostic Secrets of the Naasenes,* 45–47.

71. Gaffney, *Gnostic Secrets of the Naasenes,* 214.

72. *The Elucidation,* 370–74.

73. Von Zatzikhoven, *Lanzelet.*

74. Loomis, *Celtic Myth and Arthurian Romance.*

75. Chrétien de Troyes, *Arthurian Romances,* line 216.

76. Chrétien de Troyes, *Arthurian Romances,* lines 285–86.

77. Lachet, *Sone de Nansay.*

78. *The Elucidation,* 262–64.

79. *The Elucidation,* 375–80.

80. Matarasso, *The Quest of the Holy Grail.*

81. *The Elucidation,* 381–82.

82. Magill, "Part 1 of the *Voeux du Paon* by Jacques de Longuyon."

83. Skeels, *The Romance of Perceval in Prose.*

CHAPTER 4. THE MAIDENS OF THE WELLS AND THE FAERY ACCORD

1. Von Zatzikhoven, *Lanzelet;* Layamon, *The Arthurian Section of Layamon's Brut.*

2. Matthews, J., *The Grail: A Secret History.*

3. Harf-Lancner, *Les Fées au Moyen Age.*

4. Duffy, *The Erotic World of Fairy.*

5. Gervase of Tilbury, *Otia Imperialia.*

6. Gervase of Tilbury, *Otia Imperialia.*

7. Knight, *The Book of Melusine of Lusignan.*

8. Marie de France, *French Medieval Romances.*

9. Matthews and Matthews, *Ladies of the Lake.*

10. *Third Continuation,* trans. CM.

11. Conlee, *The Prose Merlin.*

12. *The Elucidation,* 35–57.

13. Gervase of Tilbury, *Otia Imperialia,* chapter 60, trans. CM.

14. Büsching, "Das Oldenburger Horn," 380–83.

15. Stokes and Windisch, *Irische Texte,* trans. CM (italics added).

16. Gervase of Tilbury, *Otia Imperialia.*

17. Matthews and Matthews, *Encyclopedia of Celtic Wisdom,* 408ff.

18. Koble, *Le Lai du Cor.*

19. Burgess and Brook, *French Arthurian Literature.*

20. *The Elucidation,* 127–36; Koble, *Le Lai du Cor,* trans. CM.

21. *The Elucidation,* 383–86.

22. *The Elucidation,* 414.

23. *The Elucidation,* 582.

24. Von dem Türlin, *The Crown.*

25. *The Mabinogion.*

26. *The Elucidation,* 3–10; Matthews, C., *King Arthur's Raid on the Underworld.*

27. Matthews, J., *At the Table of the Grail.*

28. Bromwich, *Trioedd Ynys Prydein.*

29. Bromwich, *Trioedd Ynys Prydein.*

30. *The Elucidation,* 205–6.

CHAPTER 5. IN THE LAND OF WOMEN

1. Matthews, C., *The Spells of Women.*

2. Matthews, C., *The Spells of Women;* Pomponius Mela, *De Situ Orbis* 3.6, trans. CM.

3. Pomponius Mela, *De Situ Orbis* 3.6, trans. CM; Strabo, *Geography* 4.4, 4.6, trans. CM.

4. Matthews, C., *Celtic Book of the Dead.*

5. Harf-Lancner, *Les Fées au Moyen Age.*

6. *The Mabinogion.*

7. Matthews, C., *King Arthur's Raid on the Underworld,* 125.

8. *The Elucidation,* 405–10.

9. Bryant, *Complete Story of the Grail,* 61.

10. Bryant, *Complete Story of the Grail,* 57–76.

11. Harward, *The Dwarfs of Arthurian Romance,* 8.

12. *The Mabinogion,* 248.

13. *The Mabinogion,* 249.

14. *The Mabinogion,* 249.

15. Gowans, *Am Bròn Binn.*

16. Carmichael, *Carmina Gadelica,* vol. 2, from an unknown singer in 1866, the wife of a schoolmaster in North Uist, who had it from the singing of her mother, trans. CM.

17. Isidore of Seville, *The Etymologies,* 199.

18. Kirk, *Secret Commonwealth.*

19. Harward, *The Dwarfs of Arthurian Romance,* 41.

20. Saint Augustine, *City of God,* 3, 14.

21. Saint Thomas Aquinas, *Summa Theologiae,* Q. 65, Art 7, obj. 3.

22. Carmichael, *Carmina Gadelica,* 2:252–53, 1972.

23. Newstead, *Bran the Blessed,* cf. 122ff.

24. Weingartner, *Graelent and Guingamor.*

25. Virgil, *Aeneid,* 6:893–98.

26. Best and Bergin, *Lebor na h'Uidre,* 302–4.

27. Chrétien de Troyes, *Arthurian Romances,* line 26.

28. Baring-Gould, *Life of St. Gildas.*

29. Chrétien de Troyes, *Arthurian Romances.*

30. Roach, *The Didot Perceval,* 218855–56, trans. CM.

31. Newstead, *Bran the Blessed.*

32. Roach, *The Didot Perceval,* 18363–74, trans. CM.

33. Roach, *The Didot Perceval,* 18487–514.

34. Roach, *The Didot Perceval,* 19400.

35. Roach, *The Didot Perceval,* 19564–77.

36. *Pwyll Prince of Dyfed,* in *The Mabinogion.*

CHAPTER 6. GRAIL KINGS AND ANTI-KINGS

1. Wolfram von Eschenbach, *Parzival;* Peredur in *The Mabinogion;* Brugger, "Bliocadrin."

2. Chrétien de Troyes, *Perceval: The Story of the Grail,* 214.

3. Chrétien de Troyes, *Perceval, The Story of the Grail,* 256–57.

4. De Boron, *Merlin and the Grail,* 22.

5. De Boron, *Merlin and the Grail,* 35.

6. De Boron, *Merlin and the Grail,* 36.

7. De Boron, *Merlin and the Grail,* 42.

8. De Boron, *Merlin and the Grail,* 94.

9. De Boron, *Merlin and the Grail,* 113.

10. De Boron, *Merlin and the Grail,* 147.

11. Von Eschenbach, *Parzival, a Knightly Epic,* chapter 9.

12. Weston, *Sir Gawain at the Grail Castle.*

13. Weston, *Sir Gawain at the Grail Castle.*

14. Chrétien de Troyes, *Perceval: The Story of the Grail,* 180.

15. Spaan, "The Otherworld in Early Irish Literature."

16. Von Eschenbach, *Parzival,* 312–13.

17. Malory, *Le Morte d'Arthur,* book 2, chap. 15.

18. Matarasso, *The Quest of the Holy Grail.*

19. Chrétien de Troyes, *Perceval: The Story of the Grail,* 38.

20. Bryant, *Complete Story of the Grail,* 479.

21. Chrétien de Troyes, *Perceval: The Story of the Grail,* 213.

22. Malory, *Le Morte d'Arthur,* book 3, chap. 15.

23. Matthews and Matthews, *Taliesin: The Last Celtic Shaman.*

24. Chrétien de Troyes, *Arthurian Romances,* verses 318–1726.

25. Beaujeu, *Le Bel Inconnu.*

26. Houdenc, *Meraugis de la Portugeis,* verse 2232.

27. Houdenc, verse 4342

28. Lachet, *Sone de Nansay.*

29. Arthur and Corbett, *The Knight of the Two Swords.*

30. Chrétien de Troyes, *Perceval: The Story of the Grail,* 244, verse 898.

31. Chrétien de Troyes, *Perceval, The Story of the Grail,* verses 38165–931.

32. Bryant, *Complete Story of the Grail,* 506.

33. Bryant, *Perceforest,* 44–45.

34. *The Elucidation,* 92–94.

35. Bryant, *Perceforest,* 68.

36. Bryant, *Perceforest,* 46.

37. St. Matthew 13:30.

38. Best and Bergin, *Lebor na h'Uidre.*

CHAPTER 7. THE CAUSES AND CONSEQUENCES OF THE WASTELAND

1. Chrétien de Troyes, *Perceval: The Story of the Grail,* 39.

2. Chrétien de Troyes, *Perceval, The Story of the Grail,* 51.

3. Bryant, *Complete Story of the Grail,* 210.

4. Chrétien de Troyes, *Perceval, or the Story of the Grail,* 76.

5. Bryant, *Complete Story of the Grail*, 61.

6. Chrétien de Troyes, *Perceval, or the Story of the Grail*, 105.

7. *The Elucidation*, 92–94.

8. Byrne, *Irish* Kings and *High Kings*.

9. Spaan, "The Otherworld in Early Irish Literature," trans. CM.

10. Macalister, *Echtra an mhadra Mhaoil*.

11. Cross and Slover, *Ancient Irish Tales*.

12. Malory, *Le Morte d'Arthur*, book 8.

13. Chrétien de Troyes, *Perceval, or the Story of the Grail*, 37.

14. *Lancelot-Grail*, vol. 3, ep. 149, p. 164.

15. Chrétien de Troyes, *Perceval, ou le Conte du Graal*, 6022–29, trans. CM.

16. *The Elucidation*, 99–115.

17. Macalister, *Echtra an mhadra Mhaoil*.

18. *The Elucidation*, 248–55.

19. *The Elucidation*, 219–24.

20. Von dem Türlin, *The Crown*, lines 13004 et seq.

21. Von dem Türlin, *The Crown*, lines 13183–86.

22. Matthews, C., *King Arthur's Raid on the Underworld*.

23. *The Mabinogion*, 40.

24. *The Mabinogion*, 45.

25. Matthews, J., *At the Table of the Grail*.

26. *The Mabinogion*, 57.

27. *The Mabinogion*, 155.

28. *The Elucidation*, 300–14.

29. Roach, *The Didot Perceval*, 17348–60, trans. CM.

30. Saint John 19:36.

31. Matthews, C., *King Arthur's Raid on the Underworld*, 2008.

32. *The Mabinogion*, 39–40.

33. Matthews, C., *King Arthur's Raid on the Underworld*, 2008, ll. 13–17.

34. Bromwich, *Trioedd Ynys Prydein*, 95.

35. Malory, *Le Morte d'Arthur*, book 7.

36. Vermaseren, *Cybele and Attis*.

37. Matthews, J., "The Grail before the Grail."

38. Genesis 18:1–15.

39. Matthews, C., *King Arthur's Raid on the Underworld*.

40. Matthews, C., *Sophia: Goddess of Wisdom*.

41. Geoffrey of Monmouth, *Vita Merlini*.

42. Chrétien de Troyes, *Perceval: The Story of the Grail*, 130.

43. *The Elucidation,* 30–31.
44. *The Mabinogion,* 96.
45. Matthews, J., *At the Table of the Grail.*
46. *The Mabinogion,* 56.
47. *The Elucidation,* 402–4.
48. *The Elucidation,* 426–28.
49. Lachet, *Sone de Nansay.*
50. *The Elucidation,* 401–16.
51. *The Elucidation,* 405–10.
52. *The Elucidation,* 417–18.
53. Bromwich, *Trioedd Ynys Prydein,* 90–93 (triad 36).
54. *The Mabinogion,* 93.
55. *The Mabinogion,* 93.
56. Bromwich, *Trioedd Ynys Prydein,* 92.
57. *The Elucidation,* 32–33.
58. *The Elucidation,* 141–44.
59. Hopkins, "Gods Grandeur," in *The Major Works.*
60. Matthews, C., *Sophia: Goddess of Wisdom.*
61. "Life of Adam and Eve," verse 2. Gospel of Nicodemus.
62. "Life of Adam and Eve," verse 2.
63. "Life of Adam and Eve," verse 3.
64. "Life of Adam and Eve," verse 4.
65. Charles, "Apocalypse Mosis," chapt. 50, v. 1 from *The Apocrypha and Pseudepigrapha of the Old Testament.*
66. Matarasso, *The Quest of the Holy Grail;* Malory, *Le Morte d'Arthur.*
67. Bryant, *Complete Story of the Grail,* 214.
68. Skeels, *The Romance of Perceval in Prose.*

CHAPTER 8. IN THE PLACE OF THE ANCIENT HEART

1. Newman, *Symphonia,* 156; Hildegard of Bingen, *Scivias,* book 3, vision 13, chapter 2b.
2. *The Elucidation,* 345–46.
3. Bryant, *Complete Story of the Grail,* 30.
4. Matthews and Matthews, *King Arthur: One Hero, Many Faces.*
5. *The Elucidation,* 205–8.
6. *The Elucidation,* 383–400.
7. Gantz, *The Cattle Raid of Fróech.*
8. Matthews and Matthews, *Encyclopedia of Celtic Wisdom.*

9. Matthews and Matthews, *Encyclopedia of Celtic Wisdom,* trans. CM.

10. Matthews and Matthews, *Encyclopedia of Celtic Wisdom,* trans. CM.

11. *The Mabinogion.*

12. Jones, *Welsh Folklore and Folk-Custom.*

13. Chrétien de Troyes, *Arthurian Romances,* italics added.

14. Chrétien de Troyes, *Arthurian Romances,* italics added.

15. Chrétien de Troyes, *Arthurian Romances,* italics added.

16. *The Mabinogion,* 126.

17. Bryant, *Complete Story of the Grail,* 94–98.

18. Bryant, *Complete Story of the Grail,* 175.

19. *The Mabinogion.*

20. Matthews, C., *Mabon and the Guardians of Celtic Britain.*

21. Matthews, C., *Mabon and the Heroes of Celtic Britain.*

22. Matthews, C., *King Arthur's Raid on the Underworld.*

23. *The Elucidation,* 256–64.

24. Bryant, *Complete Story of the Grail,* 226.

25. *The Mabinogion,* 254.

26. *The Elucidation,* 248–55.

27. *The Elucidation,* 268–72.

28. Davies and Matthews, *This Ancient Heart.*

29. Roach, *The Didot Perceval,* 16175–82, trans. CM.

30. Roach, *The Didot Perceval,* 16165–69.

31. *The Elucidation,* 406–25.

32. *The Elucidation,* 429–43.

33. Evans-Wentz, *The Fairy Faith in Celtic Countries,* 44.

34. *The Mabinogion.*

35. Geoffrey of Monmouth, *History of the Kings of Britain,* book 2, chap. 7.

36. Bryant, *Complete Story of the Grail,* 41.

37. Bryant, *Complete Story of the Grail,* 41–43.

38. Matthews and Matthews, *King Arthur: One Hero, Many Faces,* chap. 3.

39. Marren, *Battles of the Dark Ages.*

40. Bowen, "(Former) Enemies at the Gate," 50; Matthews, J., *Sir Gawain: Knight of the Goddess.*

41. Matthews, C., *King Arthur's Raid on the Underworld,* lines 7–12.

42. Matthews, C. *King Arthur's Raid on the Underworld,* lines 43–46.

43. Matthews, C. *King Arthur's Raid on the Underworld,* lines 27–30.

44. Matthews, C. *King Arthur's Raid on the Underworld,* lines 31–34.

45. *The Elucidation,* 157–60.

46. *The Elucidation,* 358–59.

47. Matthews and Matthews, *King Arthur: One Hero, Many Faces,* chap. 3.

48. Matthews, C., *King Arthur's Raid on the Underworld,* lines 3–7.

49. Roach, *The Didot Perceval,* 13367–73, trans. CM.

50. Dillon, *The Cycles of the Kings.*

51. Roach, *The Didot Perceval* 13364ff.

52. *The Elucidation,* 417–18.

53. *The Elucidation,* 427–28.

54. *The Elucidation,* 465–74.

55. Bryant, *Complete Story of the Grail,* 130.

56. *The Elucidation,* 453–64.

57. Green, *Arthuriana,* 77.

58. Roach, *The Didot Perceval,* 16405–14, trans. CM.

59. *The Elucidation,* 155–56.

60. Roach, *The Didot Perceval,* 17001–10, trans. CM.

61. Roach, *The Didot Perceval,* 17072–73.

62. *The Elucidation,* 365–68.

63. *The Mabinogion; Lancelot-Grail.*

64. Roach, *The Didot Perceval,* 17157–64, trans. CM.

65. *The Elucidation,* 55–56.

66. Roach, *The Didot Perceval,* 17427–30, trans. CM.

67. Roach, *The Didot Perceval,* 17697–700.

68. Roach, *The Didot Perceval,* 17820–32.

69. Roach, *The Didot Perceval,* 17838–48.

70. Bryant, *Complete Story of the Grail,* 496–506.

71. Roach, *The Didot Perceval,* 18363–74, trans. CM.

CHAPTER 9. THE GRAIL REVEALED

1. Weston, *From Ritual to Romance,* 121; Govinda, *Foundation of Tibetan Mysticism.*

2. Matthews and Matthews, *Hallowquest.*

3. *The Eludication,* 323–30.

4. *The Eludication,* 247–60.

5. Chrétien de Troyes, *Perceval: The Story of the Grail,* 50.

6. De Boron, *Merlin and the Grail.*

7. Chrétien de Troyes, *Perceval: The Story of the Grail,* 207–9.

8. Chrétien de Troyes, *Perceval, The Story of the Grail,* 207–9.

9. Spaan, "The Otherworld in Early Irish Literature."

10. *The Elucidation,* 327–30.

11. *The Elucidation,* 304–14.

12. Bryant, *Complete Story of the Grail.*

13. Chrétien de Troyes, *Perceval, ou le Conte du Graal,* 6022–29, trans. CM.

14. Torroella, *La Faula.*

15. Matthews, C., "The Voices of the Wells."

16. St. Matthew 22: 37–40.

17. Matthews, C., *A Hundred Steps to the Grail.*

18. Chrétien de Troyes, *Perceval: The Story of the Grail,* 51.

19. Matthews, C., *King Arthur and the Goddess of the Land.*

20. Hahn, *Sir Gawain: Eleven Romances and Tales.*

21. Von Eschenbach, *Parzival, a Knightly Epic.*

22. Bryant, *Perlesvaus;* Malory, *Le Morte d'Arthur.*

23. Bryant, *Complete Story of the Grail,* 105–6.

24. Roach, *The Didot Perceval,* 13367–73, trans. CM.

25. Bryant, *Complete Story of the Grail,* 364.

26. Chrétien de Troyes, *Perceval: The Story of the Grail,* 66.

27. Isaiah 34:4.

28. Von Eschenbach, *Parzival, a Knightly Epic.*

29. Chrétien de Troyes, *Perceval: The Story of the Grail,* 160.

30. *The Elucidation,* 450–52.

31. Matthews, J., *Sir Gawain: Knight of the Goddess.*

32. Chrétien de Troyes, *Perceval: The Story of the Grail,* 121.

33. *The Elucidation,* 141–44.

34. Matthews, C., "The Voices of the Wells."

35. Sallustius, *Concerning the Gods and the Universe.*

36. *The Elucidation,* 192–93.

37. Grayson, "In Quest of Jessie Weston," 72.

38. *Krishna Myth.* Available at the website of Harekrsna.de.

39. Meyer and Robinson, *Nag Hammadi Scriptures.*

40. *The Elucidation,* 451–52.

41. *The Elucidation,* 209–212.

42. *Kore Kosmou,* 44–45.

BIBLIOGRAPHY

Arthur, Ross G., and Noel L. Corbett. *The Knight of the Two Swords*. Gainesville: University of Florida Press, 1996.

Augustine, Saint. *City of God*. Edited and translated by G. R. Evans. London: Penguin, 2003.

———. *Confessions*. Edited by Tom Gill. Alachua, Fla.: Bridge-Logos, 2003.

Baigent, Michael, Richard Leigh, and Henry Lincoln. *Holy Blood, Holy Grail*. London: Jonathan Cape, 1982.

Baring-Gould, S., ed. *Life of St. Gildas (Vita Gildae), Lives of the Saints*. Edinburgh: Grant, 1877.

Best, R. I., and O. Bergin. *Lebor na h'Uidre: The Book of the Dun Cow*. London: D. Nutt for Royal Irish Academy, 1929.

Bogdanow, Fanni. "Robert de Boron's Vision of Arthurian History." In *Arthurian Literature,* vol. 14, edited by James P. Carley and Felicity Riddy, 19–52. Woodbridge, U.K.: D. S. Brewer, 1996.

Bowen, Edward Mead. "(Former) Enemies at the Gate: Insinuations of Betrayal in *Pa Gur yv y porthaur.*" Paper presented at the 49th International Congress on Medieval Studies at Western Michigan University, Kalamazoo, Michigan. May 10, 2014. A modified version of the paper is available at Hortulus: The Online Graduate Journal of Medieval Studies (Hortulus-journal.com).

Bromwich, Rachel, ed. *Trioedd Ynys Prydein*. Cardiff: University of Wales Press, 1961.

Brown, A. C. L. "The Bleeding Lance and Phillip Flanders." *Speculum* 21, no. 3 (July 1946): pp. 303–11.

———. *The Origin of the Grail Legend*. Cambridge, Mass.: Harvard University Press, 1943.

Bruce, Christopher W. *The Arthurian Name Dictionary*. New York: Garland Publishing, 1999.

Brugger, E. "Bliocadrin." In *Medieval Studies: Studies Dedicated to Gertrude Schoepperle Loomis.* Edited by Roger S. Loomis. New York: Columbia University Press, 1927.

Bryant, Nigel, ed. *The Complete Story of the Grail.* Cambridge: D. S. Brewer, 2015.

————, trans. *Perceforest: The Prehistory of King Arthur's Britain.* Cambridge: D. S. Brewer, 2011.

————. *The High Book of the Grail: A Translation of the Thirteenth-Century Romance of Perlesvaus.* Cambridge: D. S. Brewer, 1978.

Bullock-Davies, Constance. *Professional Interpreters and the Matter of Britain.* Cardiff: University of Wales Press, 1966.

Burgess, Glyn S., and Leslie C. Brook. *French Arthurian Literature.* Vol. 5, *The Lay of the Mantel.* Woodbridge, U.K.: D. S. Brewer, 2013.

Büsching, Johann Gustav. "Das Oldenburger Horn." In *Volks-Sagen, Mächen und Legenden,* 380–83. Leipzig: Carl Heinrich Reclam, 1821.

Byrne, Francis. *Irish Kings and High Kings.* Dublin: Four Courts Press, 2001.

Cabaniss, Allen. "Joseph of Arimathea and a Chalice." *Mississippi Studies in English* 4 (1963): 61–67.

Carmichael, Alexander. *Carmina Gadelica.* Vol. 2. Edinburgh: Scottish Academic Press, 1972.

Charles, R. H. *Apocrypha and the Pseudoepigrapha of the Old Testament.* Oxford: Clarendon Press, 1913.

Chrétien de Troyes. *Arthurian Romances.* Translated by W. W. Comfort. London: Everyman, 1914.

————. *Arthurian Romances.* Edited by D. D. R. Owen. London: J. M. Dent, 1987.

————. *Arthurian Romances.* Translated by W. Kibler and C. Carroll. London: Penguin Books, 1991.

————. *Erec and Enid.*

————. *Perceval, or the Story of the Grail.* Edited and translated by Ruth Harwood Cline. Athens: University of Georgia Press, 1985.

————. *Perceval, ou le Conte du Graal.* Edited by Pierre Kunstmann. Ottawa: Nancy-University of Ottawa, Laboratoire de Français Ancien, 2009.

————. *Perceval: The Story of the Grail.* Edited and translated by N. Bryant. Cambridge: D. S. Brewer, 1982.

Conlee, John. *The Prose Merlin.* Kalamazoo, Mich.: Medieval Institute Publications, 1998.

Coombes, Annie. "Nouer les fils de ré-écriture: une visit interpolée au Chateau de Graal." *Persée* 47, no. 187 (2004): 3–15.

Corley, Corin F. V. *The Second Continuation of the Old French Perceval*. London: Modern Humanities Research Association, 1987.

Cross, T. P., and C. H. Slover. *Ancient Irish Tales*. Dublin: Figgis, 1936.

Curtin, Jeremiah. *Hero Tales of Ireland*. London: Macmillan, 1894.

Davies, Paul, and Caitlín Matthews. *This Ancient Heart*. Alresford, U.K.: Moon Books, 2015.

Dillon, Myles. *The Cycles of the Kings*. London: Oxford University Press, 1946.

Duffy, Maureen. *The Erotic World of Fairy*. London: Cardinal, 1989.

Duggan, Joseph J. *The Romances of Chrétien de Troyes*. New Haven: Yale University Press, 2001.

Elkington, David. *The Holy Grail: The Quest for the Glory and the Hidden Face of God*. Forthcoming: 2019.

Evans-Wentz, W. Y. *The Fairy Faith in Celtic Countries*. London: Henry Frowde, 1911.

Gaffney, Mark H. *Gnostic Secrets of the Naasenes*. Rochester, Vt.: Inner Traditions, 2004.

Gallais, Pierre. *Perceval et L'Initiation*. Paris: Editions de Sirac, 1972.

Gantz, Jeffrey. *The Cattle Raid of Fróech in Early Irish Myths and Sagas*. London: Penguin, 1981.

Geoffrey de la Tour Landry. *The Book of the Knight*. Edited by Thomas Wright. London: Horace Hart, 1906.

Geoffrey of Monmouth. *History of the Kings of Britain*. Harmondsworth, U.K.: Penguin, 1966.

———. *Vita Merlini*. Edited and translated by J. J. Parry. Champaign: University of Illinois Press, 1925.

Gerald of Wales. *Journey Through Wales*. Edited and translated by L. Thorpe. Harmondsworth, U.K.: Penguin, 1978.

Gervase of Tilbury. *Otia Imperialia*. Edited and translated by S. E. Banks and J. W. Binns. Oxford: Oxford University Press, 2002.

Gospel of Nicodemus from *Selections from Hengwrt Mss.* Translated and Edited by Robert Williams. London: Thomas Richards, 1892. Preserved in the Peniarth Library.

Govinda, Lama Anagarika. *Foundation of Tibetan Mysticism*. London: Rider, 1980.

Gowans, Linda. *Am Bròn Binn: An Arthurian Ballad in Scottish Gaelic*. Eastbourne: Manor Park Press, 1992.

Grayson, Janet. "In Quest of Jessie Weston." In *Arthurian Literature*. Vol. 11. Edited by Richard Barber. Cambridge: D. S. Brewer, 1992.

Green, Thomas. *Arthuriana: Early Arthurian Tradition & the Origins of the Legend*. Louth, Lincolnshire: Lindes Press, 2009.

Hahn, Thomas. *Sir Gawain: Eleven Romances and Tales.* Kalamazoo, Mich.: Medieval Institute Publications, 1995.

Hanna, Ralph. *The Knightly Tale of Golagros and Gawane.* Woodbridge, U.K.: Scottish Texts Society, 2008.

Harf-Lancner, Laurence. *Les Fées au Moyen Age.* Paris: Librarie Honoré Champion, 1984.

Harward, Vernon J., Jr. *The Dwarfs of Arthurian Romance and Celtic Tradition.* Leiden: E. J. Brill, 1958.

Heinrich Von dem Türlin. *The Crown.* Translated by J. W. Thomas. Lincoln: University of Nebraska Press, 1989.

Hermes Mercurius Trismegistus. *Kore Kosmou* (The Virgin of the World). Translated by Edward Maitland and Dr. Anna Kingsford. Createspace Independent Platform, 2008.

Hindman, Sandra. *Sealed in Parchment: Rereadings of Knighthood in the Illuminated Manuscripts of Chrétien de Troyes.* Chicago: University of Chicago Press, 1994.

Hinton, Thomas. *The Conte Du Graal Cycle: Chrétien de Troyes' Perceval, the Continuations.* Cambridge: D. S. Brewer, 2013.

———. *New Beginnings and False Dawns.* Oxford: Society for the Study of Mediaeval Languages and Literature, 2011.

Hopkins, G. M. *The Major Works.* Oxford: Oxford University Press, 2009.

Isidore of Seville. *The Etymologies.* Edited and translated by Stephen A. Barney. Cambridge: Cambridge University Press, 2010.

Izquerdo, Joseph. "The Gospel of Nicodemus in Medieval Catalan and Occitan Literature." In *The Medieval Gospel of Nicodemus: Texts, Intertexts and Contexts in Western Europe,* edited by Zbigniew Izydorcyk, 133–64. Tempe, Ariz.: Medieval and Renaissance Texts and Studies, 1997.

Jacobs, Joseph. *Celtic Fairy Tales.* London: Macmillan, 2011.

James, Montgue R., trans. *The Apocryphal New Testament.* Oxford: Clarendon Press, 1975.

John of Glastonbury. *Cronica Sive Antiquitates Glastoniensis Ecclesie: Chronicle of Glastonbury Abbey.* Edited by James Carley. Cambridge: Boydell Press, 1985.

Jones, David. *In Parenthesis.* London: Faber & Faber, 2014.

Jones, T. Gwyn. *Welsh Folklore and Folk-Custom.* London: Methuen, 1930.

Ketrick, Paul J. *The Relationship of Golagros and Gawane to the Old French Perceval.* Washington, D.C.: Catholic University of America, 1931.

Kinoshita, Sharon. *Medieval Boundaries: Rethinking Difference in Old French Literature.* Philadelphia: University of Pennsylvania, 2006.

Kirk, Robert. *The Secret Commonweath of Elves and Faeries.* Edited by Stewart Sanderson. Cambridge: D. S. Brewer, 1976.

Knight, Gareth. *The Book of Melusine of Lusignan.* Cheltenham: Skylight Press, 2013.

———. *Melusine of Lusignan and the Cult of the Faery Woman.* Lincoln, Ill.: R. J. Stewart Books, 2011.

———. *The Secret Tradition in Arthurian Legend.* Cheltenham: Skylight Press, 2012.

Koble, Nathalie. *Le Lai du Cor.* Paris: Rue d'Ulm, 2005.

Lachet, Claude. *Sone de Nansay.* Paris: Honoré Champion, 2014.

Lacy, Norris J., ed. *Lancelot-Grail: The Old French Vulgate and Post-Vulgate Cycles in Translation.* 5 vols. New York: Garland, 1993–1999.

Layamon. *The Arthurian Section of Layamon's Brut.* Edited by W. R. J. Barron. Liverpool: Liverpool University Press, 2005.

Le Bey, André. *The Romance of the Faery Melusine.* Cheltenham: Skylight Press, 2013.

Loomis, Roger Sherman. *Celtic Myth and Arthurian Romance.* New York: Columbia University Press, 1927.

Loomis, Roger Sherman, and Lura Hibbard Loomis. *Arthurian Legends in Medieval Art.* New York: Modern Language Association of America, 1938.

The Mabinogion. Edited and translated by Charlotte Guest. London: Ballantyne Press, 1910.

Macalister, R. A. *Eachtra an mhadra Mhaoil.* London: Irish Texts Society, 1908.

Madden, Sir Frederick. *Syr Gawayne: a Collection of Ancient Romance-Poems.* Toronto: University of Guelph, 1894.

Magill, Robert Alexander. "Part 1 of the *Voeux du Paon* by Jacques de Longuyon." Ph.D. diss., Columbia University, 1964.

Malory, Thomas. *Le Morte d'Arthur.* Edited by John Matthews. London: Cassell, 2003.

Marie de France. *French Medieval Romances.* Edited and translated by Eugene Mason. London: Dent, n.d.

Marren, Peter. *Battles of the Dark Ages.* Barnsley: Pen & Sword Military, 2006.

Matarasso, Pauline, trans. *The Quest of the Holy Grail.* London: Penguin, 1978.

Matthews, Caitlín. Afterword to *The Holy Grail and the Eucharist,* by Sergei Bulgakov, 147–154. Translated and edited by Boris Jakim. Hudson, N.Y.: Lindisfarne Books, 1997.

———. *Celtic Book of the Dead.* New York: St. Martin's Press, 1992.

———. *Healing the Ancestral Communion.* In *This Ancient Heart,* edited by Paul Davies and Caitlín Matthews, 76–99. Alresford, U.K.: Moon Books, 2015.

———. *A Hundred Steps to the Grail.* Oxford: Mythwood Books, 2016.

———. *King Arthur and the Goddess of the Land.* Rochester, Vt.: Inner Traditions, 2002.

———. *King Arthur's Raid on the Underworld.* Glastonbury: Gothic Image, 2008.

———. *Mabon and the Guardians of Celtic Britain.* Rochester, Vt.: Inner Traditions, 2002.

———. *Sophia: Goddess of Wisdom, Bride of God.* Wheaton, Ill.: Quest Books, 2001.

———. *The Spells of Women.* In *Verführer, Schurken, Magier (Mitterlalter Mythen).* Vol. 3, edited by Ulrich Müller and Werber Wunderlich. St. Gallen: UVK Verlagsgesellschaft, 2001.

———. "The Voices of the Wells: Celtic Oral Themes in Grail Literature." In *Household of the Grail,* edited by John Matthews. London: Aquarian Press, 1990.

Matthews, Caitlín, and John Matthews. *Encyclopedia of Celtic Wisdom.* Shaftesbury: Element, 2000.

———. *Hallowquest.* Wellingborough: Aquarian Press, 1991.

———. *Ladies of the Lake.* Wellingborough: Aquarian Press, 1996.

Matthews, John, ed. *At the Table of the Grail.* London: Watkins Books, 2002.

———. *Faeryland.* New York: Abrams, 2013.

———. *The Grail: A Secret History.* Alresford, U.K.: Godsfield Press, 2005.

———. "The Grail before the Grail: The Sources and Analogues of Robert de Boron and Chrétien de Troyes and the Transmission of the Story of the Grail." 2016. Available online at Academia.edu.

———. *Sir Gawain: Knight of the Goddess.* Rochester, Vt.: Inner Traditions, 2003.

Matthews, John, and D. Elkington. *The Journey of the Grail.* Forthcoming: 2019.

Matthews, John, and Gareth Knight. *Temples of the Grail.* Woodbury, Minn.: Llewellyn, 2019.

Matthews, John, and Caitlín Matthews. *Encyclopedia of Celtic Myth and Legend.* London: Rider, 2002.

———. *King Arthur: One Hero, Many Faces.* Rochester, Vt.: Inner Traditions, 2016.

———. *Taliesin: The Last Celtic Shaman.* Rochester, Vt.: Inner Traditions, 2002.

Matthews, John, and Caroline Wise, eds. *The Secret Lore of London.* London: Hodder, 2016.

Meyer, Marvin W., and James M. Robinson, eds. *Nag Hammadi Scriptures.* London: Harper, 2009.

Morris, Richard. *Cursor mundi: A Northumbrian Poem of the XIVth Century.* London: Early English Texts Society, 1892.

Newman, Barbara, *Symphinia: A Critical Edition of Symphonia Armoniae Celestum*. Ithaca, N.Y.: Cornell University Press, 1998.

Newstead, Helaine. *Bran the Blessed in Arthurian Romance*. New York: Columbia University Press, 1939.

———. "The Joie de la Cort Episode in Erec and the Horn of Bran." *P.M.L.A.* 51 (1936): 13–25.

Nicholson, Helen J. *Love, War and the Grail: Templars, Warriors and Hospitallers 1150-1500*. Leiden: Brill, 2001.

Nutt, Alfred. *Studies on the Legend of the Holy Grail*. New York: Cooper Square Publishers, 1965.

Paton, L. A. *Studies in the Fairy Mythology of Arthurian Romance*. New York: Burt Franklin, 1970.

Peebles, Rose Jeffries. *The Legend of Longinus in Ecclesiastical Tradition, and in English Literature, and its Connections with the Grail*. Baltimore: J. H. Furst, 1911.

Pollmann, L. *Chretien de Troyes und der Conte del Graal*. Tübingen: Max Niemeyer, 1965.

Raoul de Houdenc. *Meraugis de la Portugeis*. Edited by Michelle Szkilnik. Paris: Honoré Champion, 2004.

———. *Vengeance de Raguidel*. Paris: Ulan Press, 2011.

Renaud de Beaujeu. *Le Bel Inconnu*. Paris: Honoré Champion, 2003.

Roach, William. *The Didot Perceval*. Geneva: Slatkin Reprint, 1977.

Roach, William, and Robert H. Ivy Jr. *The First Continuation*. Philadelphia: University of Pennsyvlania, 1950.

Robert de Boron. *Le Roman de L'Estoire dou Graal*. Edited by W. A. Nitze. Paris: Honoré Champion, 1971.

———. *Merlin and the Grail*. Translated by Nigel Bryant. Cambridge: D. S. Brewer, 2001.

Sallustius. *Concerning the Gods and the Universe*. Translated by Arthur Darby Nock. Cambridge: Cambridge University Press, 2013.

Skeels, Dell R., ed. and trans. "Guingamor and Guerrehes." In *The Anthropologist Looks at Myth*. Compiled by Melville Jacobs. Austin: American Folklore Society, 1966.

———. *The Romance of Perceval in Prose* [*Didot Perceval*]. Seattle: University of Washington, 1966.

Slocum, Jonathan, and Brigitte L. M. Bauer. *Old French Online: Master Glossary*. Available online from the Linguistics Research Center, University of Texas at Austin.

Spaan, D. B. "The Otherworld in Early Irish Literature." Ph.D. diss., University of Michigan, 1969.

Steadman-Jones, Fred, Ian Pegler, and John Matthews. *The Nanteos Grail: The History of a Relic*. Forthcoming: 2020.

Stokes, Whitley, and Ernst Windisch. *Irische Texte*. Vol. 2. Leipzig: Hirzel, 1891.

Thomas Aquinas, Saint. *Summa Theologica*. Edited by Kenelm Foster. Cambridge: Cambridge University Press, 2006.

Thompson, Albert Wilder. *The Elucidation: A Prologue to the Conte del Graal*. New York: Publications of the Institute of French Studies, 1931.

Torroella, Guillem de. *La Faula* [The Tail]. Edited by Sara Vincent Santamaria. Valencia: Editorial Tirant Lo Blanch, 2001.

Ulrich von Zatzikhoven. *Lanzelet*. Edited and translated by K. T. G. Webster, with revisions by R. S. Loomis. New York: Columbia University Press, 1951.

Vermaseren, M. J. *Cybele and Attis*. London: Thames & Hudson, 1977.

Vita Adae Et Evae in Charles, R. H. *The Apocrypha and Pseeudepigrapha of the Old Testament*. Oxford: The Claredon Press, 1913.

Watt, D. E. R., ed. *A History Book for Scots*. Edinburgh: Birlinn, 2010.

Weingartner, Russel. *Graelent and Guingamor: Two Breton Lays*. New York: Garland Publishing, 1985.

Weinraub, Eugene J. *Chrétien's Jewish Grail*. Chapel Hill: North Carolina Studies in the Romance Languages and Literatures, 1976.

Weston, Jessie. *From Ritual to Romance*. New York: Doubleday, 1957.

———. *The Legend of Sir Perceval*. London: David Nutt, 1909.

———. *Sir Gawain and the Lady of Lys*. London: David Nutt, 1907.

———. *Sir Gawain at the Grail Castle*. London: David Nutt, 1903.

Williams, John [Ab Ithel, pseud.]. *Annales Cambriae*. Cambridge: Cambridge University Press, 2012.

Williams, Robert. *Selections from the Henwrt Mss*. Preserved in the Peniarth Library. London: Thomas Richards, 1892.

Wolfram Von Eschenbach. *Parzival*. Translated by Helen M. Mustard and Charles E. Passage. New York: Vintage Books, 1961.

———. *Parzival, a Knightly Epic*. Translated by J. L. Weston. London: D. Nutt, 1894.

Wulff, Frederic. *Le Lai du Cor*. Lund: C.W.K. Gleerup, 1888.

INDEX